Elon Musk

Elon Musk

RISKING IT ALL

Michael Vlismas

Jonathan Ball Publishers

Johannesburg · Cape Town · London

Originially published in South Africa in 2022 by
JONATHAN BALL PUBLISHERS
A division of Media24 (Pty) Ltd
PO Box 33977,
Jeppestown,
2043

This edition published in 2022 by
JONATHAN BALL PUBLISHERS
An imprint of Icon Books Ltd
Omnibus Business Centre,
39-41 North Road,
London N7 9DP

Email: info@iconbooks.com
For details of all international distributors,
visit iconbooks.com/trade

ISBN 978-177619-185-7
ebook ISBN 978-1-77619-162-8

Printed and bound in Great Britain
by Clays Ltd, Elcograf S.p.A.

Contents

'The questions are always more important
than the answers.'

– Ernest Shackleton

'Sometimes the questions are complicated
and the answers are simple.'

– Dr Seuss (Theodor Seuss Geisel)

Introduction

ELON Musk, the richest man on planet Earth, is doing everything he possibly can to leave planet Earth.

His journey from Pretoria boy to billionaire entrepreneur appears destined to end, as he describes it, 'out there among the stars'. Space does indeed seem to be the final frontier for Musk, and even its vastness appears not enough to contain one of the greatest geniuses of our age, one who is determined to make human beings an interplanetary species.

This is the future towards which Musk has been moving ever since the age of five, when he first realised that not everybody has a million new ideas exploding in their brains all the time, and that people thought he was strange, and that he might be locked away because of it.

The boy who grew up reading science-fiction novels and comics became the man who brought much of what he read to life. He built electric cars and space rockets. 'Science fiction should not be science fiction forever,' he has said.

From South Africa has emerged one of the greatest minds of our time, and a man shifting the entire focus of humanity with his vision. A man who has made it his life's mission to turn human beings into a multiplanetary species in the interests of conserving that rarest and most precious thing that appears not to exist anywhere else in the universe – consciousness.

The greatest challenge in writing a biography of Elon Musk is that he does not sit still. He is a moving target. A rabbit warren of ideas, theories, arguments and counterarguments. His life is a wild journey, much like the rockets he sends soaring into space. Trying to condense Elon Musk into one book feels a bit like trying to capture the expanse of the Drakensberg on your camera phone.

So I have tried to provide the story of Musk's life, and the golden threads that run through it, as a starting point for readers who want to know more about one of the most significant people of our time.

Although it is not a requirement for an unauthorised biography of this nature, I did reach out to Musk for his thoughts. He did not respond. I also reached out to his mother, Maye, who politely declined to provide input. I first reached out to his father, Errol, in May 2021. I finally received a response in February 2022. His response was as puzzling as the popular portrayal of him: 'Good day. It is not clear to me how someone who does not know Elon can write a biography on him. Elon spent his entire childhood and youth with me. I am aware of all his affairs from day one to present. Jonathan Ball Publishers were not interested in a series of articles I wrote called "Raising Elon". The matter is very confusing to me. Without any input from me any biography is pointless. Walter Isaacson (author of Steve Jobs and various biographies) is busy with the supposedly definitive biography on Elon. Isaacson asks me daily on Elon's life. Without me Isaacson is lost.'

It was a confusing response on a number of levels. First, Errol Musk has repeatedly said he has been misrepresented in the media and by his ex-wife Maye in her book. Now, given the opportunity to correct these perceived slights on his character, he does not take it. In my response to Errol, I explained that it was for precisely this reason that I had reached out to him – to get the story from his perspective.

I know nothing about the supposed Walter Isaacson biography, and Jonathan Ball Publishers did not regard the 'Raising Elon' articles Errol says he proposed to them as publishable in book form. I also explained that much like any biography of great men long dead, a personal relationship with the individual is not a prerequisite for a biography and proper research on the subject.

Errol never responded.

For my research, I went to the world that Musk inhabits – the digital space. Sifting fact from fiction was an exhaustive process, and so much of what has been written about Musk is simply perpetuated through an ongoing news cycle that just builds on the current narrative.

It is for this reason (and others) that I did not read Ashlee Vance's 2015 biography, *Elon Musk: Tesla, SpaceX, and the Quest for a Fantastic Future*. I was determined to go into this without any preconceived ideas about Musk, and rather to form my own opinions through my research on the man.

Where necessary I spoke to people around him, especially those who knew him and his family in their early days in Pretoria.

The world of Elon Musk is quite a journey.

And it's a journey that began in Pretoria, where a young boy full of ideas first opened up a science-fiction comic book – and immediately saw our future.

PART ONE

A Strange Child

UNDER a bright-blue South African sky, a five-year-old Elon Musk stands on the brown-slate *stoep* (verandah) with his younger sister, Tosca, and brother, Kimbal. From beneath a neatly cut crop of light-brown hair, his broad smile pushes his cheeks up and his eyes are almost closed. It is the smile of a young boy seemingly in his element. A young boy wearing a yellow jersey dirtied by a game of cowboys and Indians or cops and robbers, by the look of the plastic pistol in his right hand.

The year is 1976, a year when most white South African children still played outside with the directive from their parents to come home when the street lights went on, and driven by whatever their imaginations could dream up. Television had only just arrived in South Africa, and in January of that year the South African Broadcasting Corporation officially opened its television service nationwide to those who could afford this new technology. For a child, one of the only offerings was a weekly Afrikaans show called *Haas Das se Nuuskas*, in which a range of puppet animals, led by the rabbit Haas, would read the news about *Diereland* (Animal Land).

Haas was voiced by the inimitable Riaan Cruywagen, for decades the country's most trusted television newscaster.

For a youngster like Elon Musk, it was a sheltered world. A world of big gardens in quiet suburbs, and a rabbit on the television who read the news. But he didn't read the real news. While Musk and his siblings were running around in their garden with toy guns, black children were being shot at with real guns in the Soweto student uprising of June 1976. The frustration of black learners, angered by the government's provision of second-rate education and by having to learn in Afrikaans, boiled over and they streamed out of their classes into the dusty streets of Soweto on a winter Wednesday morning.

By 9 am as many as 10 000 students were protesting, and police blocked their progress.[1] About half an hour later the shooting started. Two teenage boys, one the 12-year-old Hector Pieterson, were the first to die. By evening the fighting still continued. The majority of the dead were under the age of 23. The *Rand Daily Mail* reported 54 fatalities and close to 200 injured: Petrus Gule, 15, was shot in the head; Samuel Mhlanga, 17, died from a fractured skull; Martin Tshabalala, 17, was shot through the intestine; and Robert Tyiki, 15, was shot in the heart.[2] As the uprising spread to other parts of the country, children as young as five were among the casualties.

About 60 km away from Soweto, in Pretoria, white children sat in front of their parents' television sets to watch a rabbit read the news.

But he mentioned nothing about the children in Soweto.

At the age of five, Elon Musk already knew he was different. He was certainly different to the vast majority of black children in the country by the accident of his birth. But amid the explosion of gunshots and teargas that rattled through South Africa in 1976, Musk was dealing with another kind of explosion that made him feel different in another way.

In his young mind, there was more going on than just the normal development of language and coordination and social communication skills. There was something else. There were ideas. A constant stream of exploding ideas. And questions. And it scared him, to the point that he thought 'different' might mean he was actually a little bit crazy: 'I thought I was insane because it was clear that not everybody's mind was exploding with ideas all of the time,' he later recalled. 'I thought I was kind of like a crazy kid, I suppose. I was just very curious about the world: how did we come to be here, what's the meaning of life and all of that. I always had a really intense desire to understand things and learn.'[3]

'A strange child' is how Musk has referred to himself. Intense, inquisitive and alone in his own world. But always with a bright smile beneath eyes that from his earliest childhood photos had that same searching intensity as the man who now watches his rockets blast into space.

A strange child indeed, who on Monday 28 June 1971 was born into a 'strange society', the heart of which lay in Pretoria, South Africa's capital city and Musk's childhood home.

The Pretoria that welcomed baby Musk that day was described by the American journalist Allen Drury as 'a very strange society'.[4] And Pretoria had a strange pull on Musk's family. The city's beautiful jacaranda-lined streets had once so captivated Musk's Canadian grandfather that he moved his entire family from Canada to Pretoria.

It was a strange decision for a man who was a noted free-thinker, and whose grandson would take this to entirely new levels. And yet at the same time it was perfectly understandable, for Pretoria has always had a strange and complex relationship with the history of South Africa. From its beginnings, Pretoria represented the ideals of liberty, freedom and adventure of a new nation, things that appealed to the likes of Musk's grandfather, but that would come to represent the pinnacle of isolation and conservatism by the time Musk was growing up.

Pretoria was founded with a rebel heart when the Boer general Marthinus Wessel Pretorius rode in with his band of Voortrekkers and chose to camp by the Apies River. After running battles with indigenous groups, the newcomers declared this to be their new home. In 1855, Pretoria officially became the new capital of the South African Republic, taking over from the original capital of Potchefstroom. Its name came from the great Boer general Andries Pretorius – Marthinus's father. Marthinus Pretorius was the first president of a fiercely independent corner of the subcontinent that would soon see a tremendous scramble for land, minerals and power.

For this band of people, the Great Trek – the migration of Dutch-Afrikaners from the Cape away from British rule – was finally over. And that spirit is forever embedded in the soil of the Pretoria that Elon Musk would have dirtied his boyhood hands in. But he was not an Afrikaner. He did not identify with that conservative culture. He was appalled by the policy of apartheid, which reached a turning point in Soweto in 1976. But if you grew up in Pretoria in the 1970s, it left an indelible mark on you. It shaped you in ways you would not have even noticed. For while Musk may not have directly iden-tified with Afrikaner culture, the spirit of the Voortrekkers, people described as 'pioneers' and 'pathfinders', and the city they founded would most certainly have resonated – and probably still does – with a man on a pioneering quest of his own.

Pretoria was the home of the poet and writer Eugène Marais, of the writer, artist and activist Es'kia Mphahlele, and the sculptor and artist Anton van Wouw. These are just a few of the inquiring minds that have lived here.

And on Monday 28 June 1971, it became the home of Elon Musk. In 1971, South Africa was at the height of apartheid, the policy of racial separation that had existed since 1948. Eleven years earlier, the African National Congress (ANC) and other liberation organisations had been banned by the ruling National Party government. A decade before Musk's birth, South Africa had become a republic and withdrawn from the Commonwealth. In 1964, it was banned from the Olympics. Seven years before Musk's birth, Nelson Mandela and other anti-apartheid activists had been sentenced to life imprisonment on Robben Island.

By 1971, South Africa had become an island in the Western world, isolated by its racial politics. And yet, for the country's white hospitals, it was a significant year. It was certainly a good year for sporting births, with Lance Klusener (cricket), Joost van der Westhuizen, Jannie de Beer and Pieter Rossouw (rugby), and Amanda Coetzer and Wayne Ferreira (tennis) among the future sports stars born in 1971. Klusener would go on to make his Test debut for South Africa just five years after the country was readmitted to international cricket and would begin to bridge the two worlds between white and black in South Africa as a white sportsman fluent in Zulu, which earned him the nickname 'Zulu'. Van der Westhuizen would go on to play for the Springboks and be part of that iconic team that won the 1995 Rugby World Cup in Johannesburg, and which brought a nation together under the vision of the country's first black president, Nelson Mandela. The sports stars born that year would form part of a period in which South Africa sought to use its sporting prowess to galvanise the new Rainbow Nation while at the same time flexing the muscles of its return to the international fold. They were the bridge between two worlds.

But there was nothing to suggest that the baby boy born to Errol Musk, a highly successful mechanical engineer, and Maye Musk, a beautiful model and dietitian, on that Monday in June 1971 would emerge as one of the greatest entrepreneurs, engineers, inventors and innovators the world has ever seen. Nor that he would go on to bridge worlds of his own fantastic imagination. Or that Pretoria would one day lay claim to being the cradle of the richest man on planet Earth. A man who would single-handedly redirect public thinking back to space exploration and the conservation of not only the planet but its most dominant species – human beings. A man who by virtue of his mother's work ethic, borne of the hardships she would undergo, and his father's ruthless drive and determination would seek to bring value to society in everything he undertook. Yet also a man of polarising opinions surrounded by controversy and critics. His audacious takeover bid in 2022 for Twitter, for instance, was greeted with glee in some quarters and fear and loathing in others.

His mother would help to frame his vision and view of success when she told him, 'Being successful is what you can share with other people to make them feel good.'

Musk would later define this as 'What are the set of things that can be done to make the future better? There need to be things that make you look forward to waking up in the morning. You wake up in the morning and you look forward to the day … look forward to the future.'5

In 1971, in Pretoria, the future was uncertain.

A Family of Pioneers

ON the Monday of Musk's birth, in the leafy eastern suburbs of
Pretoria, Prime Minister John Vorster addressed the official opening
of the congress of the Afrikaanse Studentebond at the Aula of the
University of Pretoria. At the end of his speech, he left the students
with this challenge: 'You will have to find solutions that cannot be
found today.'[1] Vorster was referring to questions of race and the rising political tension at South African universities, and the role the
country's white youth would play in this.

A continent away, in the United States, the National Aeronautics
and Space Administration (NASA) had launched a solution to its
own question: is there life on other planets? This question would
captivate Musk far more than the prevailing issues of race in South
Africa at the time.

Exactly one month before Musk's birth, NASA launched the
Mariner 9 spacecraft. And they pointed it at Mars. When Musk
was about five months old, Mariner 9 made history by becoming
the first spacecraft to orbit another planet, beating its rival, the
Soviet Union's Mars 2, and sending back the first global mapping

of the surface of Mars and valuable images of the Red Planet.

In every sense, Musk was born at a time when humanity was grappling with one of its oldest questions: are we alone? And he was born into a South African society that was asking another question: how do we live together?

Much like these questions, Musk's birth was not an easy one.

'It started with three days of false labor, which means contractions all day that disappear at night,'[2] his mother recalls in her memoir *A Woman Makes a Plan*. 'The birth was hard, as he had a large head and was a big boy, eight pounds, eight ounces. I wanted a natural birth without painkillers … All the agony was forgotten when he arrived. I was so happy. He was this beautiful little cherub. I couldn't believe anything was so beautiful. He would lie next to me and I would just stare at him. It was the most wonderful thing that ever happened.'[3]

It wasn't long before Maye also realised her first born was different: 'From the age of three he just reasoned with me so well and I didn't know how he could figure out things. I sent him to school early because I told them he needed more stimulation.'[4]

After his own realisation at the age of five that his world was not the world of most five-year-olds, Musk says he was 11 when he'd already started forming in his mind what he now calls 'The essence of my philosophy': 'I had sort of an existential crisis when I was 11 – just trying to figure out what it's all about. And I came to the conclusion that we don't really know the answer, but if we increase the scope and scale of civilisation then we have a much better chance of understanding the meaning of life and why we're here or even what are the right questions to ask. So, therefore, we should strive to expand the scope and scale of consciousness to better understand the questions to ask about the answer that is the universe.'[5]

Musk was starting to formulate his philosophy in relation to the world around him. In the prevailing political context of South Africa at the time, issues of race and freedom would have dominated. But Musk's mind was drifting further than this. And for him, it was first a search for the right questions to ask.

As a boy, the questions abounded in his head. To start answering these questions, it was first to science-fiction comics and novels that he turned. Then it was his father's set of the *Encyclopaedia Britannica*, which he devoured to such an extent that his family nicknamed him 'Encyclopaedia'. And then, most significantly, it was sitting in front of a blinking green cursor on a computer screen for the first time. Ideas and questions flooded his childhood brain.

'My conclusion was that I'm strange,' he said.

But, considering his eccentric family, he was hardly strange at all.

In 1950, a red Bellanca aircraft flew over Pretoria. In the cockpit sat Dr Joshua Norman Haldeman, the son of John Elon Haldeman – after whom Elon Musk is named – and one of Canada's most respected chiropractors. He was also an accomplished aviator and avid explorer, a man who flew to far-off places and loved searching for lost worlds, and who would no doubt pass these qualities on to a grandson who would do the same.

It was Haldeman's penchant for exploration that took him to Pretoria, where he put down the family's roots in Africa.

Musk's maternal grandfather was born in a humble log cabin on the prairie of Minnesota in 1902. It was a hard life, perhaps not too dissimilar to the veld around Pretoria in the early 1900s – except for the bitter, freezing winters. And in the late 1800s, the prairie farmers of Minnesota endured devastating hail storms and plagues of grasshoppers.[6] The journalist Eugene Virgil Smalley, writing in 1893, described prairie life: 'The silence of death rests on the vast landscape, save when it is swept by cruel winds that search out every chink and cranny of the buildings, and drive through each unguarded aperture the dry, powdery snow.'[7]

The early death of children in these harsh conditions was all too common. But in the home of young Joshua Haldeman, it was to his father, John, that death came calling. When Joshua was two, his father was diagnosed with diabetes and given only six months to live.[8] His mother, Almeda Jane Haldeman, a nurse and schoolteacher, was not one to simply resign herself to the challenges of life. She took them head-on. This was a woman who had come into the world prematurely and had had to be incubated in a warm oven.[9] She had an inquiring mind despite her father's refusal to send her to school because she was a girl. She would go on to live through the Great Depression and the uncompromising life of a homesteader. So when her husband was given no hope of a cure for his diabetes from any of the traditional medical interventions of the time, Almeda Jane decided to look into a field of medicine known as chiropractic care, then in its infancy. After travelling with her husband to Minneapolis to visit a chiropractor, she decided to pursue this new field herself in the hope of being better able to treat him. Even in this simple act, Almeda Jane showed herself to be a pioneer and a woman of courage, for in those early days anybody practising chiropractic was liable to be imprisoned, as the medical fraternity baulked at these new practitioners who lacked a doctor's licence. In 1932 in the US, there were 450 cases of chiropractors being imprisoned, and often the same chiropractors were jailed on multiple occasions.[10]

Almeda Jane found that her treatments improved her husband's condition and extended his life expectancy by several years. With a degree from EW Lynch's Chiropractic School and Cure in Minneapolis in 1905, and having been advised to move her husband to a cold and dry climate, Almeda Jane Haldeman relocated the family to the Canadian province of Saskatchewan. She became the first chiropractor to officially practise there, and one of the first female chiropractors in the world.

John Elon Haldeman eventually passed away in 1909. Almeda re-married in 1915 and focused more on teaching. But her chiropractic interests were passed on to her son (and Elon's grandfather), Joshua, who in his own life had also witnessed the seemingly miraculous health benefits of the technique.

During an informal game of ice hockey at school, Joshua was hit on the head. The injury affected his eyesight, but after chiropractic treatment, his vision slowly returned. So it was hardly surprising that he should decide to follow in his mother's footsteps and also study to become a chiropractor. Already, the Musk family trait of looking beyond the obvious and finding new solutions to old prob-lems – whether it be alternative medicine or alternative energy – was evident.

Before he settled on a career as a chiropractor, Joshua was a farmer. But the advent of the Great Depression, which lasted from 1929 until the late 1930s, was not good for farmers. Crop prices dropped so low that it became cheaper for farmers to burn corn rather than coal in their stoves. From 1930 to 1939, 37 814 farm bankruptcies were recorded by the United States Department of Agriculture.[11] Other sources put the figure closer to 400 000 in terms of foreclosures. Joshua Haldeman suffered the same fate as these. The worst economic disaster in history claimed his land and his first marriage. Decades later, in 2008, his grandson Elon would fall into a similar vortex of trying to turn the key on a new car company – a revolutionary electric car company – in the midst of a global recession and while going through a divorce.

An estimated 15 million Americans were left jobless, penniless and hopeless by the Great Depression. In Canada, Haldeman was in a similar position. He moved around the country like a footloose adventurer, taking odd jobs as a construction worker, cowboy and rodeo performer. He and hundreds of thousands of men did the same. This was the era of the hoboes, the unemployed men who rode the railways in search of opportunity. And it birthed a new genre in American literature, described by Jack London, John Steinbeck, Jack Kerouac and many others.

Even when he did settle down and open his first chiropractic practice, Joshua never forgot his hobo days. His secretary, Vivian Doan, recalls how 'On occasion, he loved to put on his cowboy boots and entertain with his lasso or lariat. He would twirl the lariat and hop in and out and do various movements and steps as he continuously twirled the lariat.'[12]

Dr Joshua Haldeman rose to become a highly respected practitioner. He is credited with drafting Saskatchewan's 1943 Chiropractic Act, representing Canada on the Board of Control of the International Chiropractors' Association and campaigning to allow chiropractors to be commissioned as officers during World War II, and for his role as a political leader who was briefly imprisoned for his alternative views. Joshua was a follower of, and the leader of, the Canadian branch of Technocracy, a movement that proposed a system of government in which officials are selected based on their expertise or skill within a particular field. His political views led to clashes with local authorities on various occasions.

Joshua's life was a busy one as he juggled his interests in politics and economics with his chiropractic practice. He was so busy, in fact, that he didn't even have time for a proper home and lived at the local YMCA. Once again, this echoes the experience of his grandson, who, while focused on building his first US business, Zip2, would hire office space because it was cheaper than renting an apartment, and would shower at the local YMCA.

But Joshua, feeling that his life was a little one-dimensional, decided to take up dance lessons as a distraction. His instructor was Winnifred Josephine Fletcher, or 'Wyn' as she preferred to be called.

And she, rather than dancing, proved to be his greatest distraction of all. As Joshua recalled, 'Six months passed and in a weak moment I happened to say, "When will you marry me?" Without hesitation, "Tomorrow," she said.'[13] That sense of impulsiveness in love has also marked Elon's life. He proposed to his second wife, Talulah Riley, only ten days after meeting her.

The newly married Joshua and Winnifred lived in a trailer in Regina, Saskatchewan. Their first son, Scott, who was born in 1943, had an apple crate for a bed. Edith was born in 1945, then came the twins, Maye and Kaye, born in 1948, and finally another son, Angkor Lee, born in 1955. The children grew up in a happy home as Joshua's practice grew, and felt the love of parents who adored each other and their children. As Vivian Doan recalled of Joshua's lucky encounter with Wyn, 'The result was an especially happy marriage and five precious children.'

But Joshua's adventurous spirit could not be contained for long, and he was fortunate in having a wife with a similar bent for exploration. In 1947, Dr Haldeman took his first flying lesson. This was certainly proof of the Haldeman spirit of adventure. But there was also a decidedly practical motivation. The demands of his profession took him around the country on regular business trips, and so it made sense for him to learn to fly. He had his first flying lesson on 16 July 1947. Seventy years later, his grandson – infuriated by the endless delays caused by Los Angeles traffic – announced his own plans to finally solve the world's traffic problems by launching a tunnelling company with the vision of literally digging tunnels under major cities to ease congestion on the roads. More on that later.

But for Joshua, what started as a convenience soon became a passion. In 1948, at the age of 45, he qualified as a pilot. That's when he bought his beloved red Bellanca aircraft. And so began another chapter as the family soon gained fame as 'The Flying Haldemans', with Kaye and Maye affectionately known as 'The Flying Twins'. As Joshua recalled in a book of his flying exploits, *The Flying Haldemans: Pity the Poor Private Pilot* – co-authored with Wyn – 'Pictures of "The Flying Twins" were in the Edmonton (Alberta) papers and in Davenport, Iowa, papers in the one week ... At a year old "The Flying Twins" were certainly cute and attracted a lot of attention. They had their first radio appearance in Davenport over WHO-WOC.'[14]

It was this love of flying and adventure, combined with a growing disillusionment with the political system in Canada, that saw Haldeman turn his gaze towards South Africa. He had been corresponding with a Cape Town chiropractor by the name of Dr John Blackbourn, a New Zealander who had purchased what is thought to be the first chiropractic practice in South Africa – in Adderley Street – from Henry Otterholt, an American graduate of the Palmer College of Chiropractic in Davenport, Iowa, from where Joshua had graduated in 1926. Joshua had also reached out to missionary friends to get their views of the country, and they spoke highly of its opportunities.

So, in 1950, Joshua Haldeman packed up his family and his plane, and they boarded a ship for Cape Town. The twins were two at the time of the voyage.

Upon docking in Cape Town harbour, Haldeman uncrated the Bellanca and reassembled it. Then he took off for his first flight in South Africa, happy to just follow his own instincts. Vivian Doan made an astute observation when she declared, 'Nothing was impossible or unreasonable to Dr Haldeman.'[15] And this desire to talk less and do more is a trait that lives on in Elon.

Joshua's original plan was to settle the family in Johannesburg. But after flying over Pretoria, he was so captivated by the beauty of the jacaranda trees in bloom that he decided to settle the family there.

On 21 November 1950, the Haldeman Chiropractic Clinic

opened in the family's sprawling new home in Soutpansberg Road, in the suburb of Rietondale, behind the Pretoria Zoo and the Union Buildings, and just outside what was then the central business district of the city. It was a magnificent home with a beautiful garden and date palm trees, located in one of Pretoria's youngest suburbs. The Haldemans were certainly an intriguing new oddity in the largely Afrikaans city, even more so as they brought a new medical practice to a city whose residents were largely ignorant of chiropractic. In a letter to the International Chiropractors' Association dated 6 March 1951, Joshua described their new home and the opportunities for chiropractic practitioners:

> We have been busy getting settled in our new home here in Pretoria. This country is a wide open field for good chiropractors, although most people have not heard of chiropractic as there has been no advertising. I was unable to get an office downtown, so bought a place 2.5 miles from the business district. We moved in on the first of December and started to practice that day. Had good success with the first patients so the practice built up to twenty-five appointments by the 15th of January and thirty-seven by the 5th of February, without any newspaper announcements or advertising other than personal contact and booklets. We did put up two small signs on our gatepost, one in English and one in Africaans [sic]. The Africaans-English dictionary did not give chiropractic, so I went to Dr Bosman, who is in charge of making official translations for the Government, and had chiropractic and chiropractor translated officially into Africaans. These words will appear in the next edition of the dictionary. Of course, everyone can speak English, except in possibly

some of the outlying districts. Africaans is interesting and
it is the only modern language, so we are learning it. Many
good sized towns have no chiropractors at all. In Pretoria,
a city of two hundred and seventy thousand, there are two
others besides myself, a Carver and a Los Angeles graduate. South Africa is a most pleasant and interesting place to
live. The warmest we have experienced during the hot spell
is 86 degrees [Fahrenheit]. They have never had snow in
Pretoria and only an occasional light frost in cold weather.
Within driving and flying distance (we brought our plane
with us) are innumerable interesting spots to visit ... We
have found it most pleasant and interesting.[16]

It was on the front lawn of their new home in Pretoria that Maye
recalls watching people walk back and forth, and back and forth,
under her parents' gaze. As a child she believed these to be walking
competitions. They were in fact what Joshua called 'good posture
contests'. Her eccentric parents would hold garden tea parties and
invite people to enter these contests, which used to attract up to 180
contestants to their home.

The family were close, and Joshua even enlisted his children in
the business. Maye and her twin sister would help to post the month-
ly chiropractic bulletin that he sent out to his clients (they were paid
five cents an hour), and after school they would work as receptionists
in the practice (for 25 cents an hour).

Dr Joshua Haldeman made an indelible mark on the growth of
chiropractic in Pretoria, and throughout South Africa. He served as
the president of the South African Chiropractors' Association, and
was later elected an honorary life member of the association. He also
left deep roots as the cofounder of the Aircraft Owners and Pilots'
Association of South Africa, as a representative on the Civil Aviation

Advisory Council and the Air Navigation Regulations Committee of South Africa, a cofounder of the Pretoria Pistol Club and the first president of the South African Pistol Association.

Scott Haldeman, who as a baby would be taken on Joshua's flying trips – wrapped up in a blanket and placed on the back shelf of the cockpit – recalls a father with a pioneering spirit, an inquiring mind, a lust for life in all its fullness and a somewhat rebellious streak:

> His personal and family life were a reflection of his political beliefs and chiropractic philosophy. He believed in the innate ability of the body to heal itself given a natural environment and chiropractic adjustments. He would not permit smoking, insisted on regular exercise, and served only unrefined flour and sugar and natural foods. He would not permit the family to drink Coca-Cola, which at one time contained cocaine as an additive. He did not swear or allow swearing in the house and insisted the family at all times enjoy life. Haldemans were not permitted to have headaches or other symptoms, be unhappy or pessimistic, or to be dishonest. Chiropractic adjustments were given to the family for any symptom and at least once a month.[17]

But arguably his great impact was in moving his family to Pretoria, which would in time lead to the birth of Elon Musk.

By a fortunate twist of fate, when seen from a small red aircraft's cockpit, Pretoria would become the birthplace of a man who would take his grandfather's pioneering spirit to the greatest heights imaginable.

Don't Panic

IN Elon Musk's household, there is one golden rule: 'Don't Panic.' It comes from the hugely popular Douglas Adams novel, *The Hitchhiker's Guide to the Galaxy*, a personal favourite of Musk. It's also a Musk business rule.

On 6 February 2018, when Musk's space exploration company SpaceX launched its Falcon Heavy rocket, the 'dummy payload' was Musk's own Tesla Roadster, with a dummy named 'Starman' sitting in the driver's seat. The words 'Don't Panic' featured on the car's instrument display. Also printed on the car's circuit board was 'Made on Earth by humans'.

Maye Musk would likely have smiled at this as she recognised a golden thread running through their adventurous family. Her own family's motto was 'Live dangerously – carefully'. Maye's father, Joshua, was unapologetic in his desire to live a full life, to explore the unknown and to be different. And he brought this adventurous spirit with him to Pretoria. 'I grew up in a family that had an airplane and a fascination with exploration … My father was never one to do what anyone else was doing … My father always said, "There's nothing a Haldeman can't do,"[1] she wrote in her memoir.

The Haldeman kids were every bit part of these adventures with their eccentric parents, whether it was flights in their plane through Central Africa, horseback rides through Lesotho or the annual trips the family took for almost a decade after Joshua embarked on a quest to find the fabled Lost City of the Kalahari.

Haldeman was captivated by the legend of the Lost City, which had gained worldwide popularity from an 1885 book by the Canadian Guillermo Farini (real name William Leonard Hunt) in which he claimed to have discovered this Atlantis of the desert. At the time the Haldeman family settled in Pretoria, there had been a resurgence of interest in searching for the site. And among the many expeditions that set out on foot, in wagons and trucks, and even with aircraft loaned by the Union Defence Force, Haldeman was said to be the most devoted to the cause. It drew interest from the Royal Geographical Society in London, and even led the author Alan Paton, of *Cry, The Beloved Country* fame, to join a 1956 expedition and write a small book about it.

After his first expedition in 1953, Haldeman made 12 trips in search of a city he never found but whose existence he never stopped believing in. Two books about this fabled place quoted Joshua extensively on the subject. It remains a topic of debate to this day and amateur explorers still delight in leading their own expeditions, although they acknowledge that the Lost City is more likely an unusual rock formation rather than actual ruins. The notion even found its way into the imagination of hotel magnate Sol Kerzner and, drawing on other mythical African cities, served as the inspiration for the luxurious Palace of the Lost City development at Sun City.

Pierre Viljoen remembers well how these expeditions caught the imagination of South Africans. 'It made big news in those days,' recalls Viljoen, a respected Pretoria resident who through his own successful businesses in advertising and publishing would later become friends with Musk's father, Errol. He also knew the Haldeman family by reputation. Pretoria has always been a close-knit community, and successful families are known and remembered. Viljoen's intersection with the Haldemans and the Musks stretches even further to his being an old boy of Pretoria Boys High School, where Elon and his brother Kimbal would complete their schooling. Viljoen remains an active member of the school's old boys' association, and has a close relationship with Bill Schroder, the former headmaster, who himself has had interactions with Musk. The concept of six degrees of separation is very apt when it comes to Pretoria.

'The Haldemans were a very respected family in Pretoria in those days,' recalls Viljoen. 'I used to live in Queenswood and would travel past their house in Soutpansberg Road on my way into town. They had a big house with a big garden on the left-hand side, and old man Haldeman ran his chiropractic clinic from there. His wife ran a ballet and dance school there as well. Joshua and a friend of his named Ponie de Wet made it their goal to find this Lost City of the Kalahari.'

Ponie (Pieter Hugo) de Wet and his wife, Aletta (nicknamed Lettie or Lee), were close friends of the Haldemans. Ponie was himself a successful businessman and shared Joshua's passion for flying and adventure, and the two families would have dinner together every Sunday night. 'Ponie's wife ran a modelling school in Pretoria – the Lee de Wet School of Modelling. It was very well known,' says Viljoen. It was in fact here that Maye Haldeman started her own modelling career at the age of 15.

Maye also remembers the many family expeditions into the Kalahari, in what is now Botswana. She went on eight of these camping trips and recalls how some would last as long as three weeks, with her parents packing everything they needed to survive. She has a photo of her and her siblings sitting on camp chairs around a fire-place with a traditional black three-legged pot in it. All of them are reading books. In the background is the car and the Bellanca aircraft, which was nicknamed 'Winnie'.

'I think my father just loved to explore the unknown, learn about new cultures, and discover new areas; he and my mom never stopped learning. He loved bush-bashing, making his own roads through the desert,'[2] Maye recalls. Her father would 'shoot for the pot' and they lived like true pioneers among the lions, hyenas and leopards.

They were definitely an adventurous couple, and oldest son Scott recalls how his mother entered and won the South African Pistol Shooting Championships, and how his parents also entered the strenuous Cape to Algiers Motor Rally and tied for first place. In 1952, the couple flew all the way to Europe, and as far as Scotland and Norway, in their plane.

It's quite clear that Elon Musk inherited his love of adventure from his grandfather. 'My grandfather moved to South Africa because he wanted to use it as a base for exploration,'[3] he has said. And he's spoken with great pride of his grandfather's many flights, including the claim that he was the first person to fly from South Africa to Australia: 'He did this in a plane with no electronic instruments, and in some places they had diesel and in some places they had gasoline, and he had to rebuild the engine according to whatever fuel they had.'[4]

There is in fact documented proof of the trip – in a historical study of Dr Joshua Haldeman's career by the Canadian Chiropractic Association – which took place in 1954 and involved Joshua's taking a 50 000-kilometre trip up the coast of Africa, across the South Asian coast to Australia, around Australia and back to South Africa. It states that he is considered to have been the only private pilot to have made the trip in a single-engine aircraft.[5]

Maye also recalls how her father would simply map out the

Kalahari on his own with a traditional compass. There was no limit to his sense of adventure, whether it was the Kalahari or the world, as he and his wife flew themselves to international chiropractic conferences. 'Just my dad, my mom, and Winnie, flying over the Pacific in search of the world,'[6] Maye recalled.

But Joshua's love of flying would eventually claim his life. Musk was only three years old when his grandfather was killed in a flying accident in 1974 when his plane hit power lines. As Scott Haldeman, who was studying at the University of British Columbia at the time, tells the story, Joshua and a friend were coming down for a practice landing: 'There was a power line between where both poles were hidden in trees in a forest, and as they came down to land between them the wheels caught on the power line and the plane flipped over and killed them both. I think given a choice, that would have been a way he would have been very happy going.'[7]

Just as his grandfather had searched for adventure in this world, and in the fables of lost worlds, his grandson Elon would go in search of his own worlds – from the deepest reaches of a new world known as the Internet to the deepest reaches of space.

But first Elon Musk would have to negotiate the very real challenges of his own world, which would change drastically early in his life. It would have a profound impact on him. These would be some of the hardest years of his life. A boy lost in his imagination and the exploding ideas in his head would find himself lost at home as his family disintegrated, then lost at school as he first struggled to fit in and then struggled to survive.

Broken Home

MAYE Haldeman was at the lowest point of her 21-year-old life when her former boyfriend Errol knocked on the door of her Cape Town home. He was the last person she expected to see, and the engagement ring he offered her was also the last thing she ever expected from a man she'd shut out of her life.

And now here he stood, at a time in her life when she was questioning everything about herself.

After growing up in an English household, Maye had struggled through a degree in dietetics at the University of Pretoria which was only offered in Afrikaans. She had started a relationship with Errol Musk, but it had been a rocky one and she had broken it off. At the same time, her modelling career – though never her main focus – had started to take off. She won the Vaal Queen competition in 1969, and to this she added Miss LM Radio, and she was also a finalist in the 1969 Miss South Africa pageant, losing out to Linda Collett.

Maye was a stunningly beautiful young woman, and the Haldeman twins were certainly the talk of Pretoria society. But at the age of 21, the stress of her studies, the difficulty of finding a job and the challenges of her relationship with Errol saw her develop an eating disorder. When she finally secured her first job as a nutritional expert with a food company in Cape Town and had to give lectures to nurses about infant feeding, Maye weighed 93 kg.

Her relationship with Errol was over, in her mind at least.

'I was lonely – alone in Cape Town. I wasn't in a happy situation,'[1] she said in a CBS interview in August 2020. And that's when Errol came knocking. 'For two years I didn't see him and the next thing he turned up in Cape Town with an engagement ring.'[2]

Out of the blue, Errol proposed. Maye immediately turned him down. But, according to her, Errol went back to Pretoria and to her parents with the message that she had agreed to his proposal. They were surprised, as they were well aware of his turbulent relationship with their daughter. After sending Maye a telegram of congratulations, they suggested a double wedding with her twin sister, Kaye, who was about to marry her long-time boyfriend. As Maye recalls, before she even had time to comprehend what was happening, invitations had been sent out to 800 guests for the double wedding of the Haldeman twins.

It was a strange time for Maye, and indeed a difficult moment to comprehend, as she explains how she was basically cajoled into a wedding. According to Maye, much of this had to do with the limited telecommunications of the day. Telegrams were standard, and long-distance phone calls (even between Pretoria and Cape Town) were expensive and considered a luxury. The more time that passed between her turning down Errol and his telling an entirely different story to her parents, the more her initial refusal was drowned out by the impending wedding and the wave of well-intended goodwill that went with it. Conflicted between not wanting to marry Errol, wedding plans that were already in the making and a desire not to upset her parents, Maye relented. Weighed down by her low self-esteem and physically at one of the lowest points in her life, with back and knee pain as a result of her weight gain, it appears that Maye simply didn't have the energy but to go along with the plans that had been made for her, and the future that had been decided on her behalf: 'He sure timed it right. I was lonely, and I had thrown out my back and was in pain. I did not have any confidence because of all the weight I had gained. I hated the way that I looked, and I thought that no man would want to date me.'[3] Maye admitted: 'I wasn't attracted to him, but he was persistent.'[4]

Her parents sent her a telegram instructing her to quit her job and return home to Pretoria to prepare for the wedding. She honoured her parents' wishes, as many young women of the 1970s would have done. And in 1970, Maye married Errol Musk, an electrical and mechanical engineer who also lived in Pretoria. 'I thought,' she later recalled, "well, what can be worse? Marriage can't be that bad."[5]

'Then came the years when my life was hell. It's not a time in my life that I like to talk about, because it is so painful. It makes me angry and bitter. That is not what I want to be. After I talk about it, I toss and turn at night. I can't sleep.'[6]

It is a difficult time in the Musk family history, a time that is still shrouded in controversy and conflict. Errol has his version of events, and Maye her own. And Elon is vehement about the man he believes his father to be, going so far as to call him a 'psychopath'. Maye prefers to frame it as nine years of hell, but which resulted in three beautiful children whom she remains close to.

As she tells it, her marriage to Errol was indeed hell from the start. The slightest thing seemed to upset him. On their wedding day, Maye recalls, Errol was furious that their wedding was over-shadowed by the happiness of her sister and her husband, and that they were somehow forced to play second fiddle on this occasion. Then, on their honeymoon, Maye said, they used her savings to fly to Europe, and she did all the unpacking while Errol sat on a couch reading a *Playboy* magazine.

According to Maye, Errol was highly unstable. He would call her dumb and ugly. He would insult her in front of dinner guests, and if they never returned he would blame it on her inferior cooking skills.

'He was cruel in ways that didn't make sense,'[7] she said. In the same CBS interview in August 2020, Maye said, 'When I was married I was told about three times a day that I'm boring and stupid and ugly.'[8]

Perhaps the only thing they had in common was planes. Like Joshua Haldeman, Errol had bought his own plane. But even this brought with it painful memories. While pregnant with Elon, Maye recalls how she helped Errol paint his plane. But he would complain to her if she slowed down because of her pregnancy. 'You're just being lazy and weak,'[9] he reportedly told her.

She remembers how he even complained to a nurse in hospital about how uncomfortable he was while she was giving birth. The nurse told him to rub his wife's back to help ease the pain of her birth. 'What do you mean? She should rub my back,'[10] he shouted.

And when her father died in a plane crash, she said, Errol's response was to ask how much money they would receive. She said he was incensed that it would all go to her mother, and he banned her from seeing her family for two years. When her mother phoned her in secret, he would accuse her of speaking to another man.

The marriage lasted nine years.

Musk has spoken more openly about his father, but still without giving too many details as to the actual scale of the alleged abuse. He has referred to his father as 'pure evil'. In an interview with CBS's *60 Minutes*, Musk said, 'It was not a happy childhood. My father has serious issues.'[11]

He expanded on this in a wide-ranging 2017 interview with

Rolling Stone magazine: 'He was such a terrible human being ... You have no idea. My dad will have a carefully thought-out plan of evil. He will plan evil ... It's so terrible you can't believe it. In my experience there is nothing you can do. Nothing. Nothing. I wish. I've tried everything. I've tried threats, rewards, intellectual arguments, emotional arguments, everything to try to change my father for the better, and he ... no way, it just got worse.'[12]

It has been widely reported that Errol once shot and killed three intruders on his plot in Lonehill, Johannesburg. The sad reality for South Africans is that this would not constitute an act of evil so much as an act of self-defence, which Errol later said is why he was acquitted of any charges.

Errol corroborated this story in a series of posts on his personal Facebook page. Errol had a surprisingly active period on Facebook, where he seemed to reminisce quite freely about a number of elements in his life. And then at other times, as you trawled through his feed, you would find posts supporting conspiracy theories around anything from 9/11 to aliens building the pyramids and COVID-19 vaccines. The comments to his Facebook posts were often the most illuminating as long-lost friends kept contact and recalled favourite memories. And it was in one such series of comments that Errol corresponded with his childhood friend Bobby Snodgrass.

Errol wrote: 'You [Bobby] have always been there for me. Especially when I arrived in Villieria [an Afrikaans suburb in Pretoria] and we had to contend with the vicious Dutchmen [South African slang for Afrikaners]. You showed me how. I was very innocent and completely unprepared ... The things I learned there helped me defend myself and my daughter from six gunmen who broke in ... Fifty-two shots at me (the shells were counted by the police), two from me. Three dead. The Snodgrass way!'[13]

There is one element of Errol's lifestyle that is a common theme, and that all who know him agree upon. 'Errol started succumbing to the allure of girls from about Standard 5 [Grade 7], so our jaunts to the local creek and *kleilat* [a game played with reed sticks and mud balls] fights came to an abrupt halt,' Snodgrass said in my personal correspondence with him. He and Errol have been friends since childhood.

'We lived a few houses apart in the same Pretoria suburb. I was also friendly with Maye. As primary school kids, we got up to all sorts of mischief. There were about three girls in the vicinity of our residence who caught Errol's eye, and he once told me he would prefer to have a girlfriend from the neighbourhood as well as one from school who was from another suburb.'

In an interview with Britain's *Mail on Sunday*, Errol admitted his mistakes: 'I had a very pretty wife, but there were always prettier, younger girls. I really loved Maye, but I screwed up.'[14]

It appears that this ultimately caused the rift between him and Elon. And when Errol later fathered a child with his stepdaughter, Jana Bezuidenhout, the entire family seemed to cut him off.

Snodgrass confronted Errol on his relationship with his step-daughter: 'I exchanged quite a few messages castigating him on crossing the line of "incest", but he convinced me that it was quite acceptable.'

In response to a Facebook message from Snodgrass about this, Errol wrote back: 'I was married to her mother for two years from 1992 to 1994. Her mother remarried several times so there must be several stepfathers. I only saw Jana for the first time in about 2015, after about ten years … when she contacted me and asked for help as she and her boyfriend were "desperate" and she was contemplating the worst. I helped from then on but saw very little of her as they lived far away. Only when her boyfriend threw her out of his rented room onto the street, with her belongings, did I suggest she come here. She stayed for about four days before her boyfriend begged her to return. But without sounding trite, it takes two to tango.'[15]

The story of Errol Musk is filled with controversy, intrigue and, depending on who you speak to, a substantial amount of myth. Following Musk's revelations about his father in *Rolling Stone*, and on being asked for comment by the writer, Errol emailed the following response: 'I've been accused of being a Gay, a Misogynist, a Paedophile, a Traitor, a Rat, a Shit (quite often), a Bastard (by many women whose attentions I did not return) and much more. My own (wonderful) mother told me I am "ruthless" and should learn to be more "humane". But I love my children and would readily do whatever for them.'[16] Maye, though, has a different recollection of Errol's mother, who she says actively encouraged his hurtful nature.

Those who knew Errol in his younger days paint the picture of a highly intelligent and successful man with obvious flaws. But a man unique in every sense, much like his son Elon. 'Errol's parents, Jock and Cora, smoked heavily. And Jock drank like a fish. He was a functional alcoholic,' recalled Snodgrass in our correspondence. 'His mother was the smart one. Michael, his younger brother by five years, never took to drink or cigarettes. Michael is still my dermatologist, and during our annual mole patrols and reminiscences of yesteryear's pranks and frivolities, we always come to the same conclusion about Errol's massive IQ and depleted EQ.'

Errol's IQ was certainly never in question and found its outlet in both business and politics. Errol was politically active in the Pretoria community as an opponent of apartheid and a member of the Progressive Federal Party (PFP), the forerunner of today's Democratic Alliance. At the age of 25 he was elected as a city councillor for Sunnyside, the youngest at the time. 'This made me the first progressive English-speaking Pretoria city councillor in 24 years, and the first person to run a successful campaign and win against the apartheid National Party government at that time,'[17] Errol wrote on his Facebook page.

He recalled how John Vorster, who on the day of Elon's birth was appealing to Afrikaans students at the University of Pretoria to apply their minds to a race solution for South Africa, used to call him 'Boet' (Brother), while PW Botha addressed him as 'Geagte mnr. Musk' (Dear Mr Musk).

'I was active in opposing the Nationalist Party and their apartheid. I did not run away. I made an effort and an attempt to address change as best as I could. Not only did I attempt to enter the political spectrum to try and change the status quo, I actually successfully ran for other positions and was elected. Sadly, it was always a David and Goliath situation at the time. But it clearly demonstrates my views and a desire to change South Africa. Please appreciate that in those days opposition to the apartheid regime was done at considerable risk to me and my family.'[18]

It was during this time of political activity that Pierre Viljoen first crossed paths with Errol Musk: 'It was in the mid-Seventies. I was friendly with Hansie Steyn, the owner of the famous Steyn's Garage in Pretoria. They were also a very prominent Pretoria business family. Hansie hosted a dinner for Errol at his home in The Willows. He said Errol had just become the youngest city councillor, and he invited me to join them. That's where I first met Errol.'

According to Viljoen, there was nothing obviously untoward about the man he met: 'He was a bright guy and was doing well. He'd married into the Haldeman family. Errol said to me he knew very few people socially because he worked so hard. I invited Errol to a social occasion at my house and we became friendly, but only on a social basis.

'I never had any business dealings with him. I've subsequently heard all these stories about him, and I suppose people put their best foot forward in a social setting, but I found him to be a fairly happy and social guy. He loved a party…He never spoke about why his marriage broke down. But he was fond of the ladies. Errol was full of life. He was a forceful sort of guy in that one had the feeling that he was a go-getter. He wasn't shy to talk about his successes. He had many business interests.'

Errol's business success coincided with the 'golden' years in Pretoria, and indeed South Africa. Golden years that were quite literally carried by the gold the country's mines produced. In the 1970s, South Africa was the world's leading producer of gold, and it accounted for over 21 per cent of the country's GDP.

'It was after World War II, and the Sixties and Seventies were the golden years of the country then. Of course, that's if you were a privileged white family. The war was over, the economy was booming, the gold price was good, farming was good, and things were developing,' says Viljoen. There was a wave of optimism and success, and Pretoria's social scene was buzzing. For a successful young businessman with political ambitions such as Errol Musk, it was the perfect environment in which to see and be seen.

Snodgrass also remembers Errol as a gifted man who was a tremendous success. As he posted in a series of messages on Errol's Facebook page, 'Errol became hugely successful because he was a brilliant engineer. Elon was fortunate to have inherited Errol's gifted genes and became even more successful. If ever there was a family that made the world a better place for everyone then it must be the Musks … Elon has a great imagination, just like his dad; growing up with Errol was like being on another planet. As kids we were just not smart enough to separate Errol's facts from his fiction. Elon obviously, like the proverbial apple, takes after his father. Having said that, if it wasn't for his unrealistic imagination I very much doubt whether he could have achieved what he has accomplished so far, and I am sure he will put someone on Mars in our lifetime … I grew up with Errol and became very frustrated when as kids he would talk about aliens and spaceships rather than joining us in a game of soccer or cricket … Indeed Errol is a wise father. He inculcated, both genetically and by example, the gift of imagination in Elon's DNA. Everything Elon has accomplished bears some of Errol's genes and influence.'[19]

There is no doubt that the children of Errol and Maye Musk enjoyed a privileged childhood in Pretoria in those years, although Errol baulks at the suggestion that Elon in particular owes his success to this. According to Errol, his own opposition to apartheid and Elon's decision leave South Africa at 17 for Canada is enough indication that the family did not directly benefit from the apartheid system.

Responding to an article on the website *Business Insider* on 28 February 2021, which he said was factually incorrect, Errol wrote: 'I believe this [Elon's decision to leave South Africa] is a clear indication of his willingness to not support the political suppression in the country. Let me add that for a young man aged 17 to make this decision may sound easy and simple but it was not, and yet he stuck to his guns. What is factual is that both my sons refused to serve in the legislated mandatory military service of South Africa as we all deemed this to be inappropriate.'[20]

One of the many stories that swirl around Errol refers to his alleged ownership of an emerald mine in Zambia, which has been said to be a contributing factor to Elon's success. Errol admits that, for a time, he did own a share in a Zambian emerald mine. But, according to him, this lasted for about five years: 'Initially the trade was fairly good, but it collapsed in 1989 when Russia began producing perfect lab emeralds at one tenth the price. Income from this source consequently abruptly died.'[21]

But he rejects any suggestion that Elon benefited either from this brief business partnership in Zambia or from being a white South African under apartheid: 'Neither was it [the emerald mine] beneficial to Elon's success in the USA, starting in about 1999 … It is necessary to acknowledge the wrong and oppressive nature of apartheid and we do need to recognise the pain and suffering it caused for many South Africans, but I do not feel it is fair to associate any of that with what Elon has achieved through hard work since he left South African shores as a teenager of 17.'[22]

Yet it's obvious that the very nature of being white and of means in South Africa at that time was privilege enough.

But the fact that he was somehow given a fast track to success is something that clearly rankles with Elon. The emerald-mine story, and the fact that it keeps coming up in almost any biographical material about him, is a particular source of frustration for him. It first surfaced in a *Business Insider* article in 2018. Elon has directly spoken out about it, particularly the insinuation that the mine was an 'apartheid deal' that he somehow benefited from.

Again, there is only Errol's version of events to even suggest the mine existed in the first place, although his response to *Business Insider* was corroborated by Pieter van Niekerk, who said he was a partner with Errol in a consulting engineering business in Pretoria. 'Everything he states in this article is correct,' Van Niekerk wrote on Errol's Facebook page.[23]

Intrigued by the controversy, American journalist Jeremy Arnold has pursued the story. Arnold was on a crusade of his own that strangely intersected with the world of Elon Musk. Musk has long had a negative perception of journalists, fuelled largely by what he believes is the media's lack of proper research and fact-checking. As a result of his experiences with the media, Musk has even gone so far as to suggest that he would like to establish some form of media accountability . Some of Musk's companies, surprisingly, do not even have a PR department. In a world of traditional CEOs, Musk is that rarest of individuals, one who handles most of the media himself. He controls the narrative. He decides when to speak and when not to. And most often, he will do so not through press releases or media launches but through Twitter. Even trying to get hold of him for an interview is an almost impossible task.

As a journalist, Arnold shares a similar concern for the role journalism and journalists are playing in this new world where more people than ever in history have access to information. And the quality of that information is a concern. Arnold has spent several years showcasing examples of what he calls 'bad explanations' by the media. And he has focused exclusively on the mainstream media, the sources people are told to trust implicitly – from the BBC to *The New York Times*. Arnold has made it his personal mission to correct this. He picks the biggest media outlets because they are the most public, and he believes that if he can show the errors or inconsistencies in their reporting, there is a greater chance of something being done to improve the situation.

So with outlets such as *The Independent* newspaper in the UK, *Forbes* magazine and many others continuing to perpetuate the emerald mine story that originated in *Business Insider*, Arnold went to the source – Errol himself. The result was a long-form article[24] that corrected several inaccuracies around the story, and to which Elon himself tweeted a link. He was sick of hearing that his fortune was built on the back of apartheid and mining rights in Africa.

I contacted Arnold directly, and he was happy for his investigation to be reproduced here: 'Errol had, in his own words, very limited involvement. From the way he put it to me, it was a handshake deal with a Panamanian man that resulted in something like 110 emeralds up front and then a semi-regular trickle of rough stones over a few years following. There was never formal owner-ship.'[25] From Arnold's research, there is no paperwork to corroborate any of this: 'Errol said the man in question passed away in 2019.'[26]

Elon has called all of Arnold's research accurate. Arnold even spoke to one of Elon's college roommates, Adeo Ressi, to try and get a sense of whether there was any truth to the suggestion that Musk's success was the product of a silver-spoon family background and that he rode this to the top. According to Arnold, 'the unanimous testimony I got (which fits with the public record) was that Elon was painfully thrifty and had a high appetite for unglamorous work. And I don't take these to be common qualities among those reliant on their family wealth.'[27]

Yet Errol's success, and the possible launchpad it provided for his son Elon, would always be an easy target. According to Errol, he at one point owned six houses in the wealthy Pretoria suburb of Waterkloof Ridge, from Victoria Street down to Julius Jeppe. This neighbourhood has always been among the wealthiest and a haven of old money. It is a suburb of mansions with vast gardens behind high walls. Its streets bear the names of British royalty and the wealthy pioneers who helped found and develop modern Pretoria, and are home to diplomats, business leaders and local celebrities. It boasts some of Pretoria's most expensive real estate, and Errol's claim that he once owned several houses here would be an indication of the kind of wealth he had: 'I rented to embassies as the houses were all in "Embassy Lane". In total I had six houses in Waterkloof proper. The house Maye and I lived in, and where Elon and the kids grew up, is now the headquarters of the United Nations for the Southern Hemisphere (in Victoria Street).'[28]

Errol's three children have all become wildly successful. Tosca, the youngest, is a filmmaker and cofounder of Passionflix, a streaming platform and production company specialising in romance movies. Kimbal, two years older than Tosca, is a chef and restaurateur who is leading a crusade to change the way Americans eat through increased access to 'real food' and the construction of Learning Garden classrooms in schools throughout the United States. And then there is Elon, the oldest. The richest human on Earth. And a man now devoted to making humans an interplanetary species.

For all his own success, Elon has been dogged by claims that he benefited greatly from his father's wealth, although no real evidence of this exists. He claims he received no financial support from his father whatsoever when he left South Africa. Yet Errol has claimed to have provided the seed capital for Elon's first company, Zip2.

Elon does indeed have a complicated relationship with money, which perhaps explains his frustration and often angry outbursts that nothing but his own hard work and determination brought him the fabulous wealth and success he now enjoys. He claims not to be motivated by money at all, living a fairly simple life and not indulging in any personal excesses. Most of his fortune he ploughs back into other companies and projects. His clothes are often just a simple black T-shirt and black denim, or a plain black suit. There is the occasional purchase of an expensive car, but even here he seems more motivated by the uniqueness of the vehicle than simply buying the best on the market, such as when he bought on auction the Lotus Esprit that featured in the James Bond film *The Spy Who Loved Me*. In October 2021, infuriated by the US's complex corporate tax structure and by insinuations that billionaires such as himself are benefiting improperly from unrealised gains and using these as a means of tax avoidance, Musk did what he does best: he launched a Twitter poll asking whether he should sell a chunk of his Tesla stock. With a slight majority voting 'yes', Musk followed through and sold ten per cent of his stock, purportedly to make a point to the legislators. He tweeted that much was being made of 'unrealized gains being a means of tax avoidance'.

In those early years in Pretoria, though, his father was more focused on building his wealth than in finding ways to get rid of it. As a mechanical engineer, Errol had a similarly pragmatic approach to raising his children. He viewed Tosca, Kimbal and Elon through the lens of project management. Errol reflected, once again on his Facebook page: 'In some ways my children were projects and my job was to complete the project in the best way possible. One issue that was tantamount in my approach to my children: your brother(s) and/or sister(s) is the closest person you will ever have in your life, so never ever alienate one another. Rather cut off your right arm first. I had seen how in so many families this was not the case and the terrible results that came of it.'[29]

To illustrate his point, Errol makes a claim that Elon has subsequently denied: 'When I sent money for Zip2 I insisted that Elon include Kimbal in any venture. To do this Elon actually gave up one year, but used it wisely to obtain a second degree at UPenn [University of Pennsylvania]. The results speak for themselves.'[30]

According to Elon, 'He [my dad] was irrelevant. He paid nothing for college. My brother and I paid for college through scholarships, loans and working two jobs simultaneously. The funding we raised for our first company came from a small group of random angel investors in Silicon Valley ... He [my dad] said rather contentiously that I'd be back in three months, that I'm never going to make it, that I'm never going to make anything of myself. He called me an idiot all the time. That's the tip of the iceberg, by the way.'[31]

Yet something in his father's words did hit home. Kimbal is a board member for two of Elon's biggest companies, Tesla and SpaceX. And for all the conflict between father and son, Errol spent possibly the most time with Elon. After the divorce, Maye and the three children initially moved into their Durban holiday home. Errol moved to his smallholding in Lonehill. She then moved the family to

Bloemfontein, where she had a dietetic internship at a local hospital.

But it was at this point that Elon made a curious decision. Sparked by what he said were feelings of sorrow for his father, he decided to go and live with Errol in Johannesburg. According to Maye, they were all living in a one-bedroom flat in Bloemfontein at the time Elon left to join his father: 'Kimbal and Tosca slept in the bedroom and I slept in the living room/kitchen. It was the doctor's quarters. I stayed there while I worked in the hospital and completed my studies.'[32]

Maye said she met another man after her divorce. This too was a strange relationship for her. From the moment they met, she says, he was determined to marry her. They became engaged, and then he made another model pregnant. The couple actually moved in next door to Maye.

Asked in the CBS interview in 2020 why Elon left, Maye said: 'Elon went to live with his father when he was ten because Errol had two encyclopaedias, and then he got a computer. That was something I could never afford. Then at the age of 13, Kimbal went to live with them as well because he was missing his brother. I had them every weekend. I'd pick them up on Friday afternoon and take them back every Sunday night. Tosca didn't want to live with her father at all. I tried to let her stay weekends there, but then she'd call me crying and I'd go and pick her up.'[33]

Elon has since said it was a decision he regrets.

Based upon the many varied and sometimes contradictory views of Errol, the constant seems to be a highly intelligent man driven to succeed at any cost, a man who would belittle those he deemed inferior to him and a serial philanderer.

In my personal correspondence with Bobby Snodgrass, he said: 'Errol has many psychological flaws. I'm schooled in economics and business so human behaviour is part of the curriculum.

However, my wife did clinical psychology. While Errol was serving contractual time at Eskom, who gave him a bursary to study electrical engineering at the University of Pretoria, he was a regular visitor to our home. My wife detested his presence ... On the flip side, he has an IQ of 140 with a strong listing towards the natural sciences. He continually reminded you how stupid you are. His brother Michael was regularly called an idiot. Once, when we compared our maths results in Standard 5 [Grade 7], he always scored in the nineties and I was lucky to get in the fifties. He remarked how close I was to failing and asked me how it felt to be stupid. As a child it hurt, but we remained friends because his flip side could be very charming. I went on to graduate in economics and later did a master's *cum laude* from the prestigious University of Liverpool. The point is, I wasn't that stupid.

'As kids I was physically stronger and more athletic than Errol, who was not fat but definitely chubby and slow out of the starting blocks in track events. He was also smart enough to avoid being on the receiving end of my left jab.'

Speculating about how the break in the relationship between Errol and Elon occurred, Snodgrass said: 'Elon, as a youngster, was a sensitive and bright boy and showed much independence from the age of four. When Maye left and the two boys stayed with Errol, Errol's negative influence took its toll. I believe Elon when he says that nothing he did was good enough in the eyes of his father.'

While it may have been a financially secure childhood, Musk is adamant that 'I did not have a good childhood. It was not happy.'

Apparently deprived of any real love and affection from his father, he retreated into his own world of encyclopaedias and science fiction. Inwardly, he was growing beyond comprehension with a vision and imagination that had no borders. But outwardly, he was awkward and a loner – a 'strange child'.

As a child he often told himself, 'I never want to be alone.' Yet many of his peers at school described him as a loner.

In fact, it was the sight of a lonely Elon Musk at his new school that made him his first real childhood friend.

Educating Elon

DANNY Warnick was sitting on the steps of Hatfield Primary School in Pretoria during break and trying to solve the latest school craze – a Rubik's Cube – when the new kid walked past. The kid looked a little strange. And he looked lonely.

'So, I decided to befriend him,' says Warnick. Within a few days, his new friend Elon had helped him solve the Rubik's Cube. And from there, Danny Warnick and Elon Musk became best friends.

Warnick and his childhood relationship with Elon Musk surfaced through a school photo. In tracing the life of a man who has made his billions in technology and the Internet, it's hardly surprising that the digital world should prove to be fertile ground. In a Facebook post, Warnick shared a photo of the Standard 5 (Grade 7) class at Hatfield Primary School in 1983. 'Notice the boy second row left and the name,' he wrote on the post, 'Elon Musk'. There, wearing plain grey shorts and white-collared short-sleeve shirt, stands an awkward-looking boy, his arms stiff by his side as he stares at the camera. Already, Musk appears out of place among the smiling young faces around him. A boy sent to school a year early because of his genius, but an awkward and introverted child who just never seemed to fit in.

From that class photo, I tracked down Warnick. Among the many leads I followed from people who claimed to know Musk or his family, Warnick was one of the very few to agree to speak on the matter. Perhaps because he spoke the truth when he said he was Musk's best friend at school. The many others who boldly proclaimed on Facebook posts or in groups that they knew Musk suddenly went quiet or refused to say more when I contacted them directly. And often it became more a case of 'Well, I knew of him …'

'I think what helped is that we had the same interests,' Warnick says when we speak on the phone. 'I was also a shy, introverted kid, and he was as well. He was quite a loner. He was also quite odd-looking, and he had these huge braces. To me he was a bit like that Sheldon dude in the TV series *Big Bang Theory*.

'But Elon was a very pleasant guy once you got to know him. He was very mature for his age and not an emotional character. He was very factual, and you knew exactly where you stood with him. I'd say our friendship wasn't typical of children of that age. But we had great times.'

That's not the only thing that stood out for Warnick.

'From the moment we met I could see this guy was way above his grade in intelligence. He was very competitive in the maths class especially. We had a running competition between the two of us to see who could score the best on a maths paper. Our school principal, Mr Henry Alleman, had a PhD in maths and Elon and I really looked forward to his class while the other kids hated it. Elon always beat me in maths. He was highly intelligent in maths and science. But if you asked him to catch a bus from Hatfield to Church Square, he wouldn't be able to do that. He was socially quite awkward like that. I think his sister, Tosca, said the same thing.'

She did indeed. To his family and to a friend such as Warnick, Musk appeared quite at home in his own world, but very out of place in *the* world.

Musk arrived at Hatfield Primary School midway through Standard 2 [Grade 4]. His father had taken him out of Waterkloof House Preparatory School, a private boys' school in Brooklyn, Pretoria, where money and status were the language. Errol had decided his child might be better suited to a government school that would offer him more of the real world and 'normal people'. Musk's new school, in the Pretoria suburb of Hatfield, certainly offered such an opportunity.

Hatfield always had its own unique charm, which it retained far longer than many of the city's other suburbs because of its location on the edge of the city centre. It was a bustling residential suburb by the 1930s, and some of its landmarks became Pretoria icons. The Hillcrest Public Swimming Pool, built in 1935, was Pretoria's first public pool and for many years its only Olympic-sized pool. On hot summer days, families would come here to relax on the lawns, and it was also the venue for highly competitive school galas.

Hatfield Primary School, located on the corner of Duncan and Schoeman streets, opened its doors in 1916. Surprisingly, Musk's primary school is only a short drive away from Soutpansberg Road, where his mother grew up. Hatfield's primary and high schools developed a vibrant and youthful culture that fed into the student life of the nearby University of Pretoria.[1]

Sean Schulze attended Hatfield Primary in the time Musk was there, and remembers those years well. Sparked by the photo posted by Warnick, he remembered Musk as an intelligent and interesting boy. In a follow-up interview, Schulze was also one of the rare few able to follow through with his claims: 'I have fond memories of Elon. He was interesting company. His conversation was always a little more cerebral and meaningful than that average kid at school, and I always remember having enjoyable conversations with him. I also enjoyed playing chess with him. And I remember him being very interested in the science fiction books of Isaac Asimov.'

But so many others had hardly noticed the future billionaire in their midst, and were surprised to be reminded that they once went to school with Elon Musk. It's a theme that runs throughout Musk's school years, of a boy who passed almost unnoticed through the school halls.

Warnick, though, did notice him, and the friendship he and Musk forged was by far the closest in the short time they were together: 'I was his best friend from Grade 5 to Grade 7. Today, kids would call it BFFs. Hatfield was still very much a suburb in those days before it became the business district it is today, and his dad owned one of the houses close to the school, on the corner of Duncan and Burnett St where there is now a filling station. He used this as his office. Elon and I used to go there after school and do our homework together.

'Their home was on the plot in Lonehill, and they would drive through every day. I spent many weekends with Elon on the plot in Lonehill.'

As much as Elon fitted the mould of the nerdy, geeky type, Warnick says there was definitely another side to him: 'He definitely wasn't a sporting type at all. He never played sport in primary school. When it came to ball sense, he had two left feet. But he also wasn't the typical just stay-at-home and play TV games type. Sure, he was very much into his superhero comic books. So was I. But on the plot at Lonehill, we'd do a lot of outdoor things. They had a couple of horses, and his dad, Errol, was wealthy as far as I was concerned. Elon had everything he could've wanted.

'I came from a very average middle-class family, and his dad was quite wealthy by our standards. His dad had a passion for sports cars and luxury cars, and it was always a treat for me when we used to drive through to their plot in a Rolls Royce or a Porsche or a Maserati.

'On the plot, Elon had all the toys a boy could want. We rode around on little motorbikes and would shoot BB guns and get up to all kinds of mischief that boys do. We were also both into aviation and radio-controlled aircraft. And in the evenings we'd play chess and TV games, and read comic books.'

It was on one such occasion, while chasing around on the plot with their BB guns, that Musk accidently shot his best friend.

'He shot me in the forehead. I was so angry that I chased after him. Elon ran away and hid in the stables. When I found him, I took a shot at him as well. He started screaming like a murdered cat.'

Apart from this incident, Warnick remembers it as a very happy time. And he recalls Elon being just as happy as a child: 'He got along really well with his dad. His dad was divorced at that stage. His brother and sister were living elsewhere in South Africa. But Elon always seemed happy, and it never looked like a strained or difficult time in his life. He seemed more than happy. I only ever met his dad. I never met his other siblings or his mom. If I'm not mistaken, his younger brother Kimbal was at school in Bloemfontein at the time. It could've been Grey College, I'm not sure. I know nothing about his sister, Tosca. She was hardly ever mentioned in the time I was friends with him. I met the grandparents on a few occasions.

'In later years, when Elon moved to Canada and then the United States, I think slowly a rift started developing between him and his dad. I don't know why. His dad also had mixed fortunes, and his fair share of ups and downs.'

Warnick remembers Errol as being quite a hands-on father with Elon: 'As far as my childhood memories go, his dad always took us out on trips and we went water-skiing on the Vaal River. Errol and

Elon were both accomplished water-skiers, and they taught me. I went on to become a provincial water-skier because of them. His dad had also bought a game lodge in the Hoedspruit area and we went out there once or twice.'

And he remembers Errol as actively encouraging Elon's aptitude for maths and science, and his general curiosity about the world: 'His dad would always play car games with some maths and science involved. So he'd ask things like how far in kilometres do you think that hill is? He'd speak to us about aircraft and aviation, but on a more senior level than what you would do with most children. He'd always encourage Elon to question, and he'd put maths and science into anything he did with us. His dad really pushed the academia.'

What Musk may have lacked in genuine affection from his father was counterbalanced by an environment that stimulated his thinking and the propensity of his brain to soak up information like a sponge. Musk certainly seems to have emerged as a very potent blend of the eccentricities and adventurous, never-say-die attitude ('There is nothing a Haldeman cannot do') of his mother's family, and the logical and engineering genius of his father.

Errol certainly noticed this. In 2015, he told *Forbes* magazine: 'Elon has always been an introvert thinker. So where a lot of people would go to a great party and have a great time and drink and talk about all sorts of things like rugby or sport, you would find Elon had found the person's library and was going through their books. He'd find fun in that, not to say he wasn't a person who would party every now and then.'[2]

It also explains why Errol was hardly as concerned as the rest of the world, Tesla shareholders included, when Elon appeared on *The Joe Rogan Experience* podcast in September 2018 and smoked marijuana on camera. The incident made headlines and caused a few stock fluctuations in his companies. But Errol was unmoved: 'Elon is the most unlikely guy in the world to get high on marijuana. He hates the taste of alcohol and would have a milkshake rather than anything else.'[3] Once again, there is an echo of his grandfather's approach to life; Joshua Haldeman had a general distaste for alcohol.

Speaking on Bruce Whitfield's *Money Show* on Radio 702,[4] Errol also recalled: 'He had brilliant ideas right from the start … Elon has always been a very deep thinker. The kind of things he would come out with as a youngster were always somewhat surprising. For example, when he was very small – about three or four – he would ask me, "Where is the whole world?" These sorts of questions made me realise he is a little different.'

And Maye recalls a boy who read everything he could get his hands on: 'When Elon was young, I noticed that he read everything … Elon remembered everything that he read. He was always absorbing information. We called Elon the encyclopaedia, because he had read the *Encyclopaedia Britannica* and *Collier's Encyclopedia* and remembered everything. That's also why we called him Genius Boy. We could ask him anything.'[5]

Elon himself declared: 'I was raised by books, and then my parents.'[6]

But Maye makes a critical point in what she believes has been the difference between the genius of her son and other geniuses. According to her, Elon has been able to articulate his genius into actually accomplishing things rather than just thinking about them. It's a distinction not just poignant to her.

The science behind genius still cannot fully answer why this is the case, or, rather, why some highly gifted individuals excel and others don't.

Perhaps the most important attempt to answer this question has been the Study of Mathematically Precocious Youth (SMPY), founded by psychologist Julian Stanley at Johns Hopkins University in Baltimore. The study began in 1971, the year Elon Musk was born, and is considered one of the longest-running longitudinal studies of gifted youth.

Stanley's inspiration was a child named Joseph Louis Bates. A local computer science instructor who was running a summer pro-gramme for children had noticed what she called Bates's 'extreme intellectual precocity' and had alerted Stanley. In 1996, in a paper titled 'In the Beginning: The Study of Mathematically Precocious Youth',[7] Stanley wrote, 'I was somewhat hesitant and perhaps even reluctant at first to get involved: there were too many other pressing duties. But I did, and my life and career were never to be the same again.'

Stanley exposed the 13-year-old Bates – or Joe, as he called him – to a series of college-grade aptitude tests, specifically the Scholastic Aptitude Test (SAT), which is the standard college entrance exam in the United States. 'His scores were startlingly excellent,' he wrote. This recalls the computer aptitude test that Elon took at the University of Pretoria at the age of 17. A letter dated 17 May 1989 from the university's Office of the Director: Information Management stated, 'The results were outstanding.' Musk scored an A+ in both operat-ing and programming, despite being a year younger than the other students taking the test.

Stanley discovered something similar with Joe as he exposed him to even more difficult tasks: 'Joe thrived and went on to receive his BA and Master's degrees in computer science at age 17. Then, still 17, he became a doctoral student at Cornell University.'

Over the next two decades of Stanley's research, the SMPY grew from 450 students to 150 000 annually. The children who typically qualified to be part of the study were those who could complete a year-long syllabus of algebra in three weeks. The SMPY later grew from just identifying and developing gifted students to tracking the careers of these students, and it has been the subject of over 400 academic papers and several books.

'We have the evidence to show that if you provide services to gifted children, we can detect differences 40 to 50 years later,'[8] says Camilla Persson Benbow, who was one of Stanley's psychology students and now leads the SMPY, with David Lubinski. The now 50-year-old study still has the same goal: to gather data that shows the connection between early intellectual ability and adult achievement. In a sampling of over 1 600 gifted children, the study found that 560 went on to earn PhDs. The same group registered 681 patents and wrote 85 books and 7 752 scholarly papers.[9]

According to the researchers, 'The findings here indicate that above-level testing at an early age is a helpful tool for identifying individuals with profoundly high ability who have the potential to make great contributions to society in adulthood.'[10] Or, put another way, 'Whether we like it or not, these people really do control our society.'[11] So says Jonathan Wai, a psychologist at the Duke University Talent Identification Programme (TIP), which partners with the SMPY. According to David Lubinski, 'This population is the one that has the most promise to solve some of the most complex problems of our time'[12] – problems such as sustainable energy, carbon dioxide production, electric cars and, ultimately, a second Earth on Mars.

It's quite clear that Musk would have easily qualified for such a study, and would have been classed as a gifted child. It's also clear that Errol's care created an environment of excellence and study that was possibly pushed very hard and at the expense of a more nurturing relationship.

'[I instilled in Elon a work ethic of] "Make every minute count. No gap weekends, never mind gap years,"'[13] said Errol. Musk has retained this almost inhuman work ethic. Maye had a hand in it as well, although hers was born out of sheer necessity while trying to raise three children alone after her divorce. 'I think they saw me working all the time,'[14] she said of what her kids may have learned from her.

Musk admitted in 2018 that the demands of juggling both Tesla and SpaceX saw him working over 120 hours a week and often sleeping on his factory floor. He has since, he said, cut this back to 80 to 90 hours a week. What drives this punishing work schedule seems to be a combination of factors. 'I care a lot about the truth of things, and trying to understand the truth of things,' Musk has said. 'I seem to have a high innate drive, and that's been true since I was a little kid.'[15]

Yet he also admits to being driven by fear. 'The drive overrides fear, but I still feel the fear. It's kind of annoying. I wish I felt it less … I feel fear more strongly than I would like.'[16]

Fear of failure? Fear of disappointing others? Or perhaps a fear that time is running out? 'I have more ideas than time to implement.'[17]

Sometimes, it might even be a fear of his own mind and the constant explosion of ideas. In conversation with Joe Rogan, Musk said: 'I don't think you'd necessarily want to be me. I don't think people would like it that much. It's very hard to turn it off. It might sound great if it's turned on, but what if it doesn't turn off? … It's like running the engine with no resistance.'[18]

It may well even be that there has been an innate drive since childhood to measure up to his father's expectations. Errol's approach to raising Elon may well have unlocked genius, but it most likely also unlocked feelings of resentment that Musk still harbours towards his father to this day.

Nevertheless, Errol provided one critical component that became the launchpad for Musk's inquiring mind and supreme intelligence. And that was giving him access to his first computer.

'When computers came out at the very beginning, it started off with him (Elon) saying he wanted to go on a course to use these new computers,'[19] Errol recalled to Bruce Whitfield.

'When I inquired about these courses, it was under the auspices of Hyperama, and experts were coming from England and all over. I inquired and they said they weren't taking any children. But Elon persisted. This was when he was 11. I was doing some engineering work for Hyperama, and I managed to book Elon a seat at the inaugural lecture for R75, which was a lot of money in those days. It was hosted at the University of the Witwatersrand in Johannesburg.

'He went and they told me he had to sit on the side and keep quiet. He had to dress appropriately, so he was there with a jacket and tie and his primary-school grey trousers. I left him there and went to get a hamburger with Kimbal. It was a three-hour-long lecture, and when we came back and everybody came out, there was no Elon. We waited and waited and finally went into the halls and found the lecture hall. There was Elon with his jacket and tie off and sleeves rolled up in his long grey flannels, four feet high, talking to all these blokes from England. When I walked up, one of these professors, who didn't even bother to introduce himself, said this boy needs to get his hands on one of these computers. So, we got one, thank God at a discount, and with that computer he taught himself, using Disk Operating System, which is DOS, to program. Then in the mid-Eighties I remember him showing me a box with a red light on it and he would say, "This is a modem. With this, computers can talk to one another. If that computer is on the line, then I can talk to a computer in England and ask it questions." He was always switched on.'[20] That blinking red light certainly switched on Musk's brain to the potential of computers and, as he admitted to Joe Rogan, it has never switched off since.

Musk remembers the moment he first set eyes on a computer:

'When I was ten years old, I went into a store in South Africa and saw a Commodore VIC-20. I thought this was the most awesome thing I'd ever seen. You could write computer programs and make games. I'd played Atari and other games when I was six or seven, so the idea that I could create games was really exciting. So that was my first computer. I think it had like 8 KB of memory.'[21]

It was on this computer that Musk wrote his first computer game, called Blastar. He sold it to a computer magazine for $500. Musk was already showing himself to be quite an entrepreneur as he delivered newspapers and even dabbled in the stock market: 'I had various odd jobs … I also did a little bit of stock market stuff when I was about 15 or 16. I actually did pretty well just making bets on some stocks in South Africa. But I just made a few bets that did pretty well. I tripled my initial tiny stake and then that stopped because I just didn't like it,' he said in a 2009 podcast interview.[22]

As much as Errol was determined to encourage his son's genius, Musk's childhood friend Danny Warnick suggests it might have been Errol's age-old penchant for a pretty girl that ultimately got in the way of their relationship: 'I don't mean to be nasty when I say this, but I think Errol was a bit of a playboy. I spent many a weekend with them over a period of two to three years, and often there was another lady in the house. I don't think Elon approved of that.'

Danny Warnick lost contact with Musk after primary school. He went to the Glen High School in the east of Pretoria, while Musk went to Bryanston High School in Johannesburg. The last time they met, Warnick recalls how Musk wasn't particularly keen on going to Bryanston High School: 'I saw him once or twice after primary school. We didn't have cellphones then. The last time I saw him was some time in Grade 8 [Standard 6]. We'd spent the weekend on the plot in Lonehill. I drove with him and his dad on the Monday morning, and his dad dropped him off at Bryanston High and then took me home. Even then, he wasn't keen to go to school. He wasn't picked on in primary school, but in high school he was singled out. As I said, he was kind of odd-looking with these big braces, and because of that, you know what kids are like. He reminds me of that typical nerd versus jock story.'

After school, Warnick became involved in the motor industry and is now manager of a Mercedes-Benz dealership and owner of his own motor vehicle brokerage company in Pretoria. 'I'm not close to what Elon has become,' he jokes, adding that he is now happy to watch Musk's astounding success from the sidelines: 'It actually started filtering through about ten years ago. I come from a large family with four sisters and they all knew Elon was my friend. You'd see articles here and there about him. But then one of my sisters said Elon Musk is in the newspapers and media quite a bit. It was when he sold his company Zip2. I always thought he'd do well, but now here's this guy reaching for the stars. I thought, damn, I should've stayed in contact with him.'

A soft-spoken man, Warnick now has no contact whatsoever with the Musk of his past. He expresses some sadness that Musk has cut all of his ties to South Africa and never even mentions the country of his birth: 'I haven't had contact with him since primary school. He doesn't seem very concerned or interested in South Africa. He never mentions the country. I don't know if he has a dislike for it or if it just doesn't feature on his radar.'

And he says he feels uncomfortable about suddenly popping up on Musk's radar as a long-lost friend. But the past did bump into him. It was while walking around Pretoria's Brooklyn Mall that Musk's past stared him right in the face: 'I bumped into his father, Errol, a couple of years ago at the Brooklyn Mall. He gave me Elon's personal email address. At that stage Elon was already very well known. I sent him an email, and never heard back from him. But I kind of feel that now that he's a rock star, I don't want to just all of a sudden rekindle that friendship.'

A friendship that began on the steps of Hatfield Primary School, and around the shared desire to solve a puzzle. A Rubik's Cube.

But there is one particular memory of Elon Musk that Warnick treasures: 'When we had our graduation at Hatfield Primary School, I won the maths cup for that year. I still remember the name of it. It was called the Barrowman Cup. For some reason, that final year I was able to pip Elon to the post on that one. He was mad as hell about that.'

The other memory, of an unhappy Elon Musk being driven to Bryanston High School that last Monday morning Warnick saw him, would prove just as poignant.

For Elon Musk, high school in Bryanston would present a far greater challenge than any maths competition.

Broken Bones

IN 2013, Elon Musk graced the cover of *Time* magazine as one of 'The 100 Most Influential People in the World'. On 15 May 2013, Bryanston High School issued a post on Facebook congratulating Musk: 'Congratulations to past Bryanstonian, Elon Musk, on making the *Time* Magazine's 100 Most Influential People in the World list (and cover) for 2013.'

As proud as the school was of one of its former pupils, Musk's memories of his time at Bryanston High School are hardly pleasurable.

That morning in January 1984, when Danny Warnick remembers Musk being dropped off at Bryanston High to begin Grade 8 [Standard 6], began a period in his young life that was not only one of his most harrowing but also very nearly killed him.

The awkward, shy, geeky-looking kid was now no longer just a passing amusement and slight oddity. In a culture and environment that turned a blind eye to bullying as simply 'boys being boys' or a rite of passage towards manhood, Musk became a target. He was bullied relentlessly and viciously. Being younger than many of his peers didn't exactly help: 'I was almost beaten to death, if you would call that bullied,' he said in a *60 Minutes* interview.[1]

Former students of Bryanston High School from that era have spoken out on social media about the out-of-control culture of bullying that existed at the school. Many have mentioned by name gangs of individuals who prowled the hallways; for those who suffered at their hands, the physical scars may have been temporary, but the emotional scars have lasted a lifetime.

Some saw it as simply a part of growing up, something to be endured, and something as much a part of the fabric of the school system as homework or teachers shouting. Others dismissed it as 'Africa is not for sissies'. But for Musk, it quite literally was a matter of survival, as he was mercilessly targeted by a gang of bullies: 'For the longest time, I was the youngest and the smallest kid in the class because my birthday just happens to fall on almost the last day that they will accept you into school, June 28th. And I was a late bloomer. So, I was the youngest and the smallest kid in class for years and years. The gangs at school would hunt me down – literally hunt me down,'[2] he said.

The worst beating he ever suffered put him in hospital. While sitting at the top of a flight of stairs, he was kicked in the head by a group of seniors. As he tumbled to the bottom, the bullies set on him there as well. Musk was beaten so badly he had to be taken to the Sandton Mediclinic.

Errol confirmed this in a note to the South African financial journalist Alec Hogg. When he read of what Elon had suffered, Hogg wrote an article about the experiences of his own son, Travis, with bullies: 'My late son Travis, similar to the schoolboy Elon Musk in many ways, was also bullied mercilessly at school. Too smart for his own wellbeing, he often suffered the consequences of a quick mouth and late developing body. His mother was so incensed she gave one of the bullies a clout. But even that didn't help. But as tough a time as Travis had of it, Elon Musk's Bryanston bullies set new levels of schoolyard brutality.'[3]

Errol's note to Hogg described how Elon 'was so injured I never recognised him at Sandton Clinic. He was in hospital for two weeks. I laid a charge of assault but the Randburg police declined to prosecute saying it was just "skoolseuns wat rondspeel" (schoolboy highjinks). The school itself was non-committal. Elon was 12. I removed him immediately, driving at first daily to Pretoria Boys High.'[4]

The emotional effect of the bullying was obviously long-lasting. But even on a physical level, it left its mark on the future billionaire. In 2013, Errol wrote on Facebook: 'Elon has recently had corrective surgery inside his nose from being beaten up as a kid at school in the Old South Africa. Elon always gave as good as he got but in the Old South Africa things were rough among whites and NO ONE fought fair. Two held you down while another pommelled your face with a log and so on. New boys were forced to fight the school thug on their first day at a new school. The hatred was endemic.

'Among "adults" a polite glance at someone when entering a bar (if you were stupid enough to go into a bar, which were "men only" then) could get you three days in intensive care. Make that three months if your glance was remotely arrogant. Anybody doubt me on this? Then you weren't here.'[5]

It seems that, in this instance, Musk and Errol have much in common. Errol has recounted how he too was bullied at school: 'I also went to Rietondale [High School in Pretoria], after Hamilton [Primary School, also in Pretoria]. Hamilton in town before that was a nightmare for six months. I came out from England at the time. I'm still looking for Malcolm Watt. Please contact me if you read this, Malcolm. I owe you a broken nose, maybe a bit more. Rietondale was one of the worst of all with the Fishbachs, the Stoltzes and the Larks. I had to fight John Fishbach on my first day there, ten rounds. I was beaten to shit. Hey, I wore sandals. All English kids did. They beat me for that, p....d in my bag and books. Next time I saw Fishbach he was lying drunk in a gutter in Durban. He asked me for sixpence to help him out.'[6]

Errol summed up the way to survive as 'Look down, don't stand out, you know.'[7]

When a reader questioned him about the Facebook post, he responded: 'As for the bars in the Sixties. Hey, I was at the Plaza with my friends when someone kicked a guy called Joe to death outside in the queue. You were not there. Elon went to school in the Eighties. He was in hospital for two weeks, beaten to within an inch at Bryanston. Get real.'[8]

What Errol describes of his school years in Pretoria certainly resonates. In those years, there were running battles between English and Afrikaans kids. While the country was split by the racial divide between black and white, the whites were further split between English and Afrikaans. As an English boy growing up in an Afrikaans suburb, Errol would have certainly been a target as a 'Soutie' or 'Rooinek'. Pretoria, always a more Afrikaans society, had its own culture wars in this sense. Johannesburg, though, was another world entirely. While separated by less than 65 km of national highway, Pretoria and Johannesburg have always been worlds apart. Johannesburg was more English, but it had its fair share of thugs as well, and the Portuguese, Greek and Lebanese gangs were some of the most feared in the city.

Coming from the largely conservative society of Pretoria to Johannesburg would have been a major adjustment for Musk. Lonehill, where Errol had his plot, is less than ten kilometres away from Bryanston, so it made sense to consider Bryanston High School for Elon.

But as much as Musk was a victim, he didn't adopt a victim mentality. Musk said he took up karate and learned to defend himself: 'I started dishing it out as hard as they'd give it to me ... It taught me a lesson: If you're fighting a bully, you cannot appease a bully ... You punch the bully in the nose. Bullies are looking for targets that won't fight back. If you make yourself a hard target and punch the bully in the nose, he's going to beat the shit out of you, but he's actually not going to hit you again.'[9]

Interestingly, this experience seems to have hardened his resolve to do something positive for other people. When he was asked during the *Rolling Stone* interview what his greatest fear was, he said it was the extinction of human civilisation.[10] 'I'm pro-human. I love humanity. I think it's great,' he said when he appeared on *The Joe Rogan Experience*.[11]

After the news broke about Musk's bullying at Bryanston High School, principal John Skelton issued a statement: 'Initially I felt very sad after reading what had apparently happened to him,' Skelton told *News24*.[12] 'The culture of our school is honour, dignity and respect. Every human being is unique and special ... Bullying was accepted as a part of growing up and now we know the impact. In the 1990s, people started realising that bullying is a very destructive force.'[13] In response, Errol, also speaking to *News24*, said: 'South Africa is seen as a jock culture. It might produce intellectual people, but it is not an intellectual culture.'[14]

When Elon was moved to Pretoria Boys High School, where the discipline was stricter, Errol recalls that the bullying stopped.

Many people have speculated that it is this period in Musk's life that led to his severing his ties with South Africa. And it has also led to a great misconception regarding Boys High.

It was widely reported that Musk was approached by former headmaster Bill Schroder for funds to help with several new building projects at the school. This was part of a worldwide drive among old boys to fund projects, such as the building of a new school hall, library and computer centre. It was reported that Musk made a R1 million donation, and then requested of Schroder that the school never, ever contact him again.

But Schroder, who was headmaster at the school between 1990 and 2009, said this was incorrect. In a full statement released to the media, Schroder confirmed that Musk had donated R1 million to the school. He confirmed that when he approached Musk for a second time, he again donated funds to the school. But he corrected what he felt was a lie about the former pupil: 'I was the Headmaster of Pretoria Boys High School from 1990 to 2009 and subsequent to my retirement was asked to head a fundraising exercise over a four-year period. As such, I feel it is important to set the record straight in terms of donations received from Elon Musk, who matriculated at Boys High in 1988.

'It is true that Elon Musk did, at my request, give a donation for R1 million. What is not true is that he disliked the country or the school so intensely that he told me not to approach him again. I, in fact did, and he sent a second donation per that request. I lost contact with him for a while as he changed PAs and on re-establishing contact, a new network for consideration of donations had been put in place and it must be understood that people with that amount of wealth have teams of people who deal with huge numbers of requests for donations. At that point we received nothing further from him.

'It is well documented in a number of biographies that Elon was bullied and an unhappy schoolboy in a school in Johannesburg and was moved to Pretoria Boys High in Grade 10 (Standard 8). There is no evidence that he was poorly treated at Boys High, and when he matriculated he went to Canada, where his mother was living.

'Possibly what upsets me more is that the size of his donation was

leaked somehow. I did the fundraising alone with the help of my secretary of 20 years and one of the bases of the fundraising was that the
amount of a donation was treated in the strictest confidence. I only
targeted alumni and close friends of the school and believe that our
success in raising R32 million in four years was based on the confi-
dentiality factor. Until the publication of this article, the only thing
a member of the Pretoria Boys High community would know is that
Elon Musk did donate as his name appears on a donor board together
with his year group, making no differentiation between some who
gave R100 or R1 million.'[15]

By all accounts, Musk enjoyed his time at Boys High. Kimbal
later joined him at the school. I also attended Boys High and was
five years behind Musk. The school's entire ethos of producing gen-
tlemen who are an asset to South Africa is inculcated in everything it
does. Masters wear gowns, and it is drilled into boys from the minute
they start their schooling there that you stand when an adult enters
a room, you greet teachers and visiting adults as Ma'am and Sir and
not Mr or Mrs, you are never seen in public in uniform where your
socks are around your ankles or your tie is not properly knotted,
and you generally conduct yourself as a school that first opened its
doors in 1901 demands of you by the weight of its history and legacy. For those who have never attended a traditional boys' school, it
can seem an entirely foreign concept. Even the grade system is different. Whereas in those days you were in Standard 6 when you started
high school, and these days you are in Grade 8, at Pretoria Boys High
it has always been Form I. The grades are referred to as forms. The
more disciplined environment of a boys' school indicates that Musk's
bullying did not continue when he arrived at Boys High. It was, of
course, not a perfect school. No school is. But Boys High has always
been determined to celebrate each boy, whether he be a sports star,
an academic genius or a cultural phenomenon. It is a school that,

no matter a boy's background, does not accept what a boy is, and believes far more in what a boy can become.

And it was here, among the pine trees and in the main building, designed by Patrick Eagle, who also designed the Supreme Court building in Johannesburg, that Musk's obsession with space, as well as his genius, became even more clear.

It is quite apparent in the physics marking book of Daniela Albers, Musk's science teacher in Form 5B in 1988. There, in blue ink, it records that 'Musk, E' averaged 80 per cent that year. He gained an academic distinction, beating his closest rival by 13 per cent. According to Albers, the physics quizzes included a 'test on electricity' or electrical circuits, in which Musk beat 20 class rivals. Albers also tested her students on momentum, free fall and inertia – all things a future rocket scientist should know about. Musk just missed out on first place in an exam on momentum but tied for first place on his understanding of Newton's three laws of motion.

Years later, Albers was one of millions who watched SpaceX's first launch, headed by her former pupil from a class that sat at the end of a block in a school on a hill in Pretoria. As Albers had been my science teacher as well, I contacted her to ask for her recollections of Musk: 'For me watching the SpaceX launch, I obviously felt quite proud, thinking, "Gee, hopefully I played a small part." But to be honest, I think he's such an intelligent person he probably could have done it without me,' she said.

And then she reflected on that boy in her class: 'He was a very quiet boy, who sat at the back of the class and just got on with his work. Obviously, he was the highest marked in the class, with a distinction for science at the end of the year.'

But she has a very clear and lasting memento of Elon Musk, one that remained in her class for many years after he left: 'I re-member him bringing a beautiful model of a rocket into class for a project.' And yet she also admitted that she wasn't sure if it was in fact his rocket, because Musk was such a quiet boy who kept largely to himself.

There is every indication that, in high school, Musk remained the shy and introverted boy he had been in primary school. David Johnson, a fellow Boys High pupil at the time, told me: 'I remember Kimbal as a friendly, outgoing guy. Very different to Elon.' Johnson has photos from his school yearbook showing a smiling Kimbal Musk with his date at their matric dance. There is also a 1990 photo of 'Sergeant K Musk' in the school's cadet squad, and further mention of him as sergeant of No 3 Troop on the inspection parade. Similarly, he's seated in the middle in the front row of a 1990 photo of the school's Academic Ties for that year.

The opposite is true for his older brother. In his matric year (1988), Elon doesn't appear anywhere in the school's yearbook, *The Pretorian*, other than on the fourth page as part of 'The Leaving Group of 1988'. The name of 'E Musk' is listed as a member of 'Form 5B: Mrs Marshall'. Musk's name is absent from the 1988 list of 'Digni Laude – Outstanding Scholars for 1988', most notably in the categories of maths and science. But he is mentioned as having earned two matric distinctions, in science and computer studies. He does not appear on the list of Academic Ties either.

'My impression is that Elon kept to himself and was relatively quiet and reserved. I believe he was involved with the computer club at school, but otherwise was not really visible in mainstream activities,' says Gavin Ehlers, who was head boy at the school in 1988.

Even those who went to Bryanston High School struggle to remember much about Musk. In a Facebook group for former Bryanston High pupils, the comments about Musk all have a familiar theme: 'He was very quiet'; 'I cannot remember him at all'; 'He was a quiet, unassuming person.'

'I remember playing chess with him. He was quiet and kept to himself.'

The person who wrote this post was in fact on the school's chess 'A' team with Musk, and in a chess team photo is sitting just one place away from him. Yet Musk kept so much to himself that the chess player hardly remembers more than this.

The comments continued: 'I was in the same group of kids and I don't remember him at all. I wonder who he was friends with and why no one helped him ... Sad.'

'I know someone who was in Elon Musk's class. He said the bullying was out of hand and that Elon was very badly hurt.'

'Who didn't get bullied at school? Part of life. When I told my parents I was getting bullied, my father basically said, "Suck it up buttercup. Life is tough. And it is gonna get tougher. Deal with it."'

'I was in the same year as him. Very quiet kid ... was picked on a lot.'

'His nickname was "Bunny" because of his two protruding front top teeth. He was very quiet, spoke to no one and read all the time. He was teased in the class.'[16]

From his Bryanston High years, there is a school photo of him in the chess team, and another that appeared in a local newspaper where his Standard 8 (Grade 10) class is celebrated for knitting 720 blanket squares for a local charity drive. Musk is pictured top right in the photo. But other than this, Musk seems to have gone through Bryanston High School and Pretoria Boys High School in relative anonymity.

Kimbal, on the other hand, appeared the more outgoing of the two. He matriculated from Boys High in 1990, and he did so with only one distinction less than his brother – for history. An essay he wrote in Afrikaans, 'Die Geskiedenis van Oorlog' (The History of War), appeared in *The Pretorian* of 1990. And he played first-team basketball for his school.

Even Bill Schroder doesn't recall much about the boy who he would years later approach – along with a host of other Old Boys – to assist with the school's fundraising efforts. I know Schroder, affectionately called 'The Boss', from my own time at the school and in my subsequent involvement with the school. When we spoke about Musk he said, 'I remember being called by *Time* magazine to comment for a cover article they were doing about him, and I had to tell them that I couldn't really say much because I didn't know him that well. I asked some of the teachers who had been in the school a long time, and some had vague memories of him, but also not enough to feel they could comment about him.'

But after school, Musk wasted no time in realising his own ambitions. And in his mind, they lay in the United States, where the technology boom was building, and with it this new thing called the Internet that he desperately wanted to be a part of.

PART TWO

Canada Calling

FOR Elon Musk, the end of high school did not necessarily signify the sense of a new world opening up before him. For white South African males, the notion that 'the world is your oyster' had to wait a few years – two years in fact. In the meantime, they belonged to the South African government, and, in particular, to the South African Defence Force (SADF).

By the time Musk reached the end of his secondary education, compulsory conscription for military service was at its peak. All white males between the ages of 17 and 65 had to serve. The arrival of the matric certificate would usually be followed by a brown envelope containing the Notification of Allotment for National Service, which indicated that you had been called up for duty 'in accordance with the provisions of the Defence Act, 1957'. The letter provided the details of the unit you were to report to, the place of service and the duration.

Conscription was the government's response to the increasing threat, both internal and external, from communism (the dreaded *rooi gevaar*, or 'red threat') and the exiled ANC. The growing pressure on the country was beginning to bear fruit, and the South African government responded as it knew best – with the force of its efficient and well-run police and armed forces. As a result, the 1980s was one of the most violent decades in the country's history.

Following the Sharpeville massacre of 1960, the government had cracked down hard on political unrest, banning the ANC and other liberation organisations. The 1976 Soweto uprising, which took place when Musk was still a young boy, was another watershed moment. The government responded to what it perceived as a 'total onslaught' with the 'total strategy', which aimed to mobilise the whole of South African society against the threat from communism and African nationalism. But by the mid-1980s, faced with a more unified attack from various anti-apartheid groups within South Africa, the 'total strategy' was starting to lose impetus. President PW Botha was feeling the pressure from outside as a result of growing international pressure and sanctions against South Africa. Within the ruling National Party there were differing views on the way forward.

By the time Musk's Form V (Grade 12) year ended in 1988, the country was aflame as police clashed with political activists and the SADF was deployed to the townships. The ANC and its military wing, uMkhonto we Sizwe (Spear of the Nation), escalated its campaign of resistance with a series of limpet mines and bombs. The popular Sterland cinema complex in Pretoria and several Wimpy restaurants were bombed. A bomb that exploded outside the Standard Bank in Roodepoort in June, killing four and injuring 18, led *The New York Times* to call it 'the worst South African bombing in a year'.[1] Bomb drills became routine at South African schools.

South Africa was also embroiled in the Border War (1966–1990), a long-running conflict that pitted the SADF against the guerrilla forces of the South West Africa People's Organisation (SWAPO) in then South West Africa (now Namibia). From the mid-1970s, the scope of the Border War expanded, as South Africa sought to influence the outcome of Angola's independence process and subsequent civil war. The SADF made many forays into Angola, ostensibly in pursuit of SWAPO guerrillas, leading to clashes with Angola's armed forces, which were backed by the Soviet Union and Cuba. By 1988, the Border War was at its peak.

The South African government was fighting a war on its streets and on its borders. And for that it required soldiers – plenty of them. Among those who heeded the 'call-up', or compulsory conscription, there were most certainly many who saw it as their duty to defend God and country against threats both internal and external. There were also those young men who had no idea what career path to follow straight after school, and saw two years in the SADF as time to decide what they wanted to actually do with their lives. Others found a sense of community in the brown uniforms they wore, and in the bright smiles on dirty faces gathered together in photos sent home from the Border. And still others may have been attracted by the last opportunity for adventure, to test themselves and 'man up' before settling into the routine of civilian adult life.

But many of the 1791 South African soldiers who died in the Border War[2] were just boys who felt they had no choice. Their call-up papers came, and they had to go. According to historian Graeme Callister, 'For most men, obedience to conscription was not a conscious decision but simply something that had to be done, a kind of rite of passage to manhood that became as naturally part of a white South African male's life as going to school or getting a job.'[3] For Peter Dickens, whose website The Observation Post surveys the totality of South African military history, 'It was a campaign which came about in an age when service in the SADF was part of South Africa's socio-cultural make-up – this was a very normative practice.'[4] In the popular 1984 film *Boetie Gaan Border Toe*, Arnold Vosloo plays a hapless young Afrikaner who at first tries to evade conscription before finding brotherhood among his fellow troops on the Border.

But for a young white South African leaving school with a headful of exploding ideas, this was hardly a moment of freedom.

The End Conscription Campaign (ECC), which had begun in 1983, had also been banned by 1988. The government followed this with even harsher measures for those who ignored the call-up, raising the penalty from two to six years in prison. Magnus Malan, then defence minister, said at the time: 'The End Conscription Campaign is a direct enemy of the SADF. It's disgraceful that the SADF, but especially the country's young people, the pride of the nation, should be subjected to the ECC's propaganda, suspicion-sowing and misinformation.'[5] Malan went so far as to liken the ECC to the banned ANC.

It was in this climate that Musk was preparing to leave school. He would no doubt have read of Charles Bester. After finishing Standard 10 (Grade 12) at St Martin's School in Johannesburg, Bester refused to report for military service, citing his Christian beliefs. He was given a six-year prison sentence on 5 December 1988 and sent to Kroonstad prison.

According to Bester at the time, 'apartheid means separation and its application is a denial of Christ's exhortation to love one's neighbour as oneself. The role the SADF is playing in South Africa underpins the policies of division of the present government. I believe that in order for me to follow a path that will best demonstrate my love for God, my country and my fellow South Africans, I must pursue the way of reconciliation and non-violence. I will therefore refuse to serve in the SADF.'[6]

Musk's own family history, especially that of his politically active father, Errol, meant he was never going to consider fighting for the apartheid government. It was against this background of a country on the brink of civil war and his own desire to get to the US and pursue his interest in the growing technology boom that Musk made a decision. He had to leave South Africa. 'It always seemed like when there was cool technology or things happening, it was kind of in the United States. So, my goal as a kid was to get to go to America basically,' he said.[7]

But going directly to the US was not an option for Musk. Instead, he started planning on returning to the country of his mother's birth – Canada. And even this wasn't as easy as it seemed. Musk had no real contacts there, apart from very distant family whom he'd never even met. He clearly required more time to plan his exit, but it was time he didn't have, with the SADF just as eager to get its hands on him.

So Musk decided to buy himself some time by enrolling at the University of Pretoria in 1989. There is no public record of what he actually enrolled for. In May 1989, Musk was given a computer aptitude test by JLM Wiechers, the university's director of information management. As later publicly shared by Maye Musk on Twitter, Musk received an A+ in both operating and programming, with Wiechers commenting, 'The results were outstanding.'

The details of Musk's time at the University of Pretoria are quite vague, so I made contact with Professor Karen Harris, who heads up the university archives. After a few days of digging in their files, Professor Harris confirmed the validity of Musk's aptitude test, and that he had enrolled for a BCom in financial management at the university. The government did grant a deferment of conscription for those wishing to study first.

But Musk was still very much focused on getting to Canada, and it was clear he never intended to complete his BCom. As soon as he was able to purchase an air ticket, he discontinued his studies at the University of Pretoria.

Musk, not yet even 18 years old, was about to make a very brave decision. He would leave his family behind and fly to Canada on his own. You have to wonder about the conversations he would have had with his mother and father about this. These days, a child leaving home at the age of 17 remains a very complex decision, never mind in the late 1980s. Even more so considering that he left South Africa against his parents' wishes.

'In South Africa, whenever I read about technology and great innovation, it was coming from the United States. That's where I wanted to be,' Musk told the popular talk-show host Charlie Rose in a 2009 interview.[8] 'I tried to convince my parents to move there and neither of them would. They were divorced. My mother later moved back to Canada and then the US. So when I was 17, as soon as I got my Canadian passport, three weeks later I was in Canada.'[9]

Musk had planned to stay with an uncle in Montreal. However, upon arrival he was informed that the uncle was away in Minnesota. According to Musk, he had $2000, a backpack of clothes and a suitcase of books. He was 17 and stuck.

After spending a few days in the city, staying at a youth hostel, Musk reached out to Mark Teulon, a cousin of his mother's, who lived on a farm in Saskatchewan.[10] The farm was near Swift Current, 170 km west of Moose Jaw, an area rich in Musk family history. In the strangest of ways, Musk had come home. It perhaps wasn't lost on the teenage Musk that the town motto of Swift Current is 'Where Life Makes Sense'.

Musk's grandmother, Winnifred, came from Moose Jaw, and his grandfather and great-grandfather had deep roots in Saskatchewan. And so he bought himself a bus ticket and travelled more than 3000 km from Montreal to Swift Current. From there it was another 18 km to Waldeck, and the Teulon grain farm. He was an adventurer in the grand tradition of his grandfather Joshua. And already, he was an island. The boy who didn't fit in at school, who was always alone and kept to himself, who was happier being in his own head than in the crowd, was now experiencing the freedom of the wide world. He was shaping his own independent nature on the road.

Musk only spent about six weeks on the Teulons' farm, but in that time he showed himself to be more than capable of the hard and unglamorous work of farming as he helped tend to the vegetables and shovelled out the grain bins. As his childhood friend Danny Warnick observed, Musk was not a jock, but he didn't fit the typical mould of a nerd either. Clearing out the grain bins was particularly hard and hazardous work. When a bin was almost empty save for the last bit of grain at the bottom, Musk would have to climb inside, with the only light coming from the small hatch at the top. Farmers describe the bins as dark, dusty, loud and hot – and dangerous. There is the very real danger of either being hurt by the machinery that sweeps the grain or being engulfed by an avalanche of grain and dying of suffocation.

According to a report by Purdue University, more than 24 farmers are trapped in grain bins in any given year in the US Corn Belt. In fact, more accidents occur in confined agricultural spaces than in the mining industry. And on average, one in five grain bin accidents, or 'entrapments', involve teenage boys.[11] Ironically, a robot has been invented to make the process safer, which farmers put inside the grain bin to disturb any potential risk areas in the grain. If Musk had worked this job long enough, he would no doubt have invented something similar.

His cousin said Musk quickly gave you the impression that he was not your normal teenager. 'He was a pretty smart guy. We had that figured out pretty quick.'[12] Musk celebrated his 18th birthday on the farm, and has a photograph taken on the day of himself wearing a cowboy hat and a cap on top of that and holding a hammer.

After leaving the farm, Musk worked as a lumberjack and never shied away from using a chainsaw.

Almost two decades later, Elon Musk – as the founder of SpaceX and working feverishly to build rockets – would hire a bright young rocket engineer by the name of Thomas (Tom) Mueller. Mueller grew up in the small town of St Maries, Idaho, just two and a half hours from the Canadian border. He was a kid who spent most of his time in the library, reading science-fiction books. He was a kid interested in rockets. These were big dreams for a kid from a small town where the mainstay of the local economy was forestry. But Mueller's maths teacher, Gary Hines, noticed his talent. And when Mueller told him he wanted to become an aircraft mechanic, Hines responded, 'Do you want to be the guy that fixes the plane, or the guy that designs the plane?'[13] This inspired Mueller to embark on his studies as a mechanical engineer. But to pay for this, he did what everybody in town did. He did what his own father did. He did what his future boss Elon Musk did. He worked as a lumberjack.

Whether it was a quest to establish his own boundaries or his version of manhood beyond just the pages of books such as *The Lord of the Rings* or *Lord of the Flies* – which Musk has suggested everybody should read – the young South African seemed to enjoy the hard manual jobs he took. And the element of danger in them.

Another job involved cleaning out the boiler room of a lumber mill. Musk took it purely on the basis that it paid well – $18 an hour. Traditionally, manual jobs pay well because they're dangerous. Much like his experience in the grain bins, Musk would climb into the boiler and shovel out the steaming residue. He could only do this for about half an hour at a time before it became too hot, forcing him to climb out again.

But having spent time wandering around Canada doing odd jobs like his grandfather used to do, Musk decided it was time to settle down to his studies.

He enrolled at Queen's University in Kingston, Ontario, and spent his freshman and sophomore years there from 1989 to 1991. After months of backbreaking manual labour, he clearly enjoyed his newfound freedom as a student. 'I had a great time at Queen's. It was fun and interesting. I'd call them formative years,' he said in a 2013 interview with the *Queen's Alumni Review*.[14]

Musk stayed in Victoria Hall, the largest of the university's 17 residences, named after Queen Victoria. Coincidentally, the building's architecture resembles a large X; perhaps this planted a seed in the mind of the future founder of a space exploration company he named SpaceX.

Musk enjoyed every aspect of his student years, and it laid the foundation for a way of thinking and working that would become his philosophy for success. 'In the first two years at university, you learn a lot about a great many things. One particular thing that I learned at Queen's – both from faculty and students – was how to work collaboratively with smart people and make use of the Socratic method to achieve commonality of purpose,' he told the *Queen's Alumni Review*.[15]

The Socratic method, named for the Greek philosopher Socrates, involves a constant dialogue between teacher and student in which the teacher asks a range of probing questions in order to engage the students in more critical thinking and the shaping of their own views rather than just accepting the transfer of knowledge from their teacher.

Musk would later merge this philosophy with the scientific method to develop his own approach to asking questions and problem-solving. In its simplest form, the Socratic method involves the questioning of another person, whereas the scientific method involves the questioning of nature. So the Socratic method has a more inward, interpersonal focus, while the scientific method focuses outward on the world around us. For Musk, if you want to approach a project such as sending people to a new planet, you need both methods in order to effectively mobilise the massive human resources required, as well as the ability to solve the scientific questions of inhabiting a new world completely foreign to Earth.

The Socratic method also shines through in Musk's belief that when pursuing something that is important to you, you should 'seek out negative feedback, because it gets harder and harder to get as you progress in the world'.[16]

And he used this most effectively in the creation of SpaceX. As Musk told the *Queen's Alumni Review*, 'It would have been quite difficult if I'd just started off by cold-calling them (scientists and rocket engineers) and saying that I wanted to start a rocket company. What I said instead – because these people were working at Northrop Grumman, Boeing, and other big aerospace companies – was "Would you mind helping me with a feasibility study to find out if it's possible to make significant advancements in rocket technology? It will involve a few weekends and evenings of your time." I said I'd pay a decent amount for their help, and so they were enthusiastic. We had a series of meetings, and the people I recruited put a lot of thought into it and came to the conclusion that yes, it would be possible to build better rockets than had been made before.

'I essentially led them to a conclusion that *they* created. It was sort of a Socratic dialogue on a technical level. The essence of a Socratic dialogue is that people wind up convincing *themselves*. People are much more willing to change their opinion if you're not forcing it.'[17]

But, ultimately, Musk's decision to go to Queen's was an interesting one forged by a far simpler desire, but one that is no less telling in terms of his childhood and the impact it had on him. Faced with the opportunity to attend Queen's or the University of Waterloo, also in Ontario, Musk was swung not by a better academic programme or research facilities, but by a more basic desire: 'I was going to do physics and engineering at Waterloo, but then I visited the campus … and, you may not want to print this, but there didn't seem to be any girls there! So, I visited Queen's, and there *were* girls there. I didn't want to spend my undergraduate time with a bunch of dudes,' he said in his 2013 alumni interview.[18]

As innocuous as this may seem at first, it does point to an innate desire on Musk's part to find love. This is a man who perhaps finds it easier to build rockets and dream of taking people to Mars than he does to find love on Earth. 'This may sound corny, but love is the answer,' he said on the Joe Rogan podcast as he spoke about his love for humanity and belief in human goodness, and that these are things worth protecting.[19] Lauded as the man who makes science fiction reality, and as much as he has embraced and lived in that world since he was a child, Musk is very much a man in love with the idea of what it means to be human. He has said all along that his desire is not to escape Earth but rather to protect it: 'People think Mars is some kind of escape hatch for rich people. It's not like that at all.'[20] And more specifically, to protect that one thing he believes is unique in the entire universe – human consciousness.

Love and the impact it has on people pervades even some of his business motives. 'How many things can you buy that you love, you know, that really give you joy? It's so rare. So rare. I wish there were more things. That's what we're trying to do, to make things that somebody loves,'[21] he says of Tesla and the goal of producing electric cars.

'What are the set of things that can be done to make the future better? There need to be things that make you look forward to waking up in the morning. You wake up in the morning and you look forward to the day … look forward to the future.'[22] This is another

way Musk has framed the thought process behind his ideas and constant drive for innovation. It is a process surprisingly lacking in strict
capitalist desire from the world's richest man.

And perhaps recalling a father who drove him to excellence at the
expense of love, Musk has said one of his great motivators is 'doing
something useful for other people – that I like doing'.[23] Whether
it's a love of ideas, a love of innovation, a love of making the world
a better place or a love of humanity, Musk is right on point when he
says, 'Love is the answer.'

It's an answer he has searched for since he was a child, and he
has admitted that he grew up thinking, 'I never want to be alone.'[24]
It's an answer he took into every relationship and each of his three
marriages. In his interview with *Rolling Stone* he declared, 'If I'm not
in love, if I'm not with a long-term companion, I cannot be happy.'[25]

In an interview with *Business Insider* in March 2018, Errol
declared, 'What is driving Elon is trying to find the right girl, and
that is very hard, probably the hardest thing on Earth, for you or for
me, for anybody.'[26]

So there was an underlying motive to Musk's decision to finally
settle on Queen's University. And it paid off. It was here that he met
his first wife, Justine (Wilson), an 18-year-old arts student who qualified with a degree in English literature and went on to become an
author of fantasy novels.

For Musk, if love was indeed the answer, Justine posed the first
serious question of the awkward teen: how do I ask her out?

The American Dream

WHEN Justine Wilson first met Elon Musk, she was hardly impressed.

He was nothing like the kind of guy she liked to date. 'He was a clean-cut, upper-class boy with a South African accent who appeared in front of me one afternoon as I was leaping up the steps to my dorm ... He was a scientific type, at home with numbers, commerce and logic,' she wrote in *Marie Claire* magazine.[1]

Her type was more the rebellious and tortured motorbike-riding, leather-jacketed, dark and stormy hero. Justine's early recollections of Musk, though, are of somebody less obviously rebellious and more refined. She remembers him phoning her and always having classical music playing in the background: 'He would ask me out, and I would say no. And he would call me up again and ask me out, and I would say no.'[2]

After telling Justine that he had first met her at a party she knew she hadn't attended, Musk invited her out for an ice cream: 'I said yes, but then blew him off with a note on my dorm-room door. Several hours later, my head bent over my Spanish text in an overheated room in the student centre, I heard a polite cough behind me. Elon was smiling awkwardly, two chocolate-chip ice-cream cones dripping down his hands,'[3] she wrote.

Justine was attracted to the fact that Musk was never threatened by her ambition to become a novelist, and actively encouraged it: 'Previous boyfriends complained that I was "competitive", but Elon said I had "a fire in my soul". When he told me, "I see myself in you", I knew what he meant,'[4] she wrote.

They began dating, but Musk was still set on his plans to move to the US. By now, Maye, Kimbal and Tosca had joined him in Canada. They lived in a small apartment in Toronto, and Maye has recalled how they lived so frugally that she would cut their hair for them.

It appears that Musk had always planned to bring his mother and siblings to Canada. Maye had come over to visit and consider the move but had decided to return home. However, she recalls that when she came back to South Africa, Tosca had made arrangements to sell her car and home, and Maye was simply presented with the paperwork to sign. Tosca felt there was no point in waiting for them all to join Elon.

After two years at Queen's University, where his favourite class was astronomy,[5] Elon transferred to the University of Pennsylvania (often shortened to UPenn), to begin studying physics. There was also a sense that he needed to attend one of the Ivy League universities to give his studies greater gravitas. He graduated with a bachelor's degree in economics from the university's Wharton School, and a bachelor's degree in physics from the university's College of Arts and Sciences. It was at the latter that Musk was given the opportunity to test himself and flex his mental aptitude. He described his senior-year quantum mechanics course as 'the hardest class I ever took. That stuff will mess with your mind.'[6]

Elon's time at UPenn led Errol to share, years later, a story encapsulating the Musk family spirit. Cora Musk, Errol's mother, was said to be a woman who loved her cards and her gin and tonic in equal measure, and was armed with a formidable sense of humour. Writing on Facebook, Errol recalled:

> So, my mom and I are on our way to UPenn in West Philly [Philadelphia] to Elon's rented (semi-demolished) old house next to UPenn. It's Saturday night and dark. As we go along (using McNally maps those days) we get deeper and deeper into pretty bad looking places. With groups on every corner. I am hunched over the wheel. 'Gotta get outta here, gotta get outta here,' I'm thinking. We pull up at traffic lights, crowds on each corner. 'Oh sh.t', I think. My mom (75) rolls down her window.
>
> 'Hello! Hello boys!' she shouts to them on her side. The whole group comes over.
>
> Oh no! I think.
>
> My mom: 'I'm British you know?' she says to them. 'We're looking for Apple Street. My grandson Elon lives there. Do you know him? He's very clever you know. So how do we get there?'
>
> I've stopped thinking.
>
> 'Oh don't worry ma'am,' says one giant guy. 'We'll show you. It's just around the next bend. Follow us!'
>
> So, they all jog along in front of the car as we follow them. Close? It was half a mile!
>
> Finally, 'Here it is, ma'am,' they say.
>
> 'Thank you, boys,' says my mom, and rolls up her window and off we go to Elon![7]

The off-campus house was another move by Musk to develop

more than just his mental abilities. He had shared a dorm room with Adeo Ressi, a close friend to this day. It was Ressi who convinced Musk that they should rent the house in pursuit of a better social life, which the dorm wasn't providing. On the weekends, the house became a party venue as the two of them started to charge a cover fee for access to an all-you-can-drink student hangout. But amid what often was a chaotic, sometimes debauched place, a familiar theme emerged. According to Ressi, 'Elon was the most straight-laced dude you have ever met. He never drank. He never did anything. Zero. Literally nothing.'[8] This resonates with what Errol has said about his son's aversion to alcohol and preference for a milkshake.

Throughout his time at UPenn, Musk kept in contact with Justine. He also began to expand on his own ideas, specifically his plans for sustainable energy through the use of solar power. When Justine graduated, she travelled to Japan to teach English as a second language (ESL). She spent a year there, while Musk also went his own way, and they lost contact. When she returned to Canada, Justine continued to pursue her writing while working as a bartender. Musk had by then moved to Silicon Valley in California, the epicentre of global technological innovation.

There was a brief time in 1995 when Musk allegedly enrolled and was accepted at Stanford University to study energy physics. But after just two days he says he decided to defer in light of his growing interest in the development of the Internet. According to Musk, 'I talked to the chairman of the department and he let me go on deferment, and I said I'd probably be back in six months and he said he was probably never going to hear from me again, and he was correct. I've never spoken to him since.'[9]

However, the veracity of his Stanford link was challenged in court years later in 2009, when Martin Eberhard, one of the original founders of Tesla, sued Musk for what he alleged was slander pertaining to Eberhard's true role in founding the company. In documents submitted in that trial, it is claimed that 'In several national publications, Musk has allegedly misrepresented his affiliation with Stanford University, claiming to have "dropped out" of a PhD program at that university when in fact he was never enrolled at Stanford.'[10]

He may well, however, had had a letter of acceptance to attend Stanford University. In fact, Stanford president John Hennessy confirmed Musk's recollection of events: 'He arrived at Stanford to pursue his PhD in physics, but left after two days. I said, "What was wrong, Elon? Was it the food, the water, the weather?" No, he left to launch his first start-up – Zip2.'[11]

Attending university and racking up academic qualifications has never appealed to Musk, who has often been quoted as generally indifferent to the practical worth of a degree. He's even made it a requirement in his companies not to let the lack of a university degree prevent the hiring of a potential employee who shows outstanding talent. This leads to the other theory that Musk's time at university – in Canada and the United States – was more a part of his plan to get out of South Africa and into the United States. His Canadian citizenship and place at a respected Canadian university made it a lot easier to move to the United States; a Canadian passport counted for more than a South African one. Musk's transfer to UPenn and later to the Wharton School meant he could show more time spent living in the United States, fulfilling the necessary immigration requirements. An acceptance letter from Stanford would have also lent more weight to the case for his eventually becoming a US citizen. More importantly, being accepted to study at Stanford meant he could move to California and work there. All of which builds on the theory that, much like his studies at the University of Pretoria, Musk's university time in Canada and the United States was merely a vehicle for his ultimate objective – and stated childhood aim – of living and working in the United States. In itself, this is a prime example of Musk's pragmatism and ability to achieve his objectives.

At this time, Musk also worked at a videogame company in Palo Alto – ten minutes from Silicon Valley – where he wrote a multi-tasker for PC in C++ that could basically read video from a CD while running a game at the same time. The name of that videogame company, ironically, was Rocket Science Games. It was a night job; during the day he worked on ruthenium-tantalum ultracapacitors at Pinnacle Research. Quite simply, electrical energy. Already, the seeds of his interest in electric cars, which would come to fruition in Tesla, had been planted.

'But that summer I realised the Internet is going to be one of the biggest impactors on humanity, and communication will go from osmosis to humanity having like a nervous system where you could access any part of humanity's knowledge from any connection anywhere. I wanted to be a part of creating that,' he said.[12]

He tried to get a job with Netscape, creator of the first wide-ly successful browser for what was then known as the World Wide Web. 'I actually wasn't sure what I wanted to do growing up. I think at one point I thought inventing stuff or creating things would be a cool thing to do. But I wasn't really sure if that meant starting a company or whether that meant working for a company that made cool stuff,' Musk said.[13] 'In 1995, I thought the Internet would be something that would change the world in a major way and I wanted to be a part of it. Actually, what I first tried to do, was I tried to get a job at Netscape. I wouldn't actually try to start a company, I'd try to get a job at Netscape.

'I didn't get any reply. I mean I had a physics and economics de-gree, or physics and business degree, from Wharton, and I was doing grad studies in applied physics and materials science. I guess that …

I mean, I didn't have a computer science degree or several years working at a software company. For whatever reason, I didn't get a reply from Netscape and I actually tried hanging out in the lobby, but I was too shy to talk to anyone. So I'm just like standing in the lobby. It was pretty embarrassing. I was just sort of standing there trying to see if there's someone I could talk to and then I just couldn't, I couldn't … I was too scared to talk to anyone. So then I left.'[14]

Saddled with $100 000 in student debt, Musk decided that the only way open for him to become a part of the Internet revolution was to start his own Internet company. And so, with a little over $2 000 and a computer, and renting office space where he also lived because it was cheaper than an apartment, and showering at the Page Mill YMCA in Palo Alto, Musk began writing software.

From Pretoria, Musk had travelled right into the heart of his science-fiction dreams and made them a reality. He was now in the world – and the literal neighbourhood – that birthed Hewlett-Packard in the late 1930s, Bell Labs in the 1940s and Intel in the 1960s. Then, in 1969, the nearby Stanford Research Institute was involved in the creation of ARPANET (Advanced Research Projects Agency Network), a government research project. It was funded by the Advanced Research Projects Agency (ARPA), a division within the US Department of Defense. ARPANET's purpose was to link computers at the Pentagon and its research institutions via telephone lines, and using the very same device – a modem – that so captured Musk's imagination as a boy, and which he told his father about.

ARPANET eventually became the Internet. And Silicon Valley exploded with innovation. The 1970s saw the birth of technology companies such as Apple, Xerox PARC (Palo Alto Research Center), Atari and Oracle. By the 1980s, Silicon Valley was the acknowledged centre of the global computer industry. In the 1990s, eBay emerged, as did Google and Yahoo.

And into this world came a kid from South Africa.

'I just started writing software,' said Musk.[15]

And to all of these giant technology companies in Silicon Valley was added a little-known outfit called the Global Link Information Network – Musk's first technology company. The name would later be changed to Zip2. It was a company that put the Yellow and White Pages on the Internet, with maps. A searchable business directory that was primarily used by the newspaper industry, with *The New York Times* as its first client. In its most simplistic description, Musk felt that everybody should be able to find their nearest pizza place, and how to get there.

'I actually wrote the first maps and directions on the Internet – the first White Pages and the first Yellow Pages – by myself. Then we hired a few interns, and then my brother [Kimbal] joined. And another friend of mine – Greg Kouri, who has passed away. And then we got some venture funding. I thought it was crazy that these guys gave us $3 million. It was just us and some interns.'[16]

The American Dream had become real for Musk.

The seed that had been planted when he saw his first computer, the discussions a young boy had had with those experts from England addressing adults about the first computers at the University of the Witwatersrand and that magical blinking light of a modem had all brought him to this point.

From the valley of global technological innovation, Musk could now see clearly before him the mountaintops he wanted to climb.

PART THREE

Zip2

FOR Elon Musk, the face of Benjamin Franklin on the US $100 bill is more significant than at first appears.

When it came to starting his first company, Zip2, Musk did what he has always done since he was a child and wanted to learn about something. He went to books. Specifically, he read biographies and autobiographies. And the one that captured his attention was *Benjamin Franklin: An American Life* by Walter Isaacson. Franklin is a source of great inspiration for Musk: 'He was basically just a runaway kid and created his printing business. He also did science and politics. He's one of the people I most admire. Franklin is pretty awesome.'[1]

Scientist, inventor, politician, philanthropist and businessman, Benjamin Franklin (1706–1790) was also one of the Founding Fathers of the United States. He helped to draft the Declaration of Independence in 1776, represented the new nation at the court of King Louis XVI and helped produce the US Constitution. But there is another reason why Franklin's face adorns the $100 bill: he was at one point the richest man in America. *Forbes* has estimated that his net worth in today's terms would make him a billionaire. Quite clearly, Franklin was a highly successful businessman and entrepreneur.

Franklin's book *The Way to Wealth* (1758) includes many of his most famous sayings, such as 'A penny saved is a penny earned' and 'Early to bed and early to rise makes a man healthy, wealthy and wise'. Franklin's career clearly resonated with Musk, as an example of someone who married science and invention with business savvy. It was not just good enough to have a great idea; it was important to have an idea that could create value.

In 2009, when he was asked by Charlie Rose what his core skill was, Musk replied, 'If something has to be designed and invented and you have to figure out how to ensure that the value of the thing you create is greater than the cost of the inputs, then that's probably my core skill.'[2]

Musk's desire to create things of value is very similar to Franklin's own philosophy of 'doing well by doing good'.[3] Musk describes his take on this as 'I try to do useful things. That's a nice aspiration. And useful means it is of value to the rest of society. Are they useful things that work and make people's lives better, make the future seem better, and actually are better, too? I think we should try to make the future better.'[4] But Musk's belief in a 'purpose-driven company' does not just have a utopian outcome. For him, such a company has the benefit of naturally attracting the best talent in the world.

In a series of conversations with Steve Jurvetson, an American businessman and venture capitalist, at Stanford in 2015 as part of the Stanford Technology Ventures Program, Musk said: 'If there's something that's intrinsically enjoyable, and the financial rewards are good, but also it's something that's going to genuinely change the world, then that's a pretty powerful motivator. But I don't think everything needs to change the world. There's lot of useful things that people do. I think it should be a usefulness optimisation. It's saying, "Is what I'm doing as useful as it could be?" Even if something isn't changing the world, if it's making people's lives better I think that's great. If it's affecting a lot of people, even in a small way, then this is good.'[5]

Musk says it was this desire that made him decide to abandon his plans to study at Stanford. 'I wasn't sure that what I would work on in the PhD would actually be useful. It could be academically useful but not practically useful,' he said. 'And I felt that if I watched the Internet get built while I'm doing this, that would be really frustrating.'[6]

It was from the biography of Franklin and a range of other books that Musk taught himself the business skills he felt he needed. But he is by no means just a theorist on business. He knows what it means to work hard to make a company successful and often gets involved himself, sometimes to the company's success and sometimes to its detriment. 'A friend once said to me, "Starting a company is like eating glass while staring into the abyss."'[7]

Another core tenet of Musk's business philosophy is to talk less and do more.

In an interview with *The Wall Street Journal* in April 2021 he said: 'I think there might be too many MBAs running companies. There's the MBA-ization of America, which I think is not that great. There should be more focus on the product or the service itself. Less time on board meetings. Less time on financials. What's the point of a company at all? Why even have companies? A company is an assembly of people gathered together to create a product or service and to deliver that product or service. Sometimes people lose sight of that. A company has no value in and of itself. It only has value to the degree that it is an effective allocator of resources to create goods and services that are of greater value than the cost of the inputs. This thing we call profits should just mean over time that the value of the output is worth more than the inputs.'[8]

Musk's general thoughts about business and what companies represent have made him one of the most uncharacteristic CEOs of his generation. But this in turn has also made him quite difficult to contain according to the traditional constraints and bureaucracy of the business world, and the legalities involved. He is a man not entirely at ease in the boardroom and with directors to report to. The red tape of company governance, and indeed the generally established and accepted corporate and financial regulations, remain a burden for someone who wants to move fast and get on with things. As a result, Musk will always butt heads with the system. His most recent issues with tax legislation in the US and ongoing issues with investors are examples of a theme that will continue to play itself out in his career.

AFTER gaining as much knowledge as he could from his studies and books, it was time for Musk to put all of this into practice with his first company. And he chose the fledgling Internet as his launch pad. 'The Internet – that was the moment to really do something,' he recalled.[9]

While it was obvious to Musk that the Internet was going to have an enormous impact and would redefine humanity, what wasn't so obvious was how to make money out of it. 'Back in 1995 there weren't many people on the Internet, and certainly nobody was making any money at all. Most people thought the Internet was going to be a fad,' he said in an interview in 1999.[10]

But his desire was not to make money off the Internet for money's sake, so much as it was a desire to be a part of the Internet.

The Internet was the first step in his carefully thought-out plan of what he wanted to achieve. 'When I was in college, there were three areas that I thought would most affect the future of humanity. Those were the Internet, the transition to a sustainable energy and transportation sector, and the third was space exploration, in particular the extension of life to multiple planets,' he said.[11]

In Musk's mind, the Internet would turn humanity into 'a super organism'. And knowing where to buy your nearest pizza and how to navigate your way there seemed like a great addition to this super organism.

Netscape had just gone public, proving that there was indeed a way to make money off the Internet. And Musk believed it wasn't the only way. So in the summer of 1995, Musk started working on the Global Link Information Network, later to become Zip2. After purchasing a local business directory, Musk acquired access to the digital mapping software of a GPS company named Navteq. He now had two large databases, and his job was a simple one by today's standards but revolutionary back then: make them talk to each other. That's where his coding skills came to the fore. He, Kimbal (who sold his share in a painting company to join his brother in business) and Kouri launched the company with whatever money they could put together, including between $20 000 and $30 000 allegedly provided by Errol.

Musk poured himself into the work. With only one computer, he coded at night so that the computer could run the business by day. And they lived on the bare minimum. Musk loves to say he didn't only have no money, he had 'negative money. I had huge student debts.'[12]

'When you are first starting out, you really need to make your burn rate ridiculously tiny,' he said in an address to the Wharton School.[13] Or, as Benjamin Franklin put it, 'Rather go to bed without dinner than to rise in debt.'[14] Speaking on the *Knowledge@Wharton* podcast, Musk expanded on this principle: 'One lesson is, spend very little money. That was a case where I had very little money, so there really wasn't any choice. I only had a few thousand dollars. And then my brother came down and he had several thousand dollars. We just rented an office for $400 or $500 a month – some really tiny little office in Palo Alto. It was cheaper than an apartment. And then we bought futons that converted into a couch, which was sort of like a meeting area during the day. We would sleep there at night and shower at the YMCA, which was just a few blocks away. That was an extremely low burn rate. It was way cheaper than a garage. Garages are expensive. So we were able to putter along for several months until we got venture funding. I think that's a good lesson. Don't spend more than you are sure you have.'[15]

But the frugality of life for him at this point was nothing compared with the pure joy of having found his purpose. For the first time in his life, Musk felt at home. The exploding ideas in his head had found a home amid the ideas exploding around him in Silicon Valley. The strange kid who worried that he was different was now a kindred spirit in a technological neighbourhood of the strangest 'kids' on the planet, all living out the exploding ideas in their own heads. And the boy who never quite fitted in at school knew exactly who he was when he slid behind a computer screen and started tapping out code on the keyboard.

And he underpinned everything he did with his main philosophy – being useful. 'Doing something useful for other people – that I like doing,' he told Joe Rogan.[16] 'My goal is to try to make useful things, try to maximise the probability that the future is good, make the future exciting, something to look forward to.'[17]

It seems a very simple philosophy for a genius, but it's one that Musk believes in an altruistic manner. Musk shows an intense love for all that humanity represents. And it shows in his work. Whether it's creating the best user experience to find your nearest pizza place, building a user-friendly payment system, creating electric cars that are actually beautiful or building rockets that will ultimately help humanity find another home and preserve the consciousness he believes is so precious and rare, Musk has always been driven to be useful to his fellow man: 'I'm pro-human. I love humanity.'[18]

He has expressed his greatest fear as, 'the extinction of human civilisation'.[19] And, in his best version of himself, he drives this with ideas rather than ego, although ego naturally gets in the way at times. But, for the most part, Musk is exactly as his friend Danny Warnick described him: 'You knew exactly where you stood with him.'

Musk himself has said, 'If everyone's trying to trick everyone all the time, it's a lot of noise and confusion. It's better just to be straightforward and try to do useful things. You don't have to read between the lines with me. I'm saying the lines!'[20]

And Zip2 was the first real expression of this philosophy.

In the Stanford conversations, he describes the one quality every successful entrepreneur needs: 'An obsessive nature with respect to the quality of the product. So being an obsessive-compulsive is a good thing in this context.'[21]

But once again, it's the overriding human element that Musk expresses in his work and philosophy of what it takes to succeed as an entrepreneur: 'Really liking what you do. Even if you're the best of the best, there's always the chance of failure. So it's important that you really like whatever you're doing. If you don't like it, life is too short. And if you like what you're doing, you think about it even when you're not working. It's something that your mind is drawn to. If you don't like it, you really just can't make it work, I don't think.'[22]

Armed with one computer, Musk drilled a hole in the floor of his office/apartment, connected a null modem cable to the ISP (Internet Service Provider) located directly beneath them, and connected to the Internet for $100 a month. A Benjamin Franklin.

With a small team of salespeople, they began the process of

trying to convince local businesses that Zip2 was the new Yellow Pages. Why have an expensive-to-produce telephone directory that gives you only local access when you can put yourself on the Internet for a fraction of the cost and have a global presence? With a dogged focus on spending almost nothing, even the little bit of money that trickled in was a positive for the company. As Musk says, 'When we went and talked to VCs (venture capitalists) we could actually say we had positive cash flow.'[23]

And the first to come around to what Musk and Zip2 were doing was the venture capital firm of Mohr Davidow Ventures. The firm invested around $3 million in Global Link Information Network, and changed the name to Zip2. In today's terms, we would describe it as an Internet 1.0 company. A pioneer.

Mohr Davidow Ventures took majority control of the company, and they brought in Richard Sorkin to replace Musk as CEO. Sorkin was a former NASA intern who had made commercialisation of new technology his speciality. He was older and more experienced, and the investors saw him as better suited than Musk – who remained as chief technology officer – to scaling the new business.

Under Sorkin, Zip2 no longer just targeted local businesses. He saw an opportunity to become the new classifieds for the newspaper industry. *The New York Times* was the first to take up this opportunity, followed by the *Chicago Tribune*, Knight Ridder group and the Hearst Corporation.

But the growth of Zip2 brought with it a fundamental problem for founding entrepreneurs – loss of control. Although Sorkin's business strategy was successful – Zip2 grew to partnerships with media companies in 60 of the 100 top metropolitan areas – Musk was not in total agreement with the way the business was headed. Sorkin wanted Zip2 to be the power *behind* these media companies, while Musk reportedly wanted to see Zip2 (and perhaps himself) more in the spotlight.

'There were disagreements over the priority of general visibility for the company,' Sorkin said in a 1999 interview with online magazine *Salon*.[24] The interviewer, Mark Gimein, asked Sorkin 'if it was true that Musk, in the words of another associate, wanted to see his picture on the cover of *Rolling Stone*? "Yes," he said. "For Elon that's what general visibility meant."'[25]

The relationship between Sorkin and Musk broke down as their inability to work together grew.

And at the heart of his product, a team of new engineers had been brought in to re-code what was seen as Musk's very much DIY approach to coding, which he had obviously taught himself and which, while effective, was in need of a serious upgrade as the company sought to move to the next level.

Musk became increasingly frustrated, to the point that after the engineers had re-coded the software in the day, he would reportedly jump in at night and secretly undo all of their work with his own coding again. It led to a period in which Musk was criticised for his micro-management and did not endear himself to his employees, who found him harder and harder to work with.

When Sorkin sought to merge Zip2 with a similar company, CitySearch, it was the final straw for Musk. With the board's approval, he had Sorkin removed as CEO and the much-talked-about merger failed. Musk later admitted his mistakes and said he had been naive. It set a troubling precedent for Musk, one often cited by his critics. After removing Sorkin as CEO of Zip2, Musk himself was later removed by his management team when he was CEO of PayPal. And even later in his career as CEO of Tesla in 2009, Musk had a very public legal battle with Martin Eberhard, the founder of Tesla Motors, who accused Musk of orchestrating his removal from the company and trying to take sole credit for the Roadster electric car they had created together.

Musk was still clearly trying to refine what he would later talk about in the Stanford conversations as a 'purpose-driven company'. The ego clashes and boardroom battles at Zip2 in the late 1990s certainly contrast with his later view of his first company: 'We had a philosophy of best idea wins as opposed to the person proposing the idea winning because they are who they are. Everyone was an equity stakeholder. If there were two paths to take and one wasn't obviously better than the other; rather than spending time trying to figure out which one was better we would just pick one and do it. Often it's just better to pick a path and do it than to just vacillate on a choice.'[26]

Derek Proudian was brought in to replace Sorkin as CEO. On the streets of Silicon Valley, Zip2 was seen as a company in trouble. Proudian had worked with the creators of ARPANET before joining Mohr Davidow Ventures in the early 1990s. But Proudian was a venture capitalist, not a CEO. He was there to invest in companies, not to run them.

Proudian describes his extensive experience in investing in start-ups as 'making a bet on people',[27] and he was clearly happy to accept the CEO role based on the risks involved, and what he says is an answer to what he looks for in a start-up: 'Can they convince me that market opportunity is big enough that you can build a sizable company in that area?'[28] Zip2 convinced Proudian. And Proudian in turn convinced the Compaq Computer Corporation.

In 1999, Compaq announced that it was purchasing Zip2 for roughly $300 million. According to *The New York Times*, the acquisition was Compaq's 'effort to make its Internet search engine, AltaVista, more competitive with rivals like Yahoo, Lycos and Excite'.[29] Musk was 27 years old when he received a reported $22 million for his seven per cent share in Zip2. 'That was certainly a better outcome than I had ever expected,' he said.[30]

Some who have criticised Musk's corporate aptitude see Zip2 as the start of this pattern in his career. In his 1999 *Salon* interview,

Mark Gimein noted: 'On the corporate report card, Musk's grade for "Plays well with others" would have been a solid F.'[31] And others were, and still are, critical of Musk's strategy of teaching himself whatever he doesn't know and learning as he goes along – whether it be Internet coding or how to build rockets.

But Musk has never put himself forward as anything else and is completely open about this side of his personality. Going back to his belief in the scientific method, Musk has described his process as follows:

1. Ask a question.
2. Gather as much evidence as possible about it.
3. Develop axioms based on the evidence, and try to assign a probability of truth to each one.
4. Draw a conclusion based on cogency in order to determine: are these axioms correct, are they relevant, do they necessarily lead to this conclusion, and with what probability?
5. Attempt to disprove the conclusion. Seek refutation from others to further help break your conclusion.
6. If nobody can invalidate your conclusion, then you're probably right, but you're not certainly right.

He described these points as 'really helpful for figuring out the tricky things'.[32]

As rogue as he may seem to some, in those heady early days in Silicon Valley, he was exactly what was needed. He was a maverick. He was a risk-taker. He was a creative genius. As Gimein wrote in 1999, 'Musk's ego has gotten him in trouble before, and it may get him in trouble again, yet it is also part and parcel of what it means to be a hotshot entrepreneur.'[33]

But 'doesn't play by the rules' only works for as long as there are no rules. When you become a $300-million company owned by a corporate colossus, there are suddenly plenty of rules. And that leaves no space for the maverick.

After the sale of Zip2, Musk knew it was time to move on.

He had embraced the digital revolution of the Internet, and where Zip2 started out as everything he ever dreamt of from his childhood in Pretoria, it ended up being only a taster of what was possible in this new information age. For Musk, this was akin to the moment when the young Leonardo da Vinci first stepped into the studio of his teacher, Verrocchio, and began to discover the world through art. Musk was at the vanguard of what would become known as the 'serial entrepreneurs' of Silicon Valley. But Silicon Valley was having a hard time coming to grips with who – or what – Elon Musk actually was. He wasn't an out-and-out developer, even though he could clearly code well enough. Neither was he just a businessman, although he had a track record better than most, having sold his first company for $300 million. He couldn't have been accused of just being in the right place at the right time either. For every successful start-up that made multimillionaires of their founders, hundreds of others never left their parents' garages.

As Gimein observed in 1999 following the sale of Zip2, 'There is no very obvious reason why Musk is the person to pull this off.'[34] A man with a keen interest in computers and science fiction and no media or marketing experience builds an online searchable database for the biggest media companies in the US. And for his next act, a man with only a brief education in economics, and an even more brief internship at the Bank of Nova Scotia in Canada in the early 1990s, sets his sights on transforming the banking sector. 'Actually, I've found that being an outsider helps you to think creatively about improving the way things are done. When people have been doing things the same way for years, they stop questioning their methods even if they defy common sense,' he told Gimein.[35]

If anything, Musk is a typical leader able to convince his followers that the adventure he is embarking on with them will be worth their while, will mean something and will contribute to something far bigger than themselves.

Musk has continually spoken of doing 'useful things'. He is not driven by money but by the desire to make a greater impact on humanity. Yes, this in turn drives his ego. Among the things he did with his earnings from the sale of Zip2 was to buy a McLaren F1 supercar. Apparently, he beat by a signature Ralph Lauren's attempt to purchase the same car. But he couldn't have looked more awkward and out of place with this vehicle. Later attempts to portray Musk as the inspiration behind the Tony Stark and Iron Man character in *The Avengers* only really stretch to the creative genius and rogue nature of both. The fictional Stark's playboy lifestyle and social chemistry do not line up with Musk at all.

In his biography of Leonardo da Vinci, Robert Payne gives a glimpse into what drives the minds of men like Musk when he describes Leonardo's own desire to 'discover the world, to force it to reveal its secrets and divest it of its mysteries; and like Columbus, who set out for the Indies in the belief that he was fulfilling the prophecies of Isaiah, they believed they were fulfilling a divine purpose'.[36]

Decades later, Musk would define his quest to go to Mars as far more than just space exploration. To him it is the final great attempt to preserve human consciousness against the threat of a catastrophic extinction of human civilisation. It is the conundrum of Musk and explains the inability to categorise him, as well as the inability of many people to grasp exactly what he is all about. On one hand, he wraps his mind around impossible calculations and is generally accepted as a genius. But, on the other, he speaks with an almost childlike naivety about saving the world and making things people will love. Speaking in his later role at Tesla, when General Motors (GM) abandoned its own electric car project – the EV1, produced from 1996 to 1999 – Musk did not lament a missed opportunity or a failed business venture so much as bemoan GM's inability to see the obvious. When GM forcibly repossessed the EV1 cars from their leaseholders and sent them to be crushed, Musk was struck by the fact that the leaseholders held a candlelit vigil at the crushing plant. 'When was the last time there was a candlelit vigil for a product?' Musk asked.[37] Their love for these vehicles touched him deeply, and also made him ask the obvious question: 'If people are willing to hold a candlelit vigil for the EV1, maybe it means you should have made an EV2?'

Sometimes, Musk looks at very obvious problems with a very obvious solution. He just gets it done when nobody else knows where to start, be it building a rocket powerful enough to go to Mars or deciding to dig tunnels under Los Angeles for a new traffic system. And he begins by just digging a hole in the SpaceX parking lot. Where others are weighed down by the planning phase, Musk just starts digging a hole and figures it out from there.

In his *Salon* article, Gimein astutely assessed the young Musk when he wrote, 'There is so much money to be made off the Internet, and most of the experts don't know where to start. None of the traditional talents seem to correlate with success. The only one that seems to really matter is the peculiar ability to get started. Everybody in Silicon Valley is looking for the lucky guy who can lead them to the big score. There is a talent that Musk has, but nobody can put his finger on it … Maybe Musk really has a special spark that lets him think more strategically than everybody around him. Maybe Musk really is the next big thing. Or maybe he has just managed to make his backers believe that he is the Brand X, the next superstar. In today's

Silicon Valley, the difference between being the next big thing and looking like it may not even matter.'[38]

In the mind of Musk, the next big thing was online banking: 'I felt there was still more that could be done with the Internet.'[39] The idea was very similar to Zip2, except with financial services.

Silicon Valley's 'Brand X' had a new vision.

And, appropriately, he called it X.com.

PayPal

AS with most of Musk's ideas, the genesis of X.com was to take something complex and make it easier for more people to use. 'Let's make a really convenient site that combines all of people's financial needs into one seamless, easy-to-use location,'[1] is how he described it.

After the sale of Zip2, Musk admits that he took no time off and moved immediately into identifying 'where are the opportunities in the Internet'.[2] For him, this was the financial services sector, which he believed lacked innovation. He later said something very similar about the space industry: 'The reason there hasn't been a big improvement in the space industry is because there's such a big amount of capital that's needed to start a rocket company, and the number of people that understand rocketry in the world is very small. So there are huge barriers to entry. That's why we haven't really seen the improvement that there should have been over the years.'

So in March 1999, one month after selling Zip2, Musk started X.com with $10 million of the $22 million he had received from the sale of Zip2. In a local TV interview at the time, a young Musk says, 'I could go and buy one of the islands in the Bahamas and turn it into my personal fiefdom. But I'm much more interested in trying to build and create a new company.'[3]

As Musk says in the interview, in his mind this was a series of poker games. And he was now moving to a more high-stakes version of poker. He then stands in front of an ATM and says, 'This is a traditional ATM. We're going to transform banking I think X.com could absolutely be a multibillion-dollar bonanza.'[4]

For Musk, the key lay in the fact that 'money is low bandwidth. You don't need some sort of big infrastructure improvement to do things with it. It's really just an entry into a database. The paper form of money is really only a small percentage of all the money that's out there.'[5]

According to Musk, combining a person's total financial services needs into one website was the complex part of the job. Strangely, the ability to send money over the Internet proved a far simpler problem to solve. Musk says it took them a day to create this revolutionary new service. And the key marketing tool here was that if somebody wanted to transfer money to another person who didn't have an X.com account, it sent them an email asking the other person if they wanted to sign up, which they clearly wanted to do. With that came the exponential growth of the service.

It surprised even Musk that the reaction to email payments and the electronic transfer of funds was far greater than it was to being able to consolidate all of your financial services on one platform.

But this was no surprise to another start-up by the name of Confinity and its founder, Peter Thiel. Confinity, also based in Palo Alto, was on the same track as X.com, although its approach was slightly different. They were using a device called the PalmPilot (a handheld mobile device) to transfer tokens from one PalmPilot to another, and they then created a website where you could redeem and reconcile these token payments. The website was called PayPal.

But Confinity came to the same surprising conclusion as Musk and X.com, namely, that people were far more interested in the electronic transfer of funds than in any of the other elements. It has been referred to as a happy accident, and one that saw the two companies merge in March 2000. The drive behind the merger was survival in the emerging digital world that was now moving at the click of a button, and with ecommerce developing equally fast.

About five years earlier, eBay had been founded as the first online auction website. By 2000 it already had 12 million users. According to David O Sacks, the South African-born former COO of PayPal, 'Confinity/PayPal and X.com were locked in a heated competition to gain share on eBay. Confinity initially offered a $10 signup bonus and a $10 referral bonus for each new user (the referral bonus went to the inviter). X.com then upped their bonuses to $20. Both companies probably would have run out of money competing with each other.'[6]

So the merger made sense in terms of combining market share. Initially, the new company was called X.com. But consumers felt the name was somewhat vague, and some were even concerned that it might be perceived as pornographic. And so it was that they settled on PayPal instead.

Musk was made the CEO of PayPal. But less than two years later, he was effectively ousted from the company he had helped to create. Once again, the disruptor-turned-founder had trouble with the transition from start-up to the day-to-day running of a company.

When Musk returned from a business trip to raise investment, he was greeted with the news that he was out. Musk describes one of the lessons he learned from that experience: 'It's not a good idea to leave the office when there are a lot of major things underway which are causing people a great deal of stress … That caused the management team to decide I wasn't the right guy to run the company. I could've fought it really hard, but I decided that rather than fight it at this critical time it's best to just concede ... Peter and Max [Levchin] and David [O Sacks] and the other guys, they're smart people with generally the right motivations. They did what they thought was right and I think for the right reasons. Except that the reasons weren't valid in my opinion.'[7]

The reasons, it seems, were decidedly simple. Musk was not in favour of the Linux software used to run PayPal, and instead preferred Microsoft software. This led to a rift in the management of the company, and there were even accusations that Microsoft was counterproductive and caused software operating issues.

So when Musk left the office for his investment drive, it provided the perfect opportunity to oust him and replace him with Thiel. According to Julie Anderson, the former vice president of public relations at PayPal, 'After the merger everyone tried to play nicely together at first, but – as has been widely chronicled from various perspectives – it took just a few months before the differences in opinion turned ugly. Elon took a vacation that year and I've always hated that I didn't realize they were going to oust him as CEO in time; he called that day from somewhere in Africa and asked "How bad is it?" and I said "Not that bad. I think it's going to be okay." Middle of the night I sat straight up in bed and headed back to the office; the lights were blazing and everyone was there. It was done by morning.'[8]

Thiel emerged as Musk's early competitor, then partner, then replacement, and even later an investor in both Tesla and SpaceX. Musk has said he harbours no ill feelings towards Thiel. And Thiel has praised Musk in the most unlikely of ways. In describing Musk as one of a kind, he's used a counterargument to claim that Musk is a 'negative role model' for kids because he is so hard to follow: 'If you tell a young person, "Why don't you be like Elon?" it's a negative role model where the basic response is, "Well that's too hard, I can't do that.'"[9]

Thiel was certainly qualified to spot the genius in Musk, being one himself. By the age of 12, he was a nationally ranked chess grand master. He went through Stanford University, like so many of Silicon Valley's brightest minds, where he cofounded the university's newspaper, *The Stanford Review*. With a degree in philosophy, Thiel shares much of Musk's desire to look at technology and innovation from the standpoint of how useful it can be to humanity.

He saw in Musk, and clearly in himself, the seeds of the great questions around innovation. In a 2015 talk at Columbia University's Center on Capitalism and Society, Thiel referred to this as the internal perspective on innovation: 'There is a sense in which every moment in the history of science and technology happens only once. The next Mark Zuckerberg will not be starting a social networking site. The next Larry Page will not be starting a search engine. The next Bill Gates will not be starting an operating system. If you are blindly copying these people, you're not learning from them at all … What if the key thing in innovation is always if not the miraculous at least the singular. The one-time and only one-time aspect that drives these kinds of things.'[10]

In Thiel, Musk most likely met someone so similar to himself that it proved a difficult working relationship at PayPal. In encouraging innovative thought, Thiel talks about challenging truths: 'What truths do people believe that nobody agrees with you on.'[11] Musk comes at it from his own perspective: 'I care a lot about the truth of things, and trying to understand the truth of things.' He expands on this: 'Reason by first principles rather than analogy. The normal way we conduct our lives is reason by analogy because it's mentally easier. But first principles is kind of a physics way of looking at the world. You boil things down to fundamental truths and say, "What are we sure is true?" and then reason up from there.'[12]

For Thiel, though, these matters of innovation and truth come with no hard and fast rules, especially in Silicon Valley, where he says it boils down to 'the inner reality being one of an always unique constellation of people and potentiality'.[13] For Musk, realising potentiality was the easy part. But, ironically enough, the man who would later build rockets to go into space found navigating constellations, particularly Thiel's 'unique constellation of people', far more challenging.

'There are many challenges with having the founders of these companies continue to manage them as CEOs,' says Thiel. 'There are all sorts of things they do not understand that well. They're often young and immature and there are a lot of things that go wrong. But the one big difference is they actually do believe in the thing they're working on.'[14] He relates an early example from Facebook, where he was the first outside investor. After two years of operation, they were presented with a billion-dollar acquisition offer from Yahoo. At the board meeting to discuss the offer, Facebook founder Mark Zuckerberg said it was obvious they should turn it down. What the rest of the board believed was going to be a ten-minute discussion turned into six hours, and they turned the offer down. As Thiel recalls, 'Mark said he didn't know what he would do with a quarter of a billion dollars. He would probably just start another social networking site, and as he quite liked the one he had, he didn't see why he should sell it.'[15]

As Thiel points out with the Facebook example, a diehard CEO would have done a lot of things better, but the one thing he would've done wrong was to sell Facebook to Yahoo for a billion dollars.

Similarly, Musk's personality was perfectly suited to the innovation phase of company development. Such was the difficult dynamic of his early start-ups. Reflecting on the early days of PayPal, Thiel said he would describe it as 'risky business': 'The whole thing was one frightening, insane risk after another.'[16] And into this came Elon Musk, he says, 'the man who knew nothing about risk'.[17] Clearly, even for Thiel and the great Silicon Valley innovators of the late 1990s, Musk was on a totally different trajectory in terms of his appetite for risk. Thiel, in his later role as a venture capitalist, has said that you always want to invest in entrepreneurs who speak in the future tense, although you also want to make sure they are not simply crazy.

For Thiel, the key is to find the people who 'have very powerful and definite visions of the future'.[18] People like Elon Musk. 'The internal versions of Tesla and SpaceX in Silicon Valley is that they could never succeed and people were deeply sceptical and there were so many different pieces you had to get to work together in just the right way. If you multiplied all the probabilities, it was just going to fail. You could not build a new car company – there were too many different pieces you had to get to work.'[19]

Thiel relates a conversation he had with Musk in 2008 that perfectly sums up the South African's approach to innovation: 'I asked him when had the last new successful car company been created in the United States? The answer was Jeep in 1941 … There's been no new car company in 67 years, therefore it must be a very hard thing to do and therefore you should not do it.'[20] Musk considered Thiel's argument, and then presented his alternative: 'It's been 67 years, so it must be time for a new car company.'[21]

'The conversations you would have with people like Elon and Mark is that if you talk about risk they would tell you the very definite things they are going to do and prove why there is no risk at all,'[22] says Thiel. For him, this is the far more interesting and fascinating part of Musk's personality than the genius entrepreneur or the eccentricities of his personality. As he said in 2015, the complex coordination of the many different working parts and getting them to work together, and the rebooting the traditional supply chain around that product to make it work – therein lies the true genius of men like Steve Jobs or Elon Musk.

It is exactly what Musk has done with SpaceX, namely, changing the supply chain of what makes building rockets so expensive and bringing the costs down as much as possible through innovation.

For Thiel, individuals like Musk are not spoken of enough for their 'coordinating vision to reduce risk' around their innovative ideas. For him, whether Steve Jobs was a horrible human being who sometimes mistreated his employees should not be the biggest question. Rather, it should be why these people continued to work for him and believe in his ideas. In looking at Elon Musk, it's an equally important distinction to make if you want to understand the genius rather than just understand the man.

People like Musk are not ignorant of risk. They simply believe implicitly that they have the answers. And when you work for Elon Musk, you should know what you are getting into. It's been a familiar theme for investors in Musk's companies, namely, that if you are going to invest in Tesla or SpaceX and know full well who is leading these companies and what his personality is like, then best you buckle up for a roller-coaster of a ride in a share price that will most definitely rise and fall with your CEO's tweets.

Anne Chinnery, in her role as operations manager at SpaceX, describes this quality as 'risk tolerance': 'He (Elon) didn't want to fail, but he wasn't afraid of it.'[23] Musk describes his own approach to risk and failure as 'Some actions will fail, some will succeed. You want the net useful output of your set of actions to be the highest. Failure is essentially irrelevant unless it is catastrophic.'[24] And let's be honest, if you were afraid of risk and failure, a rocket company is the last thing you would create.

For Thiel, society has become so risk-averse that the likes of Elon Musk and Steve Jobs stand like beacons among us. Their ideas seem so improbable as to scare us. And yet, by a very fine margin of understanding, it is clear that the geniuses of Silicon Valley are not these crazy eccentrics but rather are far more calculated. As Thiel notes, Bill Gates said he loves working with computers because they always do exactly as they're told. It's almost as if these are the people who, at the most extreme edge of innovation and risk, have found no risk at all in the certainty of their vision.

It blends perfectly with Musk's own journey of innovation.

The area where Musk speaks most about risk is SpaceX, but not in the most obvious context of exploding rockets. He does so in the broader context of Earth and the risk to humanity: 'I don't think we're currently doomed, to be clear. There are people on all ranges of the spectrum, from nothing to worry about CO_2 – just makes things better – to we're doomed and there's nothing we can do about it. I'm somewhere in the middle. My concern with CO_2 is not necessarily with where we are today. But if it is accelerating and we keep going and we're complacent, there is some risk of non-linear climate change. These are just risks that are not wise to take. Long-term, we're going to have to have renewable energy anyway because we'll run out of oil and gas. It has to end up with renewable and sustainable energy, it's really a question of whether we get there sooner or later. Let's get there sooner. It's obvious. How long do you want to run this experiment? Even if we say there is a point one percent chance of disaster, right now we've only got one planet. Why run that risk? It's crazy.'[25]

Musk is doing exactly what he's always done, and how Thiel has described it. He's looking to the future with the innovation of today, and explaining how he will eliminate the risk. Musk has described his greatest fear as the extinction of human civilisation. So now he's doing something about that risk: 'To be a spacefaring civilisation and for humanity to be out there among the stars and be a multiplanetary species. It's important for the long-term survival of humanity. Life insurance for life as we know it.'[26]

He takes this even further to his ultimate conclusion about the value of protecting human consciousness: 'As far as we know, this is the only place – at least in this part of the galaxy or the Milky Way – where there is consciousness. And it's taken a long time for us to get to this point. According to the geological records, Earth's been around for about four and a half billion years. Although it was mostly molten magma for about a half a billion years. The sun is gradually getting hotter and bigger. And over time, even in the absence of global warming, the sun will expand and it will overheat the Earth. My guess is there's probably only several hundred million years left. That's all we've got. If it took an extra ten percent longer for conscious life to evolve on Earth, it wouldn't evolve at all because it would've been incinerated by the sun. So it appears that consciousness is a very rare and precious thing, and we should take whatever steps we can to preserve the light of consciousness. The window has been opened. Only now, after four and a half billion years, has that window opened. That's a long time to wait, and it might not stay open for very long. I'm pretty optimistic by nature, but there's some chance that window might not be open for long, and I think we should become a multiplanetary civilisation while that window is open. If we do, I think the probable outcome for Earth is even better because Mars could help Earth one day. I think we should really do our very best to become a multiplanetary species and extend our consciousness beyond Earth. And we should do it now.'[27]

Another example of this thought process is Musk's views on artificial intelligence (AI): 'I think we should be really concerned about it … I keep sounding the alarm bell … AI is a rare case where we need to be proactive in regulation instead of reactive, because by the time we are reactive in AI regulation it's too late. AI is a fundamental risk to the existence of human civilisation.'[28]

And he offers the solution to this risk – the future plan: 'What to do about mass unemployment? This is going to be a massive social challenge. I think ultimately we'll have to have some kind of universal basic income. I don't think we're going to have a choice. I think it's going to be necessary. I want to be clear. These are not things that I wish would happen. These are simply things that I think probably will happen. If my assessment is correct, then we need to say what are we going to do about it? Some kind of a universal basic income is going to be necessary. The output of goods and services will be extremely high. With automation there will come abundance. Almost everything will get very cheap. The much harder challenge is how do people then have meaning? A lot of people derive their meaning from their employment. So if there's no need for your labour, what's the meaning? That's a much harder problem to deal with.'[29]

It's a familiar pattern for Musk. He thinks about ways to launch rockets but also about ways to do so sustainably without relying on fossil fuel, while at the same time admitting the challenges: 'We cannot stop CO_2 generation today without civilisation coming to a grinding halt and mass starvation and all sorts of terrible things happening.'[30]

He builds robots, and then thinks about the effect this will have on global unemployment and urges the world to start seriously planning for this eventuality. He's even thinking about babies: 'We have a serious issue with population collapse. It's far bigger than people realise. The social support networks were not set up for a higher ratio of retirees to workers. You don't want to have the youth effectively enslaved to take care of the elderly, which is what will happen if you have an upside-down demographic pyramid. This (the idea that Earth is overpopulated) is not true. Earth is going to face a massive population collapse over the next 20 to 30 years. Massive. Is civilisation going to die with a bang or a whimper? This is definitely going to be with a whimper. The birth rate is very low.'[31]

Musk is not playing a game of chance building companies on a whim. He's actually following a very clear path of addressing what he believes are the greatest risks to humanity, and to combat these, great risks need to be taken. Carefully.

Remember the Haldeman family motto? 'Live dangerously – carefully.'

For Peter Thiel, the greatest risks lie not with the ones the innovators and entrepreneurs themselves are taking, but rather with the ones the rest of us are not taking. For him, the tragedy is that only a handful of people like himself and Musk are 'allowed' to operate beyond society's constraints, and are somehow given the freedom to do so by the very nature of their being so different, while so many others have to conform in their thinking.

At the end of his 2015 talk, Thiel remarked: 'One of the striking things in Silicon Valley that I've noted is that so many of the great entrepreneurs seem to be suffering from a mild case of Asperger's. I think that we need to always flip this around into an indictment of our society. What does it tell you about our society, where all of us who do not have Asperger's are at a disadvantage because the social pressures are so extreme and we're talked out of our original, interesting, creative, heterodox ideas before they're even fully formed.'[32]

It's the great paradox of society that only when you are deemed to be so different to the norm – as an artist, creator or thinker – are you then left alone to pursue your own path. The rest of us have to fall in line. Elon Musk had to fight this in a school environment where being different was dangerous, but he then was able to revel in it – and use it to his advantage – in adulthood. He is considered so radically different to any other CEO that he's given the freedom to do what no other CEO would ever be given the liberty to do. He can behave in a way that no traditional company or board of directors would tolerate, simply because he's Elon Musk. Or, as he's often said, 'I'm just being me.'

Elon Musk is not crazy. But he certainly understands the value of having people think he's just a little crazy, and the freedom it gives him to do the things he wants. For Musk, the ideas of the future were taking shape in his mind. And the eventual sale of PayPal gave him the financial leverage he needed to realise them.

After being removed as CEO of PayPal, Musk remained as a board member and shareholder. In 2002, eBay purchased PayPal for $1.5 billion. Musk walked away with $180 million – exactly the capital he needed to launch his big ideas. The ones that were indeed going to change the world.

Musk wasn't the only one who felt he could now go off and leverage his big ideas. More significantly for the industry and Silicon Valley as a whole, the minds that came out of PayPal would impact the digital landscape in a myriad of influential ways. As described in Moaml Mohmmed's *PayPal Mafia*, Musk was one of several PayPal entrepreneurs who redefined the world we live in today. Thiel emerged as one of the new forces behind Facebook and a formidable Silicon Valley venture capitalist, investing in Tesla and SpaceX among others. Steve Chen and Chad Hurley left to cofound YouTube. Reid Hoffman founded LinkedIn.

Musk, the boy from Pretoria, was part of a pioneering group of roughly 20 individuals who remain Silicon Valley's most influential group of entrepreneurs and venture capitalists. Collectively, it is estimated that they have made over 1 005 investments into 646 companies.

But he wasn't the only Pretoria boy making waves in Silicon Valley. Roelof Botha, the grandson of former South African foreign minister Pik Botha, was CFO of PayPal in 2001. 'Elon recruited me to work at PayPal – I still have the original recruitment letter he signed, and my first desk at the company was right next to his,'[33] he said. 'Elon and the other guys at PayPal saw something in me and took a chance with me even though I didn't have any work experience in America ... I was given the opportunity to become the chief financial officer of the company. I was 29 years old and the chief financial officer of a billion-dollar public company in America ... people were willing to take a chance on me and my future.'[34]

PayPal was a stepping stone for Musk, like most of the 'PayPal Mafia'. With his earnings from the sale, he invested $100 million into starting up SpaceX, $70 million into Tesla and $10 million into SolarCity. But while this tremendous windfall precipitated the next phase of his career, there was another important reason that Musk decided to leave the office and make that two-week investment trip, which ultimately cost him his job as PayPal's CEO.

And it would also lead to the first great tragedy of his seemingly blessed life as America's newest dotcom multimillionaire.

PART FOUR
The Break-Ups

JUSTINE Wilson had just returned from ESL teaching in Japan, and was wondering what to do with her life. 'If Elon ever calls me again, I think I'll go for it. I might have missed something there,'[1] she told her sister. A week later, she says, Musk phoned her.

Musk and Justine rekindled their relationship. They were different in so many ways, with Musk's focus on the world of digital and Justine's on the world of books. But in one sense they were very much alike. As was the case with Musk and his traumatic period at Bryanston High, Justine knew all about bullies.

'The bullies found me early. In first grade, it was an oversized, older kid named Phil. In fourth and fifth grades, it was the equally oversized Ross, who introduced some confusion into the matter when he asked me to go with him. That was our version of what was once known as going steady ... From sixth grade on, my bullies were girls, the kind who didn't look or seem like bullies at all. They were bright, socially sophisticated, popular with kids and liked by grown-ups. They made my day-to-day life so miserable I eventually begged my parents to transfer me to another school. The fact that they were sweet, middle-class white girls didn't change the fact that they were (at least to me) domineering and mean; if anything, it helped them get away with it,'[2] she posted on her blog.

In a TEDx talk she gave in 2017,[3] Justine told the story of a visionary friend who revealed that he hated going to school because the other kids would follow him home and 'throw soda cans at his head'. She then told the tale of another visionary who told her that when he was a kid he was so painfully aware of how differently he thought to other kids that he was afraid he was insane. 'He was afraid that other people would find out about him and come from him and take him away and lock him up in an asylum.' She never mentioned Musk by name in these stories, but they are clearly similar to what Musk himself has said about his upbringing.

While he was still building Zip2, Justine flew out for several visits as they dated long-distance. She recalls one time when she took her father to meet Musk. As they walked through the office park, she says, 'We saw these lanky dudes in jeans and T-shirts – they were racing these remote-controlled contraptions around the parking lot and banging them into cars and my dad said, "Oh, are these the children of the engineers?" And I said, "No, Dad, these are the engineers."'[4]

And then, in January 2000, they married. Having denied himself a holiday for a long time, Musk decided that the two-week investment trip for PayPal later that year was the perfect opportunity to enjoy the honeymoon they hadn't had at the time of their wedding. The trip, which included Brazil and South Africa, nearly killed him as he contracted and eventually recovered from malaria. It would reinforce his long-held belief that vacations are bad for you – in his case professionally and personally.

While she was engaged to Musk and following the sale of Zip2, Justine made a poignant remark in a television interview. Asked about her fiancé's astounding success and his purchase of the McLaren F1 supercar, Justine responded, 'My fear is that we become spoiled brats. That we lose a sense of appreciation and perspective.'[5]

Musk had also bought a small aircraft. Like his father and grandfather before him.

Perspective was important to Justine. Her perspective on her own ambitions as an author, which she says Musk at first encouraged and then later in their marriage dismissed. And perspective on their relationship as it went from a college dorm to a small office space in Palo Alto, and into the stratosphere of the new dotcom multimillionaires of Silicon Valley.

Justine referred to Musk as her own private Alexander the Great in the *Marie Claire* feature she wrote in 2010. There is a certain irony in this. Errol Musk had always admired the Macedonian conqueror as among the greatest figures in history. Errol's own domineering personality also seemed to echo in the now supremely successful and wealthy Musk. At their wedding reception, Justine recalls his telling her during their dance, 'I am the alpha in this relationship.'[6] Many years later, Musk admitted in a Twitter response to a fan that his favourite class at the University of Pennsylvania had been 'Alexander and the Rise of Hellenism'.[7] The name Alexander resonated even further in their relationship. After the sale of PayPal in 2002, the Musks had their first child, a boy, whom they named Nevada Alexander.

Then the first real tragedy of Musk's adult life hit him. In the same week that news of eBay's purchase of PayPal was made public, Nevada died of sudden infant death syndrome (SIDS). Justine later recalled: 'Nevada went down for a nap, placed on his back as always, and stopped breathing. He was ten weeks old, the age when male infants are most susceptible to SIDS. By the time the paramedics resuscitated him, he had been deprived of oxygen for so long that he was brain-dead. He spent three days on life support in a hospital in Orange County before we made the decision to take him off it. I held him in my arms when he died.'[8]

Nevada's death destroyed both parents.

'Elon made it clear that he did not want to talk about Nevada's death,' Justine wrote. 'I didn't understand this, just as he didn't understand why I grieved openly, which he regarded as "emotionally manipulative". I buried my feelings instead, coping with Nevada's death by making my first visit to an IVF clinic less than two months later. Elon and I planned to get pregnant again as swiftly as possible. Within the next five years, I gave birth to twins [Xavier and Griffin], then triplets [Kai, Saxon and Damian], and I sold three novels to Penguin and Simon & Schuster. Even so, Nevada's death sent me on a years-long inward spiral of depression and distraction.'[9]

In the year after Nevada's death, Justine and Musk attended the Burning Man festival in Nevada's Black Rock Desert. It was the place where their son had been conceived, and after which they had named him. There she wrote his name on a makeshift shrine. But while Justine tapped into her writer's soul to try to deal with the death of her son, Musk was more pragmatic and simply decided to bury his feelings, in the belief that dwelling on something was not helpful at all.

And Musk clearly felt he had to move on, because he existed in a fast-paced world that was moving faster by the second. Justine recalls how their marriage was one of parties with the rich and famous, from Paris Hilton and Leonardo DiCaprio to Bono, Richard Branson, Larry Page, John Cusack and other celebrities and business icons. Justine even recalls going to a local Starbucks with actress Daryl Hannah.[10]

It seemed inevitable that something had to give, and in the end it was their marriage. She later wrote: 'Elon was obsessed with his work: when he was home, his mind was elsewhere. I longed for deep and heartfelt conversations, for intimacy and empathy. And while

I sacrificed a normal family life for his career, Elon started to say that I "read too much", shrugging off my book deadlines. This felt like a dismissal, and a stark reversal from the days when he was so supportive. When we argued – over the house or the kids' sleeping schedule – my faults and flaws came under the microscope. I felt insignificant in his eyes, and I began thinking about what effect our dynamic would have on our five young sons.'[11]

Eventually, it was a near-fatal car accident in Los Angeles in the spring of 2008 that convinced her the marriage was over. Justine recalls her first thoughts immediately after the accident as being more focused on what her husband's reaction would be rather than the fact that she had survived: 'In my mind's eye, I could suddenly see myself: a woman who'd gotten very thin, and very blonde, stumbling out of a very expensive car with the front-left wheel smashed in. I barely recognized myself. I had turned into a trophy wife – and I sucked at it.'[12]

Musk's emotional response to Justine at this time is strikingly reminiscent of his own father's attitude towards Maye.

The couple tried counselling, which failed. They were divorced in 2008. It was a very messy, very public divorce. In a blog post shortly after her divorce, Justine wrote: 'No one who knows my ex-husband would accuse him of being weak-willed. The same qualities that helped bring about his extraordinary success dictate that the life you lead with him is his life, you have to want the same things he wants, and that there is no middle ground (not least because he has no time to find it).'[13]

And in another blog post, she reflected on her marriage to Musk: 'The happiest moments of my marriage took place in the earlier years, on the Saturday and Sunday mornings when E and I went to the bookstore, then took our purchases to a café and read over coffee and just hung out. Somewhere along the line we stopped doing that. Hindsight tells me that our marriage suffered for it. But the ironic thing is, for all the glamour and adventure of the jet-set lifestyle, when I think about happiness with him I don't remember the south of France or St Barts or the Google dude's wedding on Richard Branson's private island (in fact, we had wicked fights and I sounded some true depths of misery at all those places). I think about lazily strolling down University Avenue in Palo Alto, our arms around each other's waists, in the sunlight.'[14]

Describing herself as Musk's 'starter wife', Justine received a text message from her ex-husband six weeks after he filed for divorce, informing her that he was dating the English actress Talulah Riley. Justine described Riley as 'better fitted to my ex-husband's lifestyle and personality than I ever was'.[15] According to Justine, Riley also seemed to have no problem with changing her hair colour from brunette to blonde, something she says was a strange sticking point in her relationship with Musk, who insisted that she colour her hair blonde.

Musk and Riley met at a club – the exclusive Whisky Mist – in London while he was on a business trip. According to him, she expressed a shared interest in physics. Musk was immediately taken by her, and they began dating.

He proposed only ten days after their first date. 'Elon proposed really quickly. The idea of being swept off your feet is really appealing,' Riley said.[16] But her marriage to Musk in 2010 coincided with some of his most chaotic, darkest and desperate years in business as he tried to keep Tesla, SpaceX and SolarCity alive while burning through his cash reserves at a furious rate. 'I don't know how he handles the stress. If I was him I would've died of a heart attack. You would not wish that kind of pain on your worst enemy,' Riley said at the time.[17]

Clearly, the strain took its toll on their marriage and they divorced in 2012. They married again in 2013, and divorced again in 2016. 'I will love you forever. You will make someone very happy one day,' Musk tweeted.[18] He told *Forbes* magazine, 'We took some time apart for several months to see if absence makes the heart grow fonder, and unfortunately it did not. I still love her, but I'm not in love with her. And I can't really give her what she wants.'[19]

Musk has spoken repeatedly of his desire for a stable relationship. In 2016, he began dating another actress, Amber Heard, who was still married to actor Johnny Depp. At the time, Heard and Depp were estranged because of their turbulent and allegedly violent relationship, and Heard had obtained a restraining order against Depp. Later, during a libel action brought by Depp against *The Sun* newspaper, a London court even heard text messages Musk had sent Heard offering to pay for her full-time security. According to Musk, he and Heard only started dating a month after she had filed for divorce from Depp. 'I don't think I was ever even in the vicinity of Amber during their marriage,'[20] he said.

Their relationship didn't develop, and in his seminal 2017 interview with *Rolling Stone* Musk admitted he was heartbroken when Heard ended it: 'I was really in love, and it hurt bad … It's so hard for me to even meet people. I'm looking for a long-term relationship. I'm not looking for a one-night stand. I'm looking for a serious companion or soulmate, that kind of thing.'[21]

And then in 2018, Musk was on Twitter and about to tweet a niche science joke about Roko's Basilisk – a thought experiment about AI taking over the world – and rococo, the ornate 18th-century design style. Musk had wanted to somehow combine the two and make a joke with their connection, only to discover that somebody had already done that and created a character called Roccoco Basilisk.

It was Claire Elise Boucher, a Canadian musician known as Grimes (the spelling Roccoco was hers). She had referenced it in the credits of her 2015 music video, 'Flesh Without Blood', listing Roccoco Basilisk as one of the characters she played in the video. The joke existed on Twitter for three years before somebody finally got it, namely, Elon Musk. After 'flirting' on Twitter – and with occasional moments of unfollowing each other that were quickly picked up on by Twitter followers – Musk and Grimes made their relationship public when they attended the 2018 Met Gala in New York. Musk described her as one of the most unusual people he had ever met.

In May 2020, the unmarried couple gave birth to a baby boy and announced his name to the world as X Æ A-12. Their choice of name was as unusual as their shared love for obscure AI jokes and references.

Grimes revealed via Twitter what the name represented:

X = the unknown variable.

Æ = my elven spelling of Ai (love &/or Artificial Intelligence)

A-12 = precursor to SR-17 (our favourite aircraft). No weapons, no defenses, just speed. Great in battle, but non-violent

+

(A=Archangel, my favorite song)

A California regulation prohibiting the use of numbers in personal names saw the couple later change the 12 to Xii. According to Musk, the name is pronounced 'X Ash A Twelve'. Musk has said he admires Grimes's work ethic, while she clearly admires his space aspirations and has declared herself ready to die with the red dust of Mars beneath her feet.

But once again, Musk's search for true love appeared as challenging as finding life on other planets. In September 2020, Musk announced on Twitter that he and Grimes had split, the result, he said, of their demanding work schedules. Nevertheless, in an interview with *Vanity Fair* on 10 March 2022, Musk and Grimes announced the birth of a daughter, named Y, conceived via a surrogate.

OF all the women in his life, Justine appears to have understood Musk the best. Or rather to have had the greatest understanding of the character and mind of Musk. She understood his childhood insecurities arising from being so different. And she had a keen understanding of how this translated into the visionary he would become.

In a manner that paraphrases Peter Thiel's summation of how society gives people like Elon Musk the freedom to move outside traditional constraints, Justine observed: 'Artists and entrepreneurs are a lot alike. They are both obsessed with creating something out of nothing. With pulling value from the dark. Before we call people visionaries, before they have that kind of success, we have other words for them. We call them geek or outsider, socially awkward, weird, a little different, the odd one out.

'In the beginning we don't trust them because we think they're crazy, but in the end we trust them because we know they're crazy. Crazy enough to accomplish anything and risk it all in order to bring us something new to believe in. They might make lousy husbands and terrible wives, but they bring light to the dark and they show us the universe.'[22]

In a 2016 talk she did for TEDx San Francisco, titled 'Wounded People Tell Better Stories', Justine made the following observation about her former husband and the similarly brilliant and successful people in his circles: 'Even the most golden among us, I mean they have stellar careers, but if you look at the other areas of their lives you'll see where their demons manifest themselves. Their forms of self-sabotage, their wounds … we can't choose our passion any more than we can choose our wounds ... We create a parallel world to escape the world that rejects us or which we find too painful to live in. But some people are so good at doing this and master such an amazing skill set that they take their world and they infuse it into our world, and they change the world. And these are the people we call visionaries. People who move between worlds.'[23]

Justine has been a keen observer of Musk's ability to transcend these two worlds, and offers an insight into why it makes him so successful: 'When Elon and I would travel and we had to fill out those forms at customs that want to know your occupation, Elon never wrote down CEO or King of the World, or Studly International Playboy. He wrote engineer. And he wore jeans and T-shirts to work. And whenever we went shopping for clothes, or later consulted with a stylist whose name was Martin, he would say, "No, no, you don't understand. I can't look cool or hip because I have to look like an engineer."

'One of the things he told me was that engineers could not quite figure out why it was that the suits made the big money when it was the engineers who actually built the stuff that they were selling. Meanwhile the suits would listen to the engineers talk and they would have no idea what they were saying. That's when I realised that Elon was somebody who had learned to speak both languages. He could move between the tribes because he was an engineer in a suit. And he brought together worlds. This is what a visionary does.'[24]

Musk once said that although many people thought of him as a businessman, his companies were actually vehicles for him to explore the engineering he was most passionate about – that he didn't want to have a suit telling him what he could and couldn't do.

But one of Justine's most astute observations has come through one of their sons. According to Justine, he was diagnosed with autism when he was four years old. He apparently also has a photographic memory. After explaining to her son how his photographic memory works, she says he looked at her and said: 'You mean other people don't think like that?'[25]

It was a comment that recalled something Musk once said about himself: 'There are things that seem quite clear and obvious to me, and I don't understand why they aren't so obvious to everyone'.[26] It harks back to that six-year-old boy in Pretoria who thought he was 'strange' because of all the ideas in his head.

Apart from Maye and Errol, Justine was possibly the first person not just to recognise Musk's different nature but also to understand it – a man who existed in different worlds, and who 'brought together worlds' through his visionary ideas and innovation.

And back in 2002, her then husband was about to embark on the boldest of these journeys between worlds as his vision started to extend towards the stars.

PART FIVE
Ad Astra

IN October 2001, Elon Musk and two friends – Adeo Ressi and Jim Cantrell – sat in a room with a few Russians. On the table was enough vodka to slay a Siberian tiger. And on the negotiating table, figuratively, was a desire to make a purchase. Musk wanted to buy missiles. In particular, he was looking for surplus Russian intercontinental ballistic missiles (ICBMs).

'It was a very trippy experience. It was very bizarre,' he later told CBS's *60 Minutes*.[1]

Musk's idea was part of an elaborate publicity stunt. He had his eye on buying three SS-18 missiles, one of the world's most powerful ICBMs, with a range of up to 11 000 km. First designed in the 1960s for use by the Soviet Union's Strategic Rocket Forces, the SS-18 has been through a process of refinement ever since. It was originally designed to give the Soviet Union a powerful 'first-strike' option against its enemies, with the United States the obvious target. From a land-based launch in Russia, the SS-18 would take only 30 minutes to reach the United States. It is a missile of immense proportions capable of carrying up to ten nuclear warheads. NATO (the North Atlantic Treaty Organisation) refers to it by the delightful name of 'Satan'.

Negotiating with the Russians to buy missiles was rather like negotiating with the Prince of Darkness himself. The boardroom battles of Zip2 and PayPal clearly paled in comparison to negotiating a missile contract with a bunch of Russians who don't take you seriously when you tell them you want to go into space.

And that's exactly what Musk sought the ICBMs for – to launch his space exploration plans.

Musk's idea for the missiles had come a year earlier. It was on a drive back from a weekend in the Hamptons with Adeo Ressi, and the two friends were mulling over what to do next with their careers. Musk had concluded the PayPal deal, and Ressi was busy building a fortune from his own Internet ventures.

The two started talking about space. What was at first just a fanciful discussion suddenly became an exploration of what it would actually cost to get there. When he got out of the car, Ressi perhaps dismissed the conversation as just an interesting way to pass the time on the drive. But Musk's mind had locked on to his next target. In fact, it had actually just zeroed in on his boyhood ambition. Zip2, PayPal and the entire Internet itself were just stepping stones for Musk towards his grandest idea of all – space.

And specifically Mars.

But Musk had identified funding as one of the greatest stumbling blocks to reaching space. He believed a dwindling public appetite for costly space programmes had contributed to the funding problem.

But Mars ticked two important boxes in Musk's vision. First, he could change the narrative of space exploration as being a fruitless and expensive waste of taxpayers' money and bring back an appetite for exploration. His publicly stated desire was not just to explore space for exploration's sake but to actually make humans a multiplanetary species. As always, the way Musk frames his vision is always key to how he sells it. And, second, Mars represented the furthest reaches of human space exploration by astronauts.

Under the initial name of Mars Oasis, Musk devised an idea to build a transportable biosphere, or greenhouse, and launch it on a rocket to Mars, where it would hopefully be able to grow the first interplanetary plants. Then there was also the idea to send mice to Mars and bring them back alive, as a way of convincing the public that Mars was worth going to. As Musk himself has said, 'I'd like to die on Mars, just not on impact.'

All of this would be an attempt to convince the public once more that space exploration was a good thing – and, most importantly, that it was feasible. And this recently cashed-up Internet millionaire was determined to be the one to prove this.

He had the money. He had the vision. He had the plants. He had the mice. But he had no rocket.

Musk persuaded Ressi and another engineer, Jim Cantrell, to join his fledgling team under the company name of 'Life to Mars'. Cantrell, who had the most experience in the space industry, advised them to fly to Paris and meet with Arianespace, a launch services company responsible for the launch of the majority of Europe's satellites. But the meeting with Arianespace executives proved fruitless as Musk, Ressi and Cantrell decided that the cost of the 'launch vehicle' was too expensive.

However, the meeting with Arianespace opened up another option: Russia. The French and the Russians had been collaborating in the space race since the late 1960s. Following the collapse of the Soviet Union, the new Russian space corporation Roscosmos saw Arianespace as an opportunity to enter the Western market. And Mars would become a common theme for Roscosmos, Arianespace and NASA, as it was for Musk. For the South African, the drive to go into space and the formation of SpaceX would represent the fulfilment of a journey that began in the mind of a Pretoria boy. The global space race would suck Musk into its vortex in the most unlikely of ways. Through the Internet. Or rather, the formation of the Internet, for which we have the Russians to thank.

Sputnik and the Space Race

On Saturday 5 October 1957, Americans woke to newspaper head-lines such as this: 'Satellite fired by Russia: Circling US 15 times a day'. Another headline read 'Russia wins race to launch Earth satellite'.

What became known as the 'Sputnik crisis' had begun.

It is ironic that the greatest achievements in the field of space exploration have come about because of the threat of war on Earth. From the moment Sputnik 1 was launched by the Soviet Union into low Earth orbit on 4 October 1957, the space race was on. And the Soviet Union was firmly in the lead.

The Soviets were bullish, and the Americans were fearful.

The Soviets had used an ICBM to launch Sputnik, and that sent two very clear messages to the US. First, the Soviets had something up there that could keep an eye on the US. This bothered everyone from the man mowing his lawn in Cleveland to the top military brass in the Department of Defense. Something up there in space – something Russian – was watching. The second concern was that Russia had missiles carrying nuclear warheads capable of reaching space, which in turn meant they were more than capable of reaching the US as well.

Sputnik 1 sparked an even greater panic in the West that the Soviets had become the dominant superpower. Some Americans even claimed they could hear the 'beep, beep, beep' sound made by Sputnik 1 as it passed overhead. The economist Bernard Baruch wrote an open letter to the *New York Herald Tribune* in which he issued a warning under the title of 'The Lessons of Defeat': 'While we devote our industrial and technological power to producing new model automobiles and more gadgets, the Soviet Union is conquering space. While America grumbles over taxes and cuts the cloak of its defence to the cloth of its budget, Russia is launching intercontinental missiles. Suddenly, rudely, we are awakened to the fact that the Russians have outdistanced us in a race which we thought we were winning. It is Russia, not the United States, who has had the imagination to hitch its wagon to the stars and the skill to reach for the moon and all but grasp it. America is worried. It should be.'[1]

The American public was indeed worried. Official NASA chief historian Roger D Launius wrote that the launch of Sputnik 1 had a 'Pearl Harbor' effect on American public opinion: 'It was a shock, introducing the average citizen to the space age in a crisis setting. The event created an illusion of a technological gap and provided the impetus for increased spending for aerospace endeavors, technical and scientific educational programs, and the chartering of new federal agencies to manage air and space research and development. Not only had the Soviets been first in orbit, but Sputnik 1 weighed nearly 200 pounds, compared to the intended 3.5 pounds for the first satellite to be launched in Project Vanguard [the American programme to launch a satellite into space]. In the Cold War environment of the late 1950s, this disparity of capability portended menacing implications.'[2]

The American historian Daniel J Boorstin noted: 'Never before had so small and so harmless an object created such consternation.'[3] Another historian, Walter A McDougall, added: 'No event since Pearl Harbor set off such repercussions in public life.'[4]

And when the trademark 'beep, beep, beep' signal of Sputnik 1 was broadcast by American radio stations, it was received by the public like a metronome of pure terror beeping out the coming red wave of communism they so feared. Americans had been convinced they were living in the world's greatest country at the dawn of an age of plenty and material progress. Sputnik 1's signal tolled like a death knell of the American dream.

In February 1958, President Dwight Eisenhower authorised the creation of the Advanced Research Projects Agency (ARPA, later to become the Defense Advanced Research Projects Agency, or DARPA). ARPA would lead to the creation of ARPANET and later the Internet that so fascinated Musk and provided the launchpad for his own ambitions. ARPA would become the vanguard of the US effort to surpass the Soviet Union as millions of dollars were poured into the development of science and technology.

In February 1958, the first American satellite, Explorer 1, was launched into orbit. In July 1958, Eisenhower signed the National Aeronautics and Space Act. NASA was born. It speaks volumes that only 11 years later, astronaut Neil Armstrong became the first human to walk on the moon. Space was a priority, and it received the required funding and attention.

And Mars also played a role in the space race.

In the 1960s, the Russians launched a series of probes intended to reach Mars. NASA made the first successful flyby of Mars in 1965, and Mariner 9 made the first orbit of Mars in November 1971. The Russians then raised the bar when they became the first to land probes on the surface of Mars, in November and December of

1971. However, neither of the two probes achieved a 'soft landing', and only one was briefly able to transmit signals. In 1976, NASA successfully landed Viking 1 and Viking 2, and the world was presented with the first colour images of the Red Planet.

Since then, China, India and the European Space Agency have joined NASA in successfully sending spacecraft to Mars.

But it was a project launched in the early 1990s, when NASA began working on a Mars observation balloon, that would intersect with Musk's own Mars ambitions.

The French had also been working on a Mars balloon. But the French were planning to send their balloon to Mars aboard a Russian rocket. With the opening up of the former Soviet Union in the late 1980s, the French suggested that NASA join them in a tripartite Mars balloon project with Russia. A talented young American engineer had secured a place on this project. His name was Jim Cantrell. It was the beginning of American and Russian space cooperation, which would eventually lead to the International Space Station (ISS). And it later led to cooperation of a private kind, when Cantrell suggested to Musk that he could indeed build his own rockets.

As a result of his role on the Mars balloon project, Cantrell had spent quite a bit of time in Russia working with Russian engineers, so he had a keen understanding of the lay of the land and the workings of the Russian space industry. Ironically, the biggest threat to the further exploration of Mars at the time was a new development on Earth – peace. The collapse of the Soviet Union ended the Cold War and heralded a new era of peace, but it almost stopped the space race as well. The reduction of the threat of war meant that both Russian and American defence funding to keep pushing the boundaries of space dried up.

However, this coincided with the growing privatisation of spaceflight. The space race was moving from government-centralised programmes to a multitude of private endeavours. Today, there are a range of private space companies offering everything from launch vehicles, cargo transport, crew transport, landers, rovers, orbiters, research craft, propulsion manufacturers and satellite launchers to space manufacturing, space mining, space settlement and more. The final frontier is now very much the home of cosmic capitalism, fuelled by billionaires with deep enough pockets for deep space. From Musk's SpaceX to Richard Branson's Virgin Galactic and Jeff Bezos's Blue Origin, they are opening up space like never before, and offering everything from official collaboration with NASA and government space projects to individual space travel for wealthy earthlings. But there are still perceptions to overcome.

'The general public doesn't understand the difference between getting to space and getting to orbit,' says Musk in an interview with Charlie Rose. 'There's a very big difference. To do a suborbital flight you need a terminal velocity of around Mach 3. To get to orbit you need a terminal velocity of Mach 25. It's a huge difference. There are a number of efforts in the suborbital category that certainly can grow one day to orbital. Jeff Bezos has an effort. Richard Branson is funding that development at Scaled Composites in California. We're in the orbit class. It's a lot more capital and that's where you're really pushing the ragged edge of what's physically possible. In the rocket business, the rocket company does the launch. It's not like the airline business. You don't sell the rocket, you sell the launch.'

And that was the initial aim for SpaceX – to be the cheapest launch services company on the market.

Cantrell was an early ally of Musk in this new world. In 2001, Cantrell was working as a private consultant in the space industry when Musk approached him with the idea of purchasing rockets to reach Mars. Because of Cantrell's contacts in the Russian space industry, when the door closed at Arianespace, Russia emerged as a solution, and a particularly cheap one at that, as they were said to be selling refurbished ICBMs at a fraction of the cost.

And that's how Musk, Ressi and Cantrell arrived in Moscow in October 2001. But in that first vodka-fuelled meeting, the Russians were dismissive of Musk's desire to purchase their missiles. In fact, they generally made fun of him as just another foreigner with more money than sense. One engineer reportedly spat at Musk in disgust at what he perceived to be a man too rich for his own good trying to purchase such a perfectly designed weapon of war.

It took another two trips to Russia before they finally reached some semblance of a deal. Musk brought with him the $21 million they had agreed for the three ICBMs. And that's when the Russians changed the deal, informing him that they actually meant $21 million apiece. Aware that he was being deliberately played, and not being taken seriously, Musk turned to Cantrell on the flight home and declared, 'We can build a rocket ourselves.' Cantrell urged him to do exactly that.

And so Musk did what he does so well. He read. The man nick-named 'Encyclopaedia' by his family buried himself in every bit of literature he could find about rockets, from dusty technical manuals dating back to the old Soviet Union to the latest research. Cantrell pointed him in the direction of books such as *Rocket Propulsion Elements*, *Aerothermodynamics of Gas Turbine and Rocket Propulsion*, *Fundamentals of Astrodynamics* and *The International Reference Guide to Space Launch Systems*. Light reading for rocket enthusiasts.

Musk read everything he could get his hands on. And when he was done, he was confident that he understood rocketry as well as the engineers themselves. In fact, it was said he could more than hold his own in discussions with rocket engineers. There was no doubt that Musk knew every single element of the rockets he was going to have other people build for him.

Musk had refocused his mind from the world of the Internet to the world of aerospace. He began to meet with aerospace engineers in Los Angeles. He drove out to the Mojave Desert to join the Reaction Research Society, one of Southern California's most famous experimental rocket clubs (founded in 1946), at their amateur launches. He attended meetings of Mars societies and clubs. If somebody was meeting in a room or hotel bar in Los Angeles to discuss space, it's a good bet that Musk was there with them. Many described the intensity of his new interest as quite startling. Others said that watching rocket launches was like a religious experience for Musk. And still others, many of them long-time industry insiders, were offended and insulted by the arrogance of his newfound knowledge. There was indeed a hint of the kid who was too smart for his own good.

Musk began cold-calling notable aerospace engineers and some of the most brilliant minds in rocket science, and telling them of his plans to start his own rocket company. Many of them thought he was mad. But slowly he gathered disciples, notably Tom Mueller, described as a rising star in the building of rocket engines. Mueller shared Musk's optimism about space. He also shared the negativity around his own ambitions. When Musk had told his parents he was leaving South Africa for Canada, Errol had said he'd be back in three months. Similarly, when Mueller told his family he was going to 'build rockets' and find a job in the aerospace industry, his father also said he'd be back and that 'the forests would be waiting for him' in his Idaho hometown.

Musk and Mueller first met through the Reaction Research Society. Musk had a variety of engineering questions for Mueller, as well as one profoundly important question. Cost? How cheaply could he build a rocket?

As Musk generated momentum on his plans, those closest to him did their best to convince him he was embarking on a journey of insanity rather than ingenuity. Adeo Ressi in particular came with one of the most convincing arguments of all. It didn't include a financial spreadsheet or talk of profit and loss. It was simply a carefully curated hour-long video of failed rocket launches, with the rockets blowing up spectacularly in the sky. Clearly, Ressi believed that if Musk saw how few rockets actually make it off the ground, it would convince his friend to end this futile endeavour.

It had the opposite effect. It actually strengthened Musk's resolve to find a solution. In the same way he had looked at the financial services industry and been surprised at its lack of innovation, Musk looked at the space industry and was surprised to learn that NASA had no plans to send human beings to Mars – the one thing he thought was a blatantly obvious goal. He even logged on to NASA's website and thought the fact that he couldn't find any mention of such a plan was merely an administrative oversight: 'I was trying to figure out why we had not made more progress since Apollo,' Musk said in 2003.[5]

He was right. Since the glory days of the 1960s and the 1969 moon landing, to exciting names such as Apollo and Voyager and Viking, the American space programme had lost momentum. In terms of Mars in particular, Mariner 9 had reached the orbit of Mars in 1971, and Viking 1 landed on Mars in 1976. But little had been done since then. The American space programme seemed to have stagnated.

'In the Sixties we went from not being able to put anybody into space to putting somebody on the moon and developing all the technology from scratch to do that. And yet in the Seventies, Eighties and Nineties we've kind of gone sideways. We're currently in a situation where we can't even put a person into lower Earth orbit,' Musk reasoned.[6]

In 2010, addressing a special Senate hearing into the future of American spaceflight, Neil Armstrong said: 'If the leadership we have acquired through our investment is simply allowed to fade away, other nations will surely step in where we have faltered. I do not believe that this would be in our best interests.'[7]

A year after his address, the Space Shuttle – once the flagship vehicle of space exploration and the main means of transporting American astronauts to the ISS – was grounded for the last time. The reason was simple. It had just become too expensive to go into space. It cost NASA roughly $450 million every time the Space Shuttle launched. Nothing had been done to make space exploration cheaper. Many argue that the writing was on the wall after the 2003 *Columbia* disaster, when seven astronauts were killed as the shuttle broke up upon re-entry into Earth's orbit. This was the second major Space Shuttle tragedy, following the 1986 *Challenger* disaster, and it led to the former paragon of American space exploration being mothballed for good.

Since 2011, NASA has been hitching rides with the Russians into space on their Soyuz rockets. And it's an expensive ride, coming at roughly $86 million a seat.

Clearly, something had to be done that would not only reinvigorate the interest in space but also make it far less expensive to get there. Since Musk's meeting with Mueller in the Mojave Desert, his mind had been working on how cheaply you could build rockets. It was a problem perfectly suited to his way of thinking. It was outlandish enough to pique his interest. It was disruptive enough for an industry deemed previously inaccessible to private companies. And, as his brother Kimbal observed, it was big enough. Space was big enough for the mind of Musk.

'He's a guy with unlimited ambition. His mind just needs to be constantly fulfilled. The problems that he takes on therefore need to become more and more complex over time in order to keep him interested,' said Kimbal.[8] Errol has also observed that he worries about the day his son becomes bored. Space clearly has the potential to hold Musk's interest for years to come.

What confounded Musk was that there had been no visible progress in terms of space exploration, while other technology sectors had grown by leaps and bounds. 'That just doesn't gel with all of the other technology sectors out there,' he argued. 'The computer that you could have bought in the early Seventies would've filled a room and had less computing power than a cellphone. So just about every sector of technology has improved. Why has this not improved?'[9]

Musk believed that if you went back 40 years with a vision of the future, and told people of the things that were to come, they would more likely have been surprised by the slow progress made in space than by the fact that people in the future carried supercomputers (cellphones) in their pockets: 'If you went back to 1969 when we landed on the moon, and asked the public what would the situation be in 2015, I think they would've imagined we'd have a base on the moon, a base on Mars, and be all over the solar system.'[10]

But it hadn't happened.

'So I started looking into that.'[11]

Believing it at first to be simply a funding issue, Musk came up with his Mars Oasis idea, a means of possibly drumming up public support for a privately funded robotic mission to Mars which in turn he hoped would reinvigorate the space debate and lead to greater funding for the industry.

Once again, the engineer showed a keener understanding of the mechanics of the human mind and people's perceptions than the mechanics of rocketry when he explained why he believed Mars Oasis would achieve this result: 'It would cost about $15 to $20 million. We would put a small robotic lander on the surface of Mars with seeds and dehydrated nutrient gel that would hydrate upon landing and you would have plants growing in Martian radiation gravity conditions. And you'd also be maintaining a life support system on Mars. This would be interesting to the public because they tend to respond to precedents and superlatives,' Musk said.[12]

'This would be the furthest that life has ever travelled.'[13]

And, he added, there would of course be the money shot – the photo of green plants on a red Martian background.

And that's exciting.

Musk realised that being Columbus and talking about discovering a new trade route is one thing, but there also needs to be talk of strange tribes and sea monsters to really get people interested and excited. It was science fiction and superheroes that had excited a young Pretoria boy's mind.

And this childhood excitement is at the very heart of so much of what Musk has done. Space is no different. Frankly, it's right there on the SpaceX website, under 'Mission'. In bold letters above a photo of the Earth, Musk tells us: 'You want to wake up in the morning and think the future is going to be great – and that's what being a spacefaring civilization is all about. It's about believing in the future and thinking that the future will be better than the past. And I can't think of anything more exciting than going out there and being among the stars.'[14]

Expanding on this, Musk said in 2017: 'The part that I find personally most motivating is that it creates a sense of adventure and it makes people excited about the future. If you consider two futures – one where we are forever confined to Earth until eventually something terrible happens, or another future where we are out there on many planets, maybe even going beyond the solar system, I think that second version is incredibly inspiring and exciting. There need to be reasons to get up in the morning. Life can't just be about solving problems, otherwise what's the point. There have got to be things that people find inspiring and that make life worth living.'[15]

Even Richard Branson, a man who built his fortune on marketing a vision to people, admitted in *Time* magazine in 2013: 'For a while now, space has been looking boring. News about space was reduced to budget cuts and deorbiting schedules, not research or innovation.'[16]

Musk realised that the narrative needed to change. The general public were quite rightly asking questions about what they believed to be the pointlessness of space exploration. Could that exorbitant cost not be put to better use right here on Earth? Why try and go to Mars when we cannot even feed or educate everybody on Earth properly? Shouldn't we first try to sort out problems here, such as world hunger, before we try and colonise another planet? For many, Musk and Branson and Bezos fit the mould of eccentric billionaires fuelling their egos with dreams of the final frontier. In *The Guardian* newspaper in May 2020, columnist Arwa Mahdawi declared: 'Of course billionaires like Elon Musk love outer space. The Earth is too small for their egos.'

'There are some people who find billionaires with big rockets very inspirational ... Hope for whom, I want to know? The World Bank estimates that between 40 and 60 million people will fall into extreme poverty (earning less than $1.90 a day) in 2020, thanks to COVID-19. What hope, exactly, does a rocket blasting into space provide when you can't put food on your plate?

'Seriously, if you think that billionaires are exploring space for the good of humankind then I have a bridge on Mars I can sell you. They are doing it for their ego and the commercial opportunity. They are doing it because they think they, quite literally, are the masters of the universe.'[17]

The topic of space exploration is fiercely debated everywhere from government offices and corporate boardrooms to podcasts such as *Metaphysical Milkshake*,[18] cohosted by Rainn Wilson and

Reza Aslan. *Metaphysical Milkshake* devoted an hour-long episode to debating the question, 'Should we colonise Mars?' They called in Dr Moogega Cooper, an astronomer who is also a planetary protection engineer for NASA, focusing specifically on Mars. Dr Cooper graduated from high school at the age of 16, one year younger than Musk. She describes herself as one of the 'modern-day real life Guardians of the Galaxy'. Essentially, Dr Cooper makes sure that the spacecraft we're sending to other planets are 'clean enough' so as not to adversely affect the ecosystems of other planets with pollutants from Earth.

The American astronomer Carl Sagan once summed up mankind's ancient obsession with Mars – from the Greeks and Mayans to Musk – as follows: 'Maybe we're on Mars because of the magnificent science that can be done there – the gates of the wonder world are opening in our time. Maybe we're on Mars because we have to be, because there's a deep nomadic impulse built into us by the evolutionary process – we come, after all, from hunter-gatherers, and for 99.9 per cent of our tenure on Earth we've been wanderers. And the next place to wander to is Mars.'[19]

In the podcast, Dr Cooper adds: 'It sparks the whole ethical side about how to responsibly wander to other places.'[20] But she goes on to say that the idea of colonising Mars, while important in the sense that it can stimulate a lot of innovative thought, is just not feasible in even the next 30 years. Apparently, Earth is still a pretty good place for humans to exist, and it is still the only place for our extremely sensitive bodies. Dr Cooper cites numerous studies showing the changes that occur in human physiology after time in space, 'and not all of them are good'.

According to Dr Cooper, humans could survive on Mars for a short time, but we certainly won't be thriving there: 'It's not easy to build a habitat, to survive Mars's high radiation and low temperature environments, and you're being constantly bombarded by all of the UV – it's not pleasant.'[21] Quite simply, Dr Cooper believes Mars will never be a viable second Earth, and that the focus should remain on 'protecting our own blue marble'.

Leave Mars to the Martians is another view of the debate.

Even Carl Sagan posed the question, 'There will be a time when Mars is all explored; a time after robot aircraft have mapped it from aloft, a time after rovers have combed the surface, a time after samples have been returned safely to Earth, a time after human beings have walked the sands of Mars. What then? What shall we do with Mars? There are so many examples of human misuse of the Earth that even phrasing this question chills me. If there is life on Mars, I believe we should do nothing with Mars. Mars then belongs to the Martians, even if the Martians are only microbes. The existence of an independent biology on a nearby planet is a treasure beyond assessing, and the preservation of that life must, I think, supersede any other possible use of Mars.'[22]

Make no mistake, if there is money to made off of Mars, even the Red Planet will be exploited. Musk has admitted that 'If we decide to establish a self-sustaining base on the moon or a base on Mars, that is enormous opportunity on the trillion-dollar level because then you've got basically interplanetary commerce going on. That's pretty huge.'[23] Clearly, financial reward in space is on the agenda in the next few light years.

But Musk has also defended space exploration in more philosophical ways. On 13 July 2021 he tweeted: 'Those who attack space maybe don't realize that space represents hope for so many people.'[24]

Back in the early 2000s, Musk could see that the narrative around space needed to change. Society needed to talk about space as exciting again, and people had to be shown the value of exploration for human advancement. Margaret Mead, the American anthropologist who died a year before Neil Armstrong walked on the moon, said: 'Once you raise the question that other lands than this Earth are possible to live on, that other places are possible places to found colonies, or that there may be other living creatures somewhere, you have changed the whole place of man in the universe. You've altered everything. This involves a considerable reduction of human arrogance and a tremendous magnification of human possibilities.'[25]

For Musk, the initial desire was not to start his own space exploration company as much as it was to restart the conversation around space exploration. 'Is there some way to reignite the dream of Apollo?' he asked. 'Apollo was incredibly inspiring to everyone around the world. Only a very tiny number of people went there, but vicariously we all went there. I think that's true of if we have a Mars base as well.'[26]

This raised another question in Musk's mind as to why space exploration had stagnated: 'Is it a question of we've lost the will to explore?'[27] Initially, he thought this was indeed the case. But later Musk says he came to realise that people had not lost the will to explore space. They just couldn't see a way. Most significantly, they couldn't see an affordable way. We needed to make space cheaper.

And even Musk admitted the colossal challenge involved here when he said during a lecture at Stanford in 2003: 'Space is advanced entrepreneuring. Space is a tough one for first-time entrepreneurs. You're better off starting with something that requires low capital, and space is a high capital effort.'[28]

But the challenge was perfectly suited to Musk. As Justine observed, Musk is a man capable of moving between the tribes. An engineer in a suit. And the challenge of space would require both of these qualities in astounding measures of genius and boldness.

SpaceX

ON 6 May 2002, 'Life on Mars' became the Space Exploration Technologies Corporation, or SpaceX. With a handful of employees and a factory in Hawthorne, California, Musk and his team of intrepid space engineers began the work of building their first rocket.

Their goal was the Russians, or rather, answering a question Russian space exploration had raised in Musk's mind: 'Why is it that the Russians can build these low-cost launch vehicles? We don't drive Russian cars or fly Russian planes or have Russian kitchen appliances. I felt the US is a pretty competitive place, and we should be able to build a cost-efficient launch vehicle.'[1]

To start with, Musk compiled a feasibility study that looked at all of the engineers who had been involved with the major launch vehicle developments over the last three decades. Together with his small team of hand-picked engineers, he spent a number of Saturdays poring over solutions to the problems of launch cost and reliability.

For Musk, the two were intrinsically linked: 'We really focused on reducing the cost across the board. For one thing, our overhead in a 30-person company is an order of magnitude less than it is in

Lockheed and Boeing. Every decision we made was with consideration to simplicity. That improves the reliability as well as reduces your cost. Fewer components means fewer components that can go wrong and fewer components to buy.'[2]

It is for exactly this reason that 80 per cent of what SpaceX uses to go into space is made in their own factory. 'The space supply chain is very expensive and you have very few options – often only one supplier,'[3] Musk said in an interview with *Planetary Radio*. 'If we didn't make stuff ourselves, we would be beholden to those legacy costs. If you're going to try and create a revolutionary rocket that's substantially lower cost and aspires to be higher reliability and where we intend to try and make reusability work, then it's very difficult to use much of the existing supply chain because you will inherit those costs. So we had to do it.'[4]

The final frontier is more a bank balance than a far-flung solar system, and space is indeed a black hole capable of swallowing billions of dollars in the blink of an eye. This is why, in a feature on *60 Minutes*, host Scott Pelley states matter-of-factly, 'Only four entities have launched a space capsule into orbit and successfully brought it back. The United States, Russia, China … and Elon Musk.'[5] It's a staggering declaration. Humanity's journey to the stars boils down to three countries, and one independent man.

One of the problems Musk had with the space industry was the exorbitant contracts dished out by government to the likes of Boeing and Lockheed Martin, and how this created a culture of payment for failure. It's one of the reasons space exploration has been for so long the preserve of government, because only government had the resources to keep paying for rockets that blew up. When SpaceX had grown to the point that it could secure NASA contracts, it was on the premise that these would be paid for meeting certain targets. Failure was always an option for Musk, but he quite clearly believed that the contractual basis upon which failure was still being rewarded was hampering the growth of the industry and stifling innovation.

At the age of 30, Musk and Justine moved from Silicon Valley to Los Angeles, the hub of America's aerospace industry, to launch SpaceX. He had found his factory space in Hawthorne. He had his core team, who celebrated moving into their new office space with a mariachi band, and with Musk waving around two wooden maracas. And he had his vision.

It was time to get to work on his first rocket – the Falcon 1.

SpaceX's first rocket was named after the *Millennium Falcon* from the *Star Wars* franchise. Joe Johnston, the original *Star Wars* modelmaker, had four weeks to build the model and described it as one of the most intense projects he'd ever worked on. Musk and his team had slightly more time, but building Falcon 1 would be more intense by several orders of magnitude. And it would test Musk to the absolute limit of not only his finances but his sanity as well.

Falcon 1

BEFORE Falcon 1 could fly, it needed a booster.

Musk's brief to Tom Mueller was simple: build a lightweight, efficient rocket engine that could produce the 70 000 pounds of thrust required to get a small satellite into orbit. But also, build a rocket engine that could handle temperatures of 3 371°C within its combustion chamber without melting everything around it. And also remember to build a rocket engine that could handle the complex relationship between vast amounts of fuel – a combination of liquid oxygen and kerosene – burning at insane temperatures and at a furious rate of combustion. Finally, remember that rockets are extremely thirsty, and while you need plenty of fuel to haul a chunk of steel into space, this makes the rocket heavy. It cannot be too heavy. Off you go, Tom.

Astrophysicist Paul M Sutter, the chief scientist at the Center of Science and Industry in Columbus, Ohio, and the host of *Ask a Spaceman* and *Space Radio*, explains exactly why rockets are so complex to build, and why Mueller's task was by no means an easy one. According to Sutter, everything in rocketry revolves around what is known as the 'rocket equation': 'This is a simple relationship between the energy needed to reach your destination, the energy available in the fuel and the fraction of the total rocket mass used up by fuel. If you want to go farther or heave a heavier object to orbit, you need more fuel. But more fuel adds more weight, making it much harder than you expect to get a lift. It's this "tyranny" that explains why modern rockets are in the range of 80 to 90 per cent fuel, all used to heft a comparatively small payload into space, and why staging – having multiple rocket stages used during launch – is such an important concept: by ditching dried-up rocket parts as you go, you become that much more efficient.'[1]

While the principle behind rocket engines is fairly simple, the building of them entails some of the most complex engineering known to humankind. According to NASA, humans have been making rockets – albeit in mostly primitive form – for around 2 000 years. But it's only been in the last 100 years or so that rocketry has developed to the extent of enabling space exploration.

So why has the basic design remain largely unchanged for the past 100 years?

According to Sutter, 'It turns out that 100 years ago we found a very potent combination. We found a very powerful way to efficiently and cheaply drive rockets that we basically haven't figured out how to beat.'[2]

That 'potent' combination is combining your energy source with your propellant so that they do one and the same thing. The fuel that burns up in the rocket is also, by engine design, the propellant that drives it outward from Earth and into space.

'You have a source of energy or propellant that you carry with you in your rocket and you mix them at precisely the right time to achieve thrust,' says Sutter.[3]

And all rocket design follows this same basic principle. But, as with Musk's brief to Mueller, simply adding more fuel to haul bigger payloads into space doesn't work.

Sutter states outright that he is not in the same league as the brilliant minds who design and build rockets. But he is a physicist and the physics of rocketry is something he can comment on. 'This is what's called the tyranny of the rocket equation,' he says. 'If you add more fuel you're adding more weight, which means it's more expensive. This can limit what you can send to orbit. This is why getting stuff to orbit is so expensive.'[4]

So it's hardly surprising that as brilliant as Mueller was, not even his closest friends believed he and a private company could build such an engine.

But he did.

The result was the Merlin family of engines. First came the Merlin 1A, evolving through the Merlin 1B, 1C and 1D between 2003 and 2012. The name was Mueller's choice, a liberty given him by Musk. Musk had named the rocket Falcon, and gave Mueller the honour of naming the engine – on condition that he give it an actual name and not a series of numbers like a serial code. Taking his lead from the Falcon engine, and on the advice of a colleague who was a falconer, Mueller opted for Merlin – the name of a medium-sized falcon.

Merlin was what drove the launch of Falcon 1, and has been behind SpaceX's Falcon 9 and Falcon Heavy rockets.

And Mueller is perfectly placed to explain to the average person how it all works. With a simple green pen sketch on a whiteboard, and speaking softly and methodically, Mueller describes the inner workings of Merlin: 'The combustion chamber is what generates the thrust of the engine. At the top of this sits an injector, which injects the propellants into the combustion chamber. These burn to produce the combustion that results in the thrust.

'The combustion chamber operates at 1000 psi (pounds per square inch) of pressure. It draws its fuel from tanks sitting alongside the rocket. In one tank is liquid oxygen (LOx) and the other fuel (Rocket Propellant 1). Each tank is at 50 psi.

'What takes the 50 psi in the tanks and turns it into 1000 psi in the chamber is a turbopump. The turbopump is basically two back-to-back impellers on a single shaft. The LOx comes in at 50 psi and goes out at 1400 psi. The fuel does the same, except it flows in through channels inside the chamber and at the same time acts like a radiator in a car cooling the chamber. The fuel comes out at 1500 psi.

'A turbine generates the horsepower to drive the two impeller pumps. A gas generator powers the turbine. We burn at high pressure inside the chamber and hot gases come out of the throat of the engine and out the nozzle to generate the thrust that lifts the rocket. That is 110000 pounds force of thrust. It all results in roughly 350 pounds mass per second. Nine of these Merlins are used on Falcon 9 (hence the name) first stage. They burn for just under three minutes. In that time they consume just over half a million pounds of propellant. It's a pretty thirsty device here to get into orbit,' says Mueller.[5]

And that, in a nutshell, is what Musk and Mueller and SpaceX and all the brilliant minds have tried to build, refine and improve upon.

Merlin is where it all began for SpaceX.

'This is a world-class engine. This is very easy to make, very low-cost and extremely reliable,' Mueller says.[6]

The company has since designed several liquid-propellant rocket engines, including the Merlin family, Kestrel (named after the smallest falcons), Draco and SuperDraco. Its most recent engine, Raptor, is the most powerful rocket engine ever produced.

But it's important to appreciate the engineering leaps Musk and SpaceX made to get to the first version of Merlin, then to its various iterations, and finally to Raptor, which is the engine Musk wants to get him to Mars as part of his Starship project to start a human settlement there.

It took only three years for SpaceX to build and test its first rocket engine. And the company surged forward from there, going from the liquid-propellant Merlin engines to the latest methane-fuelled, full-flow, staged-combustion-cycle Raptor. The option for methane with Raptor was made with Mars in mind, as it is a gas that can be produced on Mars.

Again, the leap in technology is significant. From the Merlin 1 to the Raptor, SpaceX has more than doubled the thrust of its engines and currently holds the world record for the highest combustion chamber pressure ever reached of 330 bar, surpassing the previous record of 300 bar achieved by the Russian RD-701 engine. This development came in less than 15 years.[7]

As an indication of just how impressive a feat this was, you need only turn to Musk's chief competition – fellow billionaire and rocket builder Jeff Bezos. During a tour of his factory in 2016, Bezos, hardly short of money or confidence, told reporters it takes six years to build a rocket engine. Musk's philosophy for his fledgling SpaceX team was clearly embraced. Eric Berger, author of *Liftoff: Elon Musk and the Desperate Early Days that Launched SpaceX*, described it as a philosophy of 'move fast, build things, and break things'.[8]

In 2008, Falcon 1 became the first privately funded liquid-fuelled rocket to reach orbit. And Musk has moved fast ever since. In 2012, Dragon (a spacecraft capable of carrying up to seven people or cargo into space) became the first private cargo-carrying spacecraft to reach the ISS. In 2015, Falcon 9 delivered 11 communications satellites into orbit. And then it completed what in Musk's mind has been the next evolutionary phase in rocketry – reusability.

It's probably not too far off to suggest that if the past 100 years of rocketry could be likened to the development of early hominids, this specific moment in December 2015 was when rocketry reached the equivalent of walking upright. The Falcon 9 first stage returned to Earth and landed – upright – in what was the first-ever orbital-class rocket landing. According to Musk, it made no financial sense to keep spending millions on one-time rockets when you should rather be figuring out a way to make them reusable. The Falcon had truly landed. In more ways than one. Suddenly, the three countries – the US, Russia and China – at the forefront of rocketry were all focused on one man and the advancements his fledgling company was making.

In 2018, Falcon Heavy – the world's most powerful operational rocket, which the company says is able of supporting missions to the moon and Mars – successfully blasted off into space. In 2019, Dragon became the first American spacecraft to autonomously dock with the ISS. And on 30 May 2020 came the *coup de grâce*: Dragon transported human beings to and from the ISS.

Musk has achieved all of this by creating his very own version of the rocket equation. Until recently, cost was not a priority for rocket builders because they were funded by governments. Their only focus was on making the biggest and most powerful rockets they could. It didn't matter that they burned through billions of dollars as quickly as their rockets burned through fuel.

But Musk made cost his main focus. And that is his greatest competitive edge over Bezos and every other private and government space company out there. Where NASA has spent roughly $152 million per launch, Musk has said that SpaceX will reach a point where it can launch both people and cargo into space at 1.3 per cent of that cost. Falcon 9 currently costs $62 million to launch, which is not quite where his target is, but it's getting there. In 2020, SpaceX announced that it was looking at a launch price tag of $30 million. Ultimately, Musk has said he foresees a Starship launch at a cost of $2 million. It sounds ludicrous, even when his own company declares that $10 million might be more realistic. And Musk has even managed to get his launches insured for less as well, in the range of $2.5 million compared with the roughly $7 million of his competitors.

Launch contracts are what keep a space company afloat. The cheaper you make those launch contracts, the more business you get. SpaceX is a prime example of Musk's alternative thinking. Back in the early 1990s with Zip2, Musk didn't build the Internet; he simply found a way to use it better. With PayPal, he didn't redesign money; he simply redesigned how it is used. And with SpaceX, Musk's goal was not necessarily just to get into space; it was to make getting into space cheaper. To achieve this, he redesigned the supply chain. Musk and his engineers have also ensured commonality of design so that there is very little difference between the rockets and their engines, further saving on development costs.

Falcon Heavy is a perfect example of the strides Musk and SpaceX have made in moving rocket engineering forward. The largest rocket ever built was NASA's Saturn V, used between 1967 and 1973 during the Apollo programme. It stands 363 ft (110 m) high. Falcon Heavy is 224 ft (64 m) high. Saturn V produces 34.5 million newtons of thrust. Falcon Heavy comes in at 934 000 newtons. But here comes the vital key differentiator. Saturn V weighs 6.2 million pounds. And in the other corner, fresh out of a Silicon Valley mind, comes Falcon Heavy at a lean 140 660 pounds. Most significantly, of Saturn V's 6.2 million pounds, 5.5 million was fuel. Saturn V is a prisoner of the tyranny of the rocket equation. Falcon Heavy is recalibrating the rocket equation. And SpaceX is writing its own rocket equation.

SPACEX has also revealed one other key element about Musk. Does Elon Musk view himself as South African or American?

Musk rarely speaks of South Africa and is only identified as South African in his many bios or the articles written about him. And it's probably safe to say that his role in reigniting the space race has shown that he feels a greater kinship with the US than with South Africa.

The success of Dragon has been described on the SpaceX website as having 'restored human spaceflight to the United States'. For Musk, the US is back in the driving seat of spaceflight. Any doubt that this is where his mind is at can be seen in his response to a comment from Russia.

In explaining his desire to make space exploration more accessible and to lower the costs, Musk used the example of American astronauts previously hitching rides to the ISS on Russian rockets at exorbitant cost, and pointed out that this was not a good outcome for the Americans. The fact that he personally felt a sense of patriotic embarrassment at this perhaps suggests where Musk's heart really lies. He has repeatedly said he would not have been able to achieve what he has achieved anywhere else but in the US.

In 2014, Roscosmos chief Dmitry Rogozin taunted the US by suggesting that its lack of means to deliver astronauts to the ISS meant it might as well consider using a trampoline, Musk clearly took the jibe to heart. He remembered it. And he waited six years to respond.

In 2020, when Dragon delivered the first US astronauts from American soil since 2011, Musk hit back. 'The trampoline is working,'[9] he said in the resultant press conference, calling it 'an inside joke'. It hit the target with devastating effect. Rogozin congratulated Musk on the achievement, but he was clearly infuriated by Musk's retort. In a column for the Russian edition of *Forbes*, Rogozin showed just how close to the mark Musk's comments had hit when he said, 'Our country was the first to send a man into space. We remain first to this day.'[10] It seemed an almost petulant response.

Finally, a clear indication of Musk's allegiance to his adopted country came in his response to a tweet from President Donald Trump. On 6 February 2018, Trump tweeted: 'Congratulations to @ElonMusk and @Spacex on the successful #FalconHeavy launch. This achievement, along with @NASA's commercial and international partners, continues to show American ingenuity at its best.' Musk's response was not, as is popularly believed, the following tweet: 'I'm from South Africa, you dumbass.' That tweet was a hoax that went viral. Musk's real response was perhaps far more revealing of his heart: 'Thank you on behalf of @SpaceX. An exciting future lies ahead!'

The rapid rise of SpaceX was certainly not without its challenges and failures. In fact, Musk believed it would fail right from the start. 'I thought that the most likely outcome was failure,'[11] he said of his decision to embark on the SpaceX journey.

Merely securing a launch site proved a significant challenge on its own. The paperwork and red tape involved make up the black hole down which all dreams disappear. 'The space industry is a very complicated regulatory structure,'[12] says Musk of his early frustrations. 'When somebody tries to build an orbital launch vehicle that is not all that distinguishable from an ICBM, there's a lot of regulation. There probably should be. You don't want to launch something and end up hitting LA. The regulatory stuff was very difficult. The environmental approvals were difficult. Much more so than we expected. In Silicon Valley, you live in a libertarian paradise with almost no regulation. What can be very frustrating is that regulation is often irrational. It doesn't make any sense. But you've got somebody there who is simply executing a set of rules, independent of whether those rules makes sense. You can try to convince them that the rules don't make sense, and they won't listen to you. Regulation is the most annoying thing. There are some restrictions which are really annoying. We are not allowed to employ anyone who doesn't have permanent residence in the United States. Basically, if they can't throw you in jail, they won't let you work on rocket stuff. If we talk to any foreign nationals, we need a technology transfer agreement from the State Department.'[13]

Initially, they managed to gain access to military test and launch sites in the United States. But having to wait in line for military or government launches to go first was too costly for the fledgling company. 'The resources were draining out of the company. Effectively, it was like being starved,' Musk told Berger in *Liftoff*.[14]

And so developed a bizarre adventurous period in SpaceX's history that feels like something of a cross between *Star Wars* and *Survivor*. Musk moved the entire operation to Kwajalein Atoll, in the Marshall Islands – about 10 000 km from the United States mainland – the site of a large missile defence and test site run by the US Army. The military had agreed to work with Musk and offered SpaceX a launch site on tiny Omelek Island. It was like something out of a war movie, or as Musk recalls when he flew over the islands in a helicopter, straight out of a scene in *Apocalypse Now*.

Kwajalein, the world's largest coral atoll, consists of 93 islands and islets. During World War II the islands formed an integral part of Japan's perimeter defence, and were the scene of the Battle of Kwajalein in January and February 1944. The relatively swift American success here proved decisive in the 'island hopping' strategy of breaching Japan's defensive perimeter. The Battle of Kwajalein punched a hole straight through the Japanese barrier; perhaps it could help Musk punch a hole through the red tape of space exploration. After the war, the US military used the atoll for nuclear weapons testing.

Having agreed a deal to make Omelek a launch site, the small team of SpaceX engineers worked hard to build two launchpads and a rocket in three and a half years. They quite literally poured the concrete for the launch site. It was a classic example of the Musk philosophy that anything is possible. The team worked in jungle-like conditions, slept in rudimentary military quarters and ate in a military canteen. They were more like a tribe than a company. The engineers wore T-shirts they'd designed themselves, which declared their motto in terms of the competition: 'Outsweat. Outdrink. Outlaunch.'[15] The tradition was that any new SpaceX employee on 'Kwaj', as it became known to the team, who managed to survive the first night would earn a T-shirt.

But as for reaching orbit, SpaceX hadn't yet got that T-shirt itself.

The first three launches of Falcon 1 failed.

The first took place on 24 March 2006 at 22:30. Years of hard work were condensed into the roughly 30 seconds that Falcon 1 took to rise above the island and soar into the sky before the Merlin engine malfunctioned and it came crashing down to earth again. In the time it takes to quickly check your email, years of hard work, hope and expectation went up in flames.

The second launch took place on 21 March 2007 at 01:10.

With the familiar count of 'Ten, nine, eight, seven, six, five, four, three, two, one, lift-off!' Falcon 1 rose above the island again. Droplets of water could be seen forming on the screen of the onboard video camera as it rose through the clouds, with the island growing smaller and smaller below it. After two minutes and 52 seconds the ground crew watched a successful stage separation of the rocket on their video screens, and gave a small cheer. At three minutes and 117 km they confirmed the second-stage engine ignition. Everything was going according to plan. Ice particles could be seen forming on the video camera's window, and in the background, the familiar blue curve of Earth. And then, in what was described as an 'upper stage control anomaly', Falcon 1 began spiralling. It had reached space, but it hadn't managed to achieve a stable orbit.

The third launch took place on 3 August 2008 at 03:34. The liftoff was perfect but the rocket failed to reach orbit when the second-stage separation was unsuccessful. 'Three failures is a lot of failures,' SpaceX operations manager Anne Chinnery told Berger in *Liftoff*. 'Hardly anyone survives that in the aerospace world.'[16]

The fourth launch took place on 28 September 2008 at 23:15. It was flawless. At 2:37 minutes and 18 seconds, a successful stage separation took place. 'Stage separation confirmed,' said a woman's voice, and there was cheering in the background. As the rocket continued to soar away from Earth, the hopes of those on Omelek Island were soaring with it. The words on the launch sheet read 'SUCCESS'. The irony is that Musk had decided on the fourth launch as purely a demonstration. As Berger recounts, even the payload was a demonstration. Officially, it is listed as RatSat – formed from the first letters of the surnames of SpaceX employees Jeff Richichi, Ray Amador and Chris Thompson.

After the third failed launch, the SpaceX team had to salvage and rebuild a Falcon 1 that was in pieces. And as with all things Musk and SpaceX, they were given almost no time to do it – one month.

Their first challenge was getting the rebuilt rocket from California back to Omelek Island. You don't just book a seat on the next flight for a rocket, and the waiting time for shipment by sea would cripple a now very wobbly SpaceX. 'We were running on fumes at that point. We had virtually no money. A fourth failure would have been absolutely game over. Done,' said Musk.[17] The US Air Force came to the rescue when they agreed to let the Falcon 1 hitch a ride on one of their C-17 transport aircraft.

But it was as if everything about this last launch would test Musk to the absolute limit. During the flight from California the rocket literally crumpled as a result of changes in air pressure inside the C-17. The onboard crew had to open up the rocket to prevent further crumpling, and the pilots had to take the aircraft up to a more stable pressure level. They managed to prevent further damage, but enough had been done by the time they unloaded the rocket at Omelek Island. With Musk confirming that SpaceX could not wait longer than a month for a successful launch, technicians managed in a week to repair what should have taken six weeks to do. And they rolled the rocket onto the launchpad in time for its 28 September 2008 launch, which Musk watched from a monitor back in California. He described it as one of the greatest days of his life.

It was the last Hail Mary that actually worked. And everybody knew what it meant to Musk.

Musk had shown himself to be more than just a billionaire with more bravado than brains when, in a memo to his deflated team after the failed launches, he wrote, 'Having experienced first-hand how hard it is to reach orbit, I have a lot of respect for those that persevered to produce the vehicles that are mainstays of space launch today. SpaceX is in this for the long haul and, come hell or high water, we are going to make this work.'[18]

But even with this successful launch, on Earth Musk was facing a world of problems. He was out of money, having sunk his entire fortune into SpaceX and two other ventures: the electric car maker Tesla and SolarCity, which sold and installed solar energy generation systems, primarily rooftop solar panels.

He was out of love, having divorced Justine and handed over his house in the process. He was out of time, having failed to secure the necessary investment capital before the global financial crisis hit.

And, for the first time in his life, Elon Musk was very close to being out of his mind.

Musk's Christmas Miracle

ELON Musk woke up on the Sunday morning before Christmas 2008. It was three months after the successful fourth launch of Falcon 1. The boy with the ideas exploding in his head suddenly found a new idea had popped up. It was one he didn't like. It was one he didn't know how to deal with it. It was one that frightened him.

'I remember waking up and thinking, man, I never ever thought I was someone who would be capable of a nervous breakdown. I thought, "Nervous breakdowns? That's ridiculous. Why would people have such a thing?" But I remember waking up and thinking, "Damn. This is the closest I've ever come." It seemed pretty, pretty dark,' he said of 2008.[1]

The pressure on Musk was indeed unbearable.

In 2002, he launched SpaceX. In 2004, he stepped into Tesla and the electric car market. In 2006, he launched SolarCity. In 2008, all of it was on the brink of failure against the background of a global economic meltdown and Musk's own dwindling financial reserves.

That year was possibly the hardest of Musk's adult life and the one that could've sunk every single dream and ambition he had. It was the year of three rocket failures. It was the year of his divorce from Justine. It was the year of the global recession. It was the year that his new business, Tesla, was, in his own words, 'haemorrhaging money'. Traditional car makers such as GM and Chrysler had received huge government bailouts to keep them alive. The venture capital market certainly didn't have the stomach for yet another car company, let alone one producing ground-breaking electric cars.

'The year 2008 was not a good time to be a car company, especially a start-up car company, and especially an electric car start-up company. That was like stupidity squared,' said Musk.[2]

'That was definitely the worst year of my life.'[3]

His new girlfriend, the actress Talulah Riley, recalled how he would wake up at night screaming and seemingly in physical pain.

In a TV interview in 2008,[4] Musk is seen sitting in his kitchen, with his kids running around. Wearing a simple T-shirt and jeans, he's busy helping one child with his phone while the others clamour for his attention. It's a typically chaotic household scene. Riley admitted rather awkwardly in the interview that after being swept off her feet by Musk, she had been brought down to earth when she stepped into a home full of screaming kids. She says there were times she wanted to leave, go back to England and never come back. And you can see that Musk is genuinely shocked by Riley's admission – shocked in an almost childlike way that she could even have thought such a thing. He asks her, with a quizzical look on his face, 'Really?' Riley laughs it off in the interview, yet here is another small example of how, during an excruciatingly painful time in his professional life, Musk is dealing with the one thing he cannot find a solution for – true love.

But Musk also seems to be providing a metaphor for his current circumstances when he says to the camera, 'There are a lot of resource conflicts when you have five kids. At any given point somebody's taken somebody's toy.'[5]

How to allocate his dwindling resources, given the reduction in his personal fortune, was a very real concern for Musk. Another was how to avoid losing all of his 'toys' in the process: 'I had a tough choice there because I could either provide all of the money for SpaceX or all of the money for Tesla and then increase the chance that one of them would survive. Or I have to split the money. But if I split the money then maybe both will die. It's almost like if you had two children and you had only so much food. What do you do?'⁶

SolarCity was another major cause for concern. Musk was chairman of the company, which had been founded by his cousins Peter and Lyndon Rive, and he saw it as a means to integrate a sustainable energy future into Tesla.

Key to this was the development of a solar roof. Instead of simply providing solar panels for roofs in the traditional sense, SolarCity was focused on making the entire roof one giant solar panel in which the roof shingles (tiles) were actually solar panels themselves. However, the concept, like the company, seemed doomed from the start. SolarCity became an almost perfect storm in which Musk's penchant for seeking out a grandiose idea to transform an industry, selling the concept to investors and then working out the details later would not succeed.

Leaving aside the SolarCity debacle for a moment, both SpaceX and Tesla were draining Musk of financial resources. SpaceX had sapped his personal fortune. Everything he had made from the sale of PayPal was gone. He was broke. A $20 million investment by Peter Thiel helped to stabilise SpaceX, but it wasn't nearly enough. The only project on their books was a satellite launch for Malaysia. But the customer would only pay in the case of a successful launch. The Falcon 1 that the SpaceX team had salvaged and barely put together in a week was their last working rocket.

It was estimated that by late 2008, Musk had about $30 million in cash left. He recalled this time: 'Even though the fourth launch of SpaceX succeeded, we were still running out of money. We had three failures and only one success. And then the financing round for Tesla had not closed. We were two or three days to closing before Christmas. I thought this could be a really bad end of the year where both companies could fail. Sleep was difficult.'[7]

Faced with his difficult decision of where to place his last bet, Musk opted to split the money he had left between SpaceX and Tesla: 'The difficulty in those situations is there are so many responsibilities that you have to the employees and to the investors who have come along. I would've been really disappointed if I would not have been able to keep my responsibilities to have the companies survive.'[8]

Juggling all of this clearly took its toll on Musk, and he worked a punishing and unsustainable schedule. 'For a long time it was over 100 hours a week,' he said of his work schedule at the time. 'That's a very high amount of pain. The difficulty and pain of work hours really increases exponentially. It's not linear. When the financial crisis hit in 2008 and 2009, it was just every day, seven days a week. Dreaming about work. It was terrible.'[9]

He hadn't even been able to attend the historic fourth launch of Falcon 1 in person because of his need to be in California trying to keep both SpaceX and Tesla alive. That year Tesla had to lay off 18 per cent of its workforce as it struggled to remain afloat.

But 2008 was also the year of Musk's very own Christmas Miracle. In those tumultuous three days over Christmas, everything changed. And it started with a phone call from space.

'NASA called and told me we'd won a $1.5 billion contract for SpaceX. I just blurted out, "I love you guys",' says Musk.[10] As he tells the story, his eyes are watering. The call came to Musk's cellphone on Monday morning 22 December. A press release was issued on 23 December, stating that SpaceX had been contracted to provide 12 flights for commercial resupply services (CRS) to the ISS. As he told Eric Berger, 'Without the CRS contract, we would have gone down as that company that made it to orbit, and then died.'[11]

Then, on Christmas Eve, Tesla's investors decided to pump more money into the business with a $40-million cash injection. In the space of only a few days, Musk and his companies had been saved. The 'toys' were safe.

There was a very clear reason why Musk couldn't decide between his 'children' – SpaceX and Tesla – opting instead to split his remaining funding between the two. It went deeper than just his loyalties to employees and shareholders. It was at the core of his vision when he started out and identified the three things he believed would have the greatest impact on humanity – the Internet, transitioning to a sustainable-energy economy and space exploration, including the extension of life to multiple planets.

THE real problem with SolarCity came in 2016 when Musk – a major shareholder in both Tesla and SolarCity – convinced his Tesla investors to purchase SolarCity to the value of $2.6 billion. In 2016, Musk unveiled what he called the Tesla Solar Roof, using the SolarCity roof concept. The idea was that the entire roof of a person's home would be able to feed energy into the Tesla Powerwall, a rechargeable lithium-ion battery unit installed in the home which would then charge their Tesla vehicles. It was going to be a seamless integration of green energy that would further transform the sector and, Musk argued, make Tesla even more dominant and self-sustaining.

But the problem was that SolarCity itself was not a successful company. In fact, it was failing at an alarming rate. It was not meeting its production demand and promises for some critical reasons that Musk surprisingly seemed to overlook, or chose to ignore. First, it didn't really have a product. Or rather, its product was not yet fully refined before it was already being sold. It has since been revealed that when he launched the solar roof in 2016, on the old set of *Desperate Housewives*, it wasn't actually a fully functioning product and Musk even had concerns about the design. Some critics have even suggested that the solar shingles Musk displayed at the launch were fake.

Second, the idea of being more than just a company providing solar panels, and rather being a company that installs solar roofs, brought with it significant challenges that Musk had not foreseen. Designing and providing solar panels is a far different prospect to designing and building roofs. As a result, unforeseen installation costs began to emerge, and these were passed on to angry consumers. As a *Vanity Fair* article observed in 2019, 'The real engineering that took place at SolarCity, in short, was financial, not environmental.'[12] And finally, the market demand for solar roofs just wasn't there at the time, with a significant slowdown in this sector.

Tesla investors, themselves concerned about their own company at the time, were sceptical about the acquisition of a company that was not just deep in debt and laying off staff at the time but essentially insolvent. In 2017, the Tesla shareholders dragged Musk to court over a deal they believed amounted to little more than a Tesla bailout of a failing company.

Musk's plans that SolarCity would become the new Gigafactory 2 in Buffalo, New York (following the original Tesla Gigafactory in Nevada, where lithium-ion batteries are produced), were also on the rocks. The company was given a highly favourable ten-year lease by the Buffalo city council on the grounds that the plant would employ a certain number of staff and create jobs in a very poor community.

In 2020, all of Tesla's directors – excluding Musk – agreed to a settlement of $60 million. A settlement was also reached with retail giant Walmart, which had sued Tesla after solar panels supplied by SolarCity caught fire at seven stores, resulting in millions of dollars in damage.

But Musk instead decided to move ahead with the trial involving the Tesla shareholders, denying any wrongdoing in this matter and determined to clear his name. During the trial, which is still ongoing, Musk repeatedly denied pressuring the Tesla board into agreeing to the merger despite evidence presented that he did indeed have a significant influence over the deal, and that he was also aware of SolarCity's financial difficulties at the time. To his credit, Musk has admitted that 'significant mistakes' were made, specifically regarding installations.

But the SolarCity debacle again brought to the fore the dichotomy of Musk. He has consistently shown himself to be an incredible innovator and engineer with an ability to make the impossible possible, and to move entire industries forward with his disruptive approach. On the whole, society needs thinkers of the calibre of Elon Musk. But such mavericks do not necessarily make good bosses or company CEOs.

Innovation is a risky business. Running a company is a far more conservative affair. If a healthy balance between the two is not there, risk becomes recklessness. When Musk urged his early SpaceX employees to follow the Silicon Valley mantra of 'Move fast and break things', it spurred them on to great innovation in rocketry. But it doesn't overlook the fact that there will be collateral damage, as things will break. Musk has shown from his earliest days at PayPal that he is a far better innovator than he is a CEO.

SOMEHOW, space had jumped the queue in the sense that Musk had founded SpaceX before he became involved in Tesla and

SolarCity. But Tesla was just as important to him and his process, and he couldn't let the company fail.

And once again, Tesla is a perfect example of the way Musk's mind works. His original intention was not to become a car manufacturer so much as it was to accelerate the shift towards electric vehicles. In his mind, the progress that had been made towards achieving this was staggeringly slow – much like the stagnation he had seen in space exploration.

The majority of the companies Musk has started or become involved with reflect his desire to force the pace of change at a macro level. It perhaps explains why Musk still views himself as more of an engineer – and proudly so – than a businessman or entrepreneur. The companies, and even their successes and profits, are merely the vehicle for Musk's desire to use them as a catalyst for greater change. A change in humanity's vision for the future. A change in humanity's approach to the present.

In essence, if you want to save the planet, create the companies that are capable of doing so. This is also where comparisons between Musk and Steve Jobs diverge. Musk has been labelled the Steve Jobs of his time, with a vision of making space travel and electric cars sexy and accessible – albeit not yet affordable – to the general population. Musk certainly knows the value of a good-looking product, or, as he has said, something you truly fall in love with.

His motivation for creating a good-looking product, in the case of Tesla in particular, goes beyond profit. If it was purely profit, Musk would never have considered starting two companies – SpaceX and Tesla – in which his most optimistic outcome for success was around ten per cent: 'If you're trying to convince people to make life more miserable for themselves, this is a hard argument to win. When we created Tesla, we said we have to make a car that's exciting and fun and looks good.'[13] 'The whole purpose behind Tesla – the reason I put so much of my time and money into helping create the business – is we want to serve as a catalyst accelerating the electric car revolution.

'The price of gas at the pump does not reflect the true cost of gasoline because you have a consumption of a public good. It's the same in fishing. Because there is no cost to fishing stocks, people just overfish and disaster ensues. Here we're not paying for the cost of the concentration of CO_2 in the oceans and the atmosphere, we're not paying for all the ancillary effects – the wars and all the other things – at the gas pumps. You effectively had a subsidy taking place at the gas pump because of that. So the only way to bridge that is with innovation, is to try to make electric cars better sooner than they would otherwise be.'[14]

Jobs wanted you to buy an iPhone so he built a company that made technology less geeky and more trendy. Musk wants you to buy a future. If he has to start an electric car company to do so, then he will. And yes, there needs to be a profit and he is not entirely utopian in acknowledging this.

It's a thought process that comes through in Musk's visions for space exploration. It is more than two decades since he first started dreaming about going to Mars. In Musk's mind, that is 19 years in which it still hasn't happened. He doesn't describe this as simply disappointing or a failure. Musk takes it personally. He calls it an outrage that humanity hasn't yet made it to Mars.

But as much as he cannot be defined as just an entrepreneur, he also cannot be classed with climate activists such as Greta Thunberg. He falls outside this spectrum as well, although he does speak a similar climate language. But as Justine so aptly pointed out, Musk's ability not to belong to one or the other tribe, but rather to move between the tribes, is his greatest asset.

According to the US Department of Energy, the first electric vehicle made its debut on the streets of Des Moines, Iowa, in 1890, not far at all from the birthplace of chiropractic and the first adjustment performed by Daniel David Palmer in 1895, which would become a part of Musk's family history as well. In the mind of Elon Musk, the lack of real progress towards a viable electric car, never mind an electric car company, was baffling. Two other entrepreneurs, Marc Tarpenning and Martin Eberhard, had felt the same.

And it was in fact they, and not Musk, who first did something about it.

Tesla

MARTIN Eberhard was recently divorced and in the market for a sports car. But his Silicon Valley background, his training in electrical engineering and a general awareness of and interest in global warming and sustainability saw his interest drift away from the traditional sports cars and more towards electric vehicles.

But first Eberhard wanted to ascertain whether the cost of owning an electric car was actually worth it. So he threw himself into calculations of every kind of vehicle on the planet powered by every kind of source available. Each time he came up with the same answer. 'Every which way I did the numbers, the electric cars were a lot better than everything else,' he said in a CNBC interview.[1]

There were a handful of electric cars on the market in the 1990s but nothing that struck Eberhard as looking more than very home-made and a little 'go-kartish'. The one that did catch Eberhard's eye was a fledgling electric car company by the name of AC Propulsion in California. They had developed an electric car called the TZero, but they were busy going out of business. Eberhard, already a highly successful entrepreneur in the tech world, invested his own money into saving the company, but still with only one goal in mind – for them to build him an electric car.

Eberhard and his good friend, Marc Tarpenning, had founded NuvoMedia in 1997. The company's flagship product was the Rocket eBook, an early e-reader that could store up to ten books in electronic form. And it was Eberhard and Tarpenning's work on improving the battery life and performance of the Rocket eBook that opened the door for their work on a better-performing electric car. The TZero was powered by a lead-acid battery. But Eberhard was turning his mind towards lithium-ion batteries, and he convinced AC Propulsion to convert the TZero to lithium-ion power.

'That's where it began,'[2] he said.

Where they went from there, though, was an entirely different challenge. As Tarpenning pointed out, their Silicon Valley mindset gave them the confidence that they could make whatever powered the car, but they weren't so confident about making the car itself. For this they partnered with English carmaker Lotus, which took care of the chassis and body for the first Tesla Roadster.

And so, on 1 July 2003, Tesla Motors Incorporated opened its doors. The company was named after Nikola Tesla (1856–1943), the Serbian-American inventor best known for his work on electromagnetic fields, and specifically for his contribution to the alternating current (AC) system.

But they ran up against resistance in the venture capital market. Quite simply, nobody wanted to invest. And that's when a chance meeting at a space enthusiasts' society brought them and Elon Musk together. In another of those seemingly unlikely coincidences that connect Elon Musk's world, Eberhard and Tarpenning were founding members of the Mars Society, a non-profit organisation founded in 1998 to disseminate information about the Red Planet. At one of their annual conferences, Musk was a guest speaker – a man with means on a mission to Mars. As Eberhard admits, 'He was intriguing. So we cornered him afterwards and talked for a while.'[3]

AC Propulsion, meanwhile, had also been chasing down Musk, trying to get him to invest in the company. But it was clear that Musk had no designs on AC Propulsion, so as part of the gentleman's agreement they had with Tesla, they said they would back off Musk and Tesla was free to approach him if they wanted.

Eberhard sent Musk an email, proposing a meeting. This was around the time Musk was trying to buy ICBMs from Russia. In their first meeting with Musk, both Eberhard and Tarpenning were blown away by not only his immediate understanding of what they were trying to do but also his acceptance of it. Every venture capital firm had shut the door on them, saying they were crazy. But it was their good fortune to sit down with somebody more 'crazy' than they were. Musk was busy trying to privatise spaceflight. He was likely the only other person on the planet who would have understood what they were trying to do. 'He totally got it,' said Tarpenning.[4]

Musk was in. In 2004, he invested $6.35 million in Tesla's Series A round of venture capital financing, and assumed the role of chairman of the board. In 2006, Musk convinced Google to invest in Tesla as part of another funding drive.

But success hinged on the car's battery pack. Making it stable and being able to produce it safely and at scale were key to the concept of a workable electric car that looked good and performed well. As usual, Musk does a great job of explaining it in layman's terms: 'A battery is multiple cells. As the batteries get bigger and bigger, they get harder and harder to deal with. The challenge is combining those cells and having thousands of them and making sure they're safe, making sure they'll last for 200 000 miles over bumps and potholes and extremes of temperature and that they're safe in a crash. That compounds the problem massively. The difficulty is at the pack level much more than at the cell level. That's the single biggest area of Tesla's expertise. The battery is the most important thing.

'The Tesla battery pack weighs about one thousand pounds and it has the energy content of two-and-a-half gallons of gasoline. But the consumption of that energy is much more efficient in an electric car. An electric motor is super-efficient at turning energy into motion. It's about 90 per cent efficient. A gasoline internal combustion engine is typically in the range of around 17 per cent or 18 per cent. Most of what it does is generate heat. It's almost become convention that the future is electric cars. The only problem is this transitional period. If you look at the pace of battery improvement, it's inevitable that the future will be entirely electric.'[5]

The idea to start with a sports car was vital to Tesla's success. A sports car would allow Tesla to achieve their first goal – a car that looked good. The sports car market is also relatively small, which makes it less capital-intensive to enter with a developing technology. The sedan market, by virtue of its sheer volume, is where the real money is made, but its very scale makes it incredibly hard to start there.

So, in 2006, Tesla unveiled its first Roadster prototype.

The supply chain proved problematic, though, especially since most of what went into the Tesla Roadster had to be designed from scratch, and existing companies were simply unwilling to take the risk of supplying a start-up. In a sense, it was exactly the same problem Musk would run into with SpaceX, which forced his hand from a cost perspective to bring the majority of the supply chain in-house.

And while sorting out the hardware issues, Musk was embroiled in 'software' issues as well. Or, more precisely, personality issues. The relationship between Musk and Eberhard deteriorated, apparently over the question of who had founded Tesla and was the real brains behind the technology. Several early interviews in which Musk was not mentioned in relation to Tesla seemed to worsen the situation. Eberhard has asserted that Musk is trying to rewrite history, and to write him out of Tesla's history in particular.

The result has been a long-standing feud between the two, interspersed with court battles and settlements. And it's a battle Musk has largely been winning, from the moment he told his 'cofounder' that his time with Tesla was up. In a scene reminiscent of Musk's own ousting as CEO of PayPal, Eberhard was dismissed as CEO of Tesla in 2007. It was a Musk-led initiative; he later described Eberhard as the worst person he'd ever worked with, and as someone who was bad for the progress of the company. Tarpenning left soon after Eberhard's dismissal, deciding that he'd enjoyed the journey and was ready to move on.

But Tarpenning encountered a side of Musk that Eberhard perhaps couldn't see or fully appreciate. Eberhard speaks with a sense of resentment at being forced out of what he believes he created, although he remains a shareholder in Tesla. 'Elon's done some pretty amazing things. I don't understand why he has to say he was a founder of Tesla. I don't understand that,' he said in the CNBC interview.[6]

Tarpenning, though, saw something else in Musk that is a common theme in his life. 'People want to do something that makes a difference,' he said as he tried to explain Musk's Tesla drive.[7] It's exactly this that lies at the heart of Musk's own philosophy about mankind. His statement that he is 'pro human'. His desire to spare humanity another mass-extinction event. And, despite the abuse he suffered from bullies as a child, his belief in the ultimate goodness of people. His philosophy that you need something exciting to wake up to in the morning. The promise of an exciting future. And in Musk's mind, SpaceX and Tesla play a key role in the future he believes humankind should strive towards: 'The fundamental goodness of Tesla … so like the "why" of Tesla, the relevance, what's the point of Tesla, comes down to two things: acceleration of sustainable energy and autonomy,' Musk has said.[8] 'The acceleration of sustainable energy is absolutely fundamental, because this is the next potential risk for humanity. So obviously, that is, by far and away, the most important thing.'[9]

Autonomy will have an equally big impact. Driver autonomy, to be specific. In the case of Tesla, its vehicles are equipped with Autopilot features that enable the vehicle to steer, accelerate and brake automatically using a combination of cameras, sensors and computers. However, Tesla makes the point that its current Autopilot features still require 'active driver supervision' and 'do not make the vehicle autonomous'.

Driver autonomy is perceived to be the next big thing in vehicle transport. According to a 2017 study conducted by Intel,[10] when we no longer have to drive ourselves and can instead be passengers, it will spark an economic boom that will be known as the new 'passenger economy'. And this is predicted to be worth $7 trillion by 2050. Intel predicts 250 million hours of commuting time will be freed up for people to do other things – entertain themselves, work more, buy more, invest more, think more, create more. This new architecture of human mobility will, futurists say, spark entire new industries and the birth of smart cities. Humanity will also be spared needless road deaths, with the study predicting that 585 000 lives will be saved between 2035 and 2045.

Futurist Greg Lindsay draws an interesting parallel between the drive towards the passenger economy and another of Musk's interests – the space race: 'Not unlike the space race of the 1960s, this is a rallying cry to the world to put its best minds on this challenge. The future of mobility, economic advancement and the emergence of new growth opportunities like the passenger economy demand ongoing dialogue ... to look at solutions through the lens of the diverse industries that will shape our future – from automakers to investors and policy makers to start-ups.'[11]

It's being referred to as 'car-venience', and predictions of what this new economy will feature include onboard beauty salons, fast casual dining, remote vending, mobile health care clinics and treatment pods and onboard movies complete with location-based advertising. Or, as Musk puts it, 'If you're on the road, you can spend time doing things that you enjoy instead of in terrible traffic.'[12]

The Tesla Roadster went into production in 2008. The Model S, an all-electric sedan, hit the market in 2012. In 2015, Tesla started introducing basic self-driving technology, such as autosteer and traffic-aware adaptive cruise control into its vehicles, using just one camera, a radar system and 12 sonar sensors. That year the company unveiled its Model X – 'The safest, quickest and most capable sports utility vehicle in history' according to the Tesla website. In 2017 came the Model 3, a 'low-priced high-volume' electric vehicle. Then a truck, the Tesla Semi, the Model Y mid-sized SUV and the Cybertruck, a type of SUV-sports crossover that looks like it was styled on the Batmobile.

On a similar financial timeline, in 2009 the Mercedes-Benz Group (formerly Daimler AG) invested $50 million for a ten per cent stake in Tesla, and the US Department of Energy agreed a $465 million loan to the company. In 2010, Musk took the company public with an initial public offering of $226 million, and Toyota invested $50 million as part of a strategic partnership to develop electric cars and parts. In May 2013, Tesla reported its first quarterly profit of $11 million. In 2017, Chinese ecommerce behemoth Tencent invested $1.8 billion in Tesla for a five per cent share of the company. In 2010, Tesla went public on the tech-heavy NASDAQ stock market at $17 a share. Its share price in September 2021 was $736.27.

By 2020, sales of Tesla vehicles had reached 500 000 units

globally. In the United States alone, 81 per cent of battery-powered electric vehicles sold were Tesla vehicles. The company has been valued at $146 billion in a projected global electric vehicle market valued at $725 billion. The Model 3 is the world's best-selling electric plug-in vehicle, with a range of 520 km. In 2010, The Tesla Roadster was billed as the fastest car on the planet, leaving most traditional supercars in the dust. According to Musk, the latest version of the Roadster goes from zero to 100 km/h in 1.9 seconds with a top speed of 400 km/h, and a range of almost 1 000 km. It will also cost you R2.8 million. That would make it faster than the current model of the McLaren supercar, and significantly faster than the earlier version that Musk purchased with his Zip2 windfall.

Musk is rapidly expanding the company's global footprint with the production of fast electric charging stations in major cities around the world, and in 2020 invested $6.42 million in setting up a plant in Shanghai to make charging poles.

As a Tesla owner, you can simply plug your car into a 120 V wall socket for a minimum of four kilometres of range for every hour of charge, or into a traditional 240 V wall socket for up to 50 km of range for every hour of charge. Purchase a Tesla wall connector and you can up this to 70 km of range for every hour of charge. A Tesla Supercharger – there are currently 25 000 of these worldwide – will get you 320 km of drive time in just 15 minutes of charging.

As quickly as it has built its footprint, Tesla has developed a passionate and almost cult-like following among owners. Apart from the various charging adaptors, you can buy merchandise and apparel, and even a Tesla Tequila, from the Tesla online shop.

Musk has even changed the model of the traditional car dealership. Once again, he was desperate to see past the old way of doing things in the automotive industry: 'The US automotive industry has been selling cars the same way for over 100 years and there are many laws in place to govern exactly how that is to be accomplished. We do not seek to change those rules and we have taken great care not to act in a manner contrary to those rules.'[13] And yet he's sought to redefine those rules. So Tesla dealerships didn't so much sell you cars as sell you a vision of the future of the car. There were no independently owned dealerships that brought in expensive middlemen for the consumer; Tesla sold directly to consumers. Musk made sure that Tesla stores were exactly this – stores, not car dealerships. Much like the Apple stores, the Tesla stores were retail experiences for a consumer to see just what is out there and what is possible.

But the consumer model of these stores has entailed lengthy legal and regulatory battles in certain US states. These difficulties prompted Musk to close many of the stores and instead pursue a more aggressive online sales model. According to the company, with a click you can now buy a Tesla, and with a click you can also return one within seven days or 1 600 km for a full refund. A limited number of stores have remained open in key locations, but more as marketing experiences for consumers to engage with the cars.

And the fans' love for Tesla is as powerful as their chargers. They are a perfect example of what Musk has always sought to achieve as an engineer – creating products that people love.

Tesla owners have developed their own lingo, and refer to traditional cars as 'ICE' (for internal combustion engine). A typical comment from a Tesla owner to a traditional car owner would be along the lines of 'Why on earth would you buy ICE over Tesla?'

Tesla fans love the Autopilot, the Netflix streaming, the touchscreen technology, the Tesla app and all the technology that makes their driving experience that much more pleasurable. It's exciting, as exciting as the future that Musk has always sought to create, and that he has always maintained is what should drive you to get out of bed in the morning. And it's also good for the Earth. 'If you want a high-performance car with a clean conscience, this is the only option,' says Musk.[14]

In short, Tesla owners pride themselves on having a car that looks good, drives good and does good. Such is the fanaticism around their love for their cars that it's hard to distinguish between their devotion to Tesla and their devotion to Elon Musk. The same people who call themselves 'Teslaholics' are also referred to as 'Musketeers'.

But, as every musketeer knows, there is always a Cardinal Richelieu who takes a different view of things, and Musk's Tesla adventure hasn't been without its skirmishes. In 2008, which was a good year for the new electric car company, when it unveiled the Tesla Roadster, it collided with the most devastating year for Musk. As we saw in the previous chapter, Musk's life was in turmoil. His business life was no different: SpaceX was floundering, and Tesla was losing money faster than its car batteries could be recharged.

Then came his eleventh-hour Christmas Miracle.

But Tesla's road ahead would still be filled with many potholes.

In 2008, an auto industry blog launched the 'Tesla Death Watch' – a countdown to what they believed was the demise of Tesla. The Tesla Death Watch was the brainchild of automotive industry analyst Edward Niedermeyer, who had long harboured suspicions about Tesla. In 2019, his book *Ludicrous: The Unvarnished Story of Tesla Motors* made the claim that 'Behind the hype, Tesla has some serious deficiencies that raise questions about its sky-high valuation, and even its ultimate survival.' The book, its cover says, 'lays bare the disconnect between the popular perception of Tesla and the day-to-day realities of the company – and the cars it produces.'[15]

Niedermeyer has had a particular issue with 'Tesla's attempt to merge Silicon Valley arrogance with automotive industry standards'.[16] And Tesla has had its own issues with Niedermeyer. In a 2016 press release headed 'A Grain of Salt' and responding to safety concerns about the Model S suspension, Tesla declared: 'Finally, it is worth noting that the blogger who fabricated this issue, which then caused negative and incorrect news to be written about Tesla by reputable institutions, is Edward Niedermeyer. This is the same gentle soul who previously wrote a blog titled "Tesla Death Watch," which starting on May 19, 2008 was counting the days until Tesla's death. It has now been 2944 days. We just checked our pulse and, much to his chagrin, appear to be alive. It is probably wise to take Mr Niedermeyer's words with at least a small grain of salt. We don't know if Mr Niedermeyer's motivation is simply to set a world record for axe-grinding or whether he or his associates have something financial to gain by negatively affecting Tesla's stock price, but it is important to highlight that there are several billion dollars in short sale bets against Tesla. This means that there is a strong financial incentive to greatly amplify minor issues and to create false issues from whole cloth. That said, sometimes Tesla does make genuine mistakes. We are not and have never claimed to be perfect. However, we strongly believe in trying to do the right thing and, when we fall short, taking immediate corrective action.'[17]

But Tesla has certainly been a wild ride for Musk.

In 2009, Tesla cofounder Eberhard began his legal battle with Musk. Indeed, much of Musk's Tesla time seems to involve legal issues. Since 2008, Tesla is reported to have been a party to over 1000 lawsuits around everything from treatment of workers to actual technical issues, and of course the bigger boardroom issues with Eberhard and SolarCity.

Musk has found himself playing PR director as much as CEO as he's addressed issues such as vehicles catching fire, alleged deaths from collisions while using Autopilot and other problems. In 2013, he went to war with *The New York Times* over what he said was a 'fake' review of the Tesla Model S, in which the writer claimed the car's battery range was not what it was said to be.

That year, a Tesla Model S caught fire while on the road. The company's stock went into a nose dive and Tesla's future was once again on the ropes. Musk was reportedly considering selling the company to Google for $6 billion.

In 2016, Autopilot malfunctioned on several cars, and in one case was said to have caused a fatal crash. In 2017, Toyota sold its stake in Tesla. That same year Tesla stock crashed again, losing about $12 billion, after the company failed to meet its production targets.

In 2018, Musk's propensity to tweet before he thinks provided the next Tesla crisis. After he tweeted that he was considering 'taking Tesla private at $420' with 'funding secured', Tesla stock soared by ten per cent. But the US Securities and Exchange Commission (SEC) sued Musk for 'false and misleading' statements to Tesla investors. Musk settled with the SEC for $20 million, as well as a $20 million fine for the company and a pledge that he would monitor his social media usage in the future. The SEC had also been tipped off by a former Tesla employee who claimed that the company supressed an internal investigation into criminal activity at its Nevada Gigafactory, which produces the batteries for Tesla vehicles, including rampant theft of copper wire and even allegations of drug trafficking. An investigation by the Drug Enforcement Administration found that a Tesla employee had links to a Mexican drug cartel. The Gigafactory was also under investigation by local police for the number of employee accidents, and even a death, that had occurred on site. It was alleged that fear of Musk's finding out, and his own concern about negative publicity and its impact on Tesla, in turn made employees fearful about reporting or acting on allegations. It is a harsh assessment to make of a CEO, who cannot conceivably know every single thing that occurs on the factory floor, criminal or not. But Musk has never been held to the standards of a normal CEO.

Also in 2018, the US Department of Justice launched an investigation into whether the company had misled investors about its production capabilities. In 2019, Musk was forced to cut Tesla staff by seven per cent, and an exodus of top executives followed. In February that year, Musk's Twitter account again drew the ire of the SEC as he tweeted that Tesla would make 500 000 vehicles that year, breaching their agreement that his tweets would be monitored.

Amid this, another fatality occurred when a Tesla driver in a Model 3 using Autopilot collided with a truck. Musk has vigorously defended all such cases, often using vehicle logbooks and making comprehensive and data-driven cases that driver error was at fault.

MUSK'S Twitter actions also caused unhappiness within his board, which reached a tipping point in June and July 2018 during the Tham Luang cave rescue. A Thai junior football team and their coach had found themselves trapped in the cave system by a rising, rain-swollen river, and in response a massive international rescue effort was mobilised. Musk took to Twitter to accuse the expatriate British spelunker Vernon Unsworth, one of the volunteer rescuers, of being a paedophile.

Musk and Unsworth had publicly argued about the best way to rescue the boys and their coach. While the 64-year-old Unsworth, a veteran cave diver, was recruiting diving specialists to rescue the boys, Musk sent a team of SpaceX and Tesla engineers and a mini-submarine to Thailand to assist with the rescue effort.

But when Unsworth branded Musk's offer a 'PR stunt' and suggested he 'stick his submarine where it hurts', Musk reacted. In one tweet he referred to Unsworth as 'pedo guy', allegedly because he resided in Chiang Rai province, an area notorious for child sex trafficking.

Journalist Ryan Mac actually spoke to Musk about this leap of judgement. At the time, Mac was a senior technology reporter at *BuzzFeed*.[18] He later joined *The New York Times* to cover accountability in the world of technology. Mac had uncovered scathing internal criticism of Facebook by its own staff, and had exposed Peter Thiel's secret funding of wrestler Hulk Hogan's court case against Gawker Media (2013–2016). Mac reached out to Musk via email for his *BuzzFeed* article, asking whether he would like to comment on having received a letter from Unsworth's lawyer. In his off-the-record response, Musk made various allegations about Unsworth's being a 'child rapist', as well as a poor diver, and said he welcomed the prospect of being sued.[19]

Mac followed up with several emails questioning Musk's facts, and also asserting that he hadn't agreed to any 'off the record' conversations himself so wouldn't treat it as such. 'Sometimes people think the words "off the record" are a magic command and, once uttered, immediately go into effect to hide what comes after. But in reality, a journalist and their source have to both agree to that condition before it can be established. Musk and I did not,' Mac wrote.[20] After several back-and-forth emails, Musk reportedly responded with a final mail to Mac: 'Get lost, you creep.'

Mac's further investigation later revealed that the 'private investigator' who had first tipped off Musk that Unsworth was a 'child rapist' was in fact a phoney. He was a convicted fraudster. And Musk had believed him.

Musk later deleted the tweet and apologised, which actually proved his greatest asset in the legal battle that ensued as Unsworth sued him for $190 million. The case was seen as ground-breaking in terms of the legal threshold for defamation on social media. And in the most unlikely way, Musk impacted on this as well. His defence lawyers argued the concept of 'JDart', an acronym for Twitter users who tweet something inappropriate that is badly received, and who then apologise and delete the tweet. A Los Angeles jury ruled in favour of Musk.

But in the course of his investigation, Mac hit on what he believed was a true glimpse into the psyche and character of Elon Musk. As he wrote on *BuzzFeed*, in going to court with an individual over what amounted to nothing more than Musk's believing he had been disrespected by Unsworth, and feeling aggrieved enough about this to engage not only his own Twitter account but also his multitude of Musketeers, who vehemently support him and actively troll anybody who doesn't, 'the billionaire entrepreneur brought the same drive that pushed electric cars into the mainstream to a legal dispute over his own bad behavior. And in typical fashion, Musk defied the odds. He won ... But in many ways, it is far more revealing of Musk than any of the technological feats that land him in the headlines. The weeklong trial showcased Musk's bending of reality, a skill that's part of his mythology but rarely seen outside his work. It's something he uses to convince an engineer to perfect a car part for days on end or push a public relations staffer to disappear a bad story, and it's often rescued him from the brink of failure.'[21]

According to Mac, Elon's version of reality is highly skewed ... 'In the case of Unsworth, he used it to convince himself that a critic was a pedophile simply because he happened to be an older white man living in Thailand. Then, when threatened with a defamation lawsuit, Musk and his lawyers built out an alternate reality: one where he played a key role in the cave rescue, where "pedo guy" was a common playground insult [in South Africa], and where he did not attempt to destroy a hero who had criticized him.'

Mac revealed that a former Tesla executive told him after the trial, 'Elon has an uncanny ability to tell a story he wants to be true, convince himself that it has to be true, and then convince others.'[22]

The court case, which should have been a trivial event in the world of Elon Musk, actually proved to be anything but. For Musk's critics, it proved their assertion that he was unhinged and suffering under the pressure of Tesla's not meeting its production targets. It was at this time that Musk was reportedly sleeping on the Tesla factory floor as he tried both to right the ship and to fend off vehement media criticism that he took personally. Investors were also famously 'shorting' Tesla stock at every opportunity.

For the Musketeers, though, the court case was a vindication that Musk had once again been unfairly treated by a media that cherry-picked its facts in order to make him and his companies look bad, and the legal system had finally proved this.

For the objective observer, it was a worrying glimpse into the psyche of a brilliant man who was displaying the same bullying tendencies that he had encountered at Bryanston High School. When Musk asserted in court that 'pedo guy' was South African slang for a creepy old white man, a number of South Africans – some of them his contemporaries – took to Twitter saying they had never heard this term used before. Mac investigated this himself and said he couldn't find any mention of this term being associated with South African slang.

THE 'hero' or 'hype' debate is one that often surrounds Musk, and Tesla provides an interesting case study. Whether Tesla actually makes a profit or not is a complicated matter. And even its profits are complicated.

Tesla is essentially a company that specialises in a very niche market of electric vehicles that cost anything from $40 000 to $150 000. Its production output is not close to that of the traditional automakers, although it is growing. In 2020, Tesla produced

510 000 cars. Volkswagen produced close to nine million cars in the same year.

Tesla reportedly enjoyed its first profitable year in 2020, sixteen years after Musk first invested in the company. It seems a long time to go without making a profit, and yet in this time Musk has managed on more than one occasion to grow investor interest and keep money flowing into a company that has been close to bankruptcy on a few occasions.

Even the very nature of 'profit' is confusing in the Tesla sense.

Regulations in 11 US states demand that automakers must sell a percentage of zero-emission vehicles by 2025. If they cannot meet this percentage, they have to buy regulatory credits from a company that does meet the requirements – a company such as Tesla, which exclusively sells electric vehicles. This has proved a huge financial boost for Tesla. CNN Business has estimated that in the five years before 2020, it accounted for $3.3 billion for Tesla.[23] Furthermore, Tesla's net income in 2020 was $721 million, but its regulatory credit income was $1.6 billion. The result was that Tesla could declare a 'profit'. It has been making more money off other car companies and its credits than from actual car sales. Then there is the bitcoin connection.

Musk has managed social media better than any other CEO who has ever sat in the corner office. And he's done it most effectively with cryptocurrencies. His tweets about the merits of certain cryptocurrencies have quite literally moved the markets. He has single-handedly determined the price of bitcoin with his tweets. At one point, Tesla purchased $1.5 billion in bitcoin. The company then sold ten per cent of this for $101 million, which enabled Tesla to make a profit. Tesla was making more money selling bitcoins than actual cars.

And yet Tesla's value has soared to the point that it is now the world's most valuable car company – above traditional giants such as Toyota, Volkswagen and BMW – despite taking several years to actually be profitable. Shares in Tesla rose 700 per cent in 2020. For what Tesla is now worth and future predictions of what it will be worth, it could buy every major car company out there. It has made millionaires out of those who invested early, spawning a group of what are now called 'Teslanaires'.

Investment analysts refer to Tesla as a 'polarising stock' because of the faith some have in it and the scepticism of others. Many feel the stock is hopelessly overvalued. Musk has famously said so himself, and has held Twitter polls asking whether people agree. In 2021, he shocked the investment world when he asked his followers whether he should sell ten per cent of his Tesla shares in order to increase his taxable income.[24] The real reason behind the sale, though, was that a massive tax bill was headed his way as a result of stock options he had received many years earlier. He had to sell those shares, or lose them. But Musk was taking a bigger swipe at the US tax system in general, stating, 'Much is made lately of unrealized gains being a means of tax avoidance.' Musk has often argued that his wealth lies not in his own cash but in his companies, and that he does not take a salary but instead holds stock. He has since had a few Twitter encounters with Senator Bernie Sanders, who is a leading proponent of further taxing the extremely wealthy as part of a call for a 'billionaires' income tax'. As the richest person on the planet, Musk is a clear target. And yet the value of Tesla continues to soar on his watch, and the kind of volatility he generates is clearly not an issue for the markets.

Even Tesla's actual identity is up for debate. Some argue that Tesla is more a tech company than a car company. And Musk has proved himself brilliant at using this to his advantage. It's a car company. It's a tech company. It's a battery company. It's a conscience company. It's a cryptocurrency company. It's a solar power company. It's a social movement. It's a hope of things to come.

Much like SpaceX, the money seems to be drawn to what Tesla can become and what the company represents as the future.

As Marc Tarpenning once put it, 'Elon is complicated. He delves into everything, which can be both a positive and a negative. He pushes on certain things in development that you kind of wonder why. Sometimes it makes sense and sometimes it doesn't. He's very much into risk. He's willing to take on financial risks for himself personally, and technology risks when he's working on something new that is a little out there but when it works it's really amazing. But of course there's lots of sort of collateral damage along the way. But it's a way to make things work.'[25]

Musk is acutely strategic. He is able to convince investors to become part of his grandiose projects. But at the same time he publicly declares that he never believed either SpaceX or Tesla would succeed, and that they would probably erode his personal fortune. It's the kind of brutal honesty that perhaps gives investors the comfort of knowing that if it didn't work out, he has at least been honest with them.

As for comments that Tesla is overvalued. Well, Musk agrees. In 2021, when Tesla's stock price reached $760, Musk tweeted that he thought the price was too high. And yet investors and the market keep following him.

So what is Tesla really worth? What is Tesla actually?

While those questions keep being asked, Mercedes-Benz, Ford, Kia and Volkswagen will continue spending billions on their own lines of electric vehicles. And on becoming what Tesla started.

In the race to build electric cars, Musk is now being followed closely by the other major car manufacturers. CNN Business estimates that in 2018 the number of electric vehicles on the road around the world reached over five million – a 40 per cent increase from the year before. The constant improvements in battery technology and the environmental incentive to produce greener batteries are major drivers of growth. In 2015, battery cost as a percentage of the retail price of a medium-sized vehicle in the US was just under 75 per cent. It is predicted to drop to around 25 per cent by 2025. Vehicle range and charging infrastructure will be the other major obstacles to overcome in the years ahead.

Tesla is still the frontrunner here in terms of sales. Musk's company took the top spot in 2017 with almost 100 000 cars sold. This put it at number one, ahead of Geely, Renault-Nissan-Mitsubishi, Hyundai, GM, Volkswagen, Mercedes-Benz, Ford and Toyota.

It remained there in 2018 with 222 000 cars sold.

But taking into account current production and research and development, CNN Business predicts that Volkswagen will take over the top spot in 2025, followed by Renault-Nissan-Mitsubishi, Geely and then Tesla.

Musk was spot-on. The future of the automobile is indeed electric. The future of Tesla lies in its ability to stay in the race. It's had a great head start. But Musk is well aware that one of the challenges of being first is that it gives everybody else something to aim at.

When it comes to the space race, Musk is doing his best to stay in front. And for now, he's winning.

The Space Barons

ON Wednesday 15 September 2021, our relationship with outer space changed forever.

Launched from the Kennedy Space Center in Florida, SpaceX's Dragon spacecraft carried four civilians into orbit for the first time in human history. These were not professional astronauts, and this was not just cargo. These were four ordinary people – who went into space.

This was a seminal moment for humanity, and for Musk.

Four civilians went into space alone. Humanity's previous interactions with space, from the first Earth orbits to the moon landings and the ISS, were indeed awe-inspiring. But on all of these occasions, the ordinary person was merely an observer. We watched in awe as professionals did what we could only dream of – that giant leap taken on our behalf.

And the giant leap taken by the crew of Inspiration4 was an equally defining one for Musk's space ambitions.

Musk has said all along that his driving ambition is to make humans a multiplanetary species. His reasons for this are both practical, to prevent a single extinction event similar to the one that wiped out the dinosaurs, and emotional, to make science fiction real and create the exciting future that has captivated him since he was a child.

To do this, he believed he first needed to reignite the conversation around space exploration and get people excited about the subject again. The next steps would be to build a private space company and make it financially viable by securing government contracts first to transport cargo and then to transport astronauts.

All of this Musk achieved with SpaceX.

Wednesday 15 September 2021 was a landmark. In a way, it was the day when the world of *The Jetsons* – an American animated series of the 1960s featuring a futuristic family living a space-age life – became a reality. Ordinary people could look to the stars and dream of a day when they could experience spaceflight without having to become professional astronauts.

It did, however, take a billionaire to book the seats on this historic first flight. Just as it was once the well-off who were able to book seats on the first commercial airliners, or to own mobile phones, and now everybody can fly and everybody has a mobile phone. It's that kind of trajectory that Musk likes to set his sights on. He was one of the first Internet billionaires at a time when the new technology was only really understood by a niche group of highly intelligent individuals. Now, five-year-olds understand the Internet and hold it in the palm of their hands.

For Musk, the speed with which you can close the gap between being the first and opening it up to everybody is where the thrill of engineering lies: get the conversation going, whether it be the Internet, electric cars or spaceflight, and then move fast. In doing so, you ensure the industry and the entire narrative move a lot faster than they would have if the grand vision had not been revealed. It is for this reason that Musk has declared he doesn't register patents.

On two separate occasions, he has said Tesla patents would be open-source. 'If somebody comes and makes a better electric car than Tesla and it's so much better than ours that we can't sell our cars and we go bankrupt, I still think that's a good thing for the world.[1]

The overarching goal of Tesla is to accelerate the advent of sustainable energy. And so if we created a patent portfolio that discouraged other companies from making electric cars, that would be inconsistent with our mission.'[2]

And yet with Musk, there is always a carefully thought-out strategy that his followers sometimes don't see. Musk announced Tesla's patent strategy shortly before Toyota ended its collaboration with Tesla in 2017 – reportedly over a clash between Tesla's risk-taking approach and the more conservative approach of Toyota – and announced its own hydrogen vehicle. By opening Tesla's patents, a move that Toyota mimicked with the patents for its hydrogen vehicle, the idea was indeed to accelerate the move to a sustainable energy vehicle. Musk, though, was tipping the scales in his favour, or rather in favour of electric vehicles over any other competing technology. With open patents, more developers could support and grow Tesla's current technology, which in turn would keep Tesla in the driving seat of the move to sustainable-energy vehicles and wouldn't shift the development focus to another source of energy, such as hydrogen. It's a subtle shift, but one that clearly shows how Musk's mind works. As altruistic as his ambitions are, Musk still works very much at the sharp end of what makes business sense.

So it's safe to say there will be a commercial benefit for SpaceX beyond just protecting human consciousness, and clearly there needs to be a return in order for the company to survive.

But the four-person crew of Inspiration4 were not concerned with such matters. The crew was led by technology billionaire Jared

Isaacman, who paid around $200 million for the privilege of being mission commander. A qualified pilot, Isaacman has vast experience in flying everything from small aircraft to fighter jets. Draken International, one of his companies, provides flight training services to the US Department of Defense. Like Musk, Isaacman never much enjoyed school and found a life in technology and adventure. But he has also displayed a keen understanding of privilege, and has used many of his flying experiences to help raise funds for charity.

In Isaacman, Musk certainly had the right ambassador for Inspiration4. In a special Netflix documentary about the mission, Isaacman reflected: 'What thoughts do I think people could potentially have on this? Well, it's a billionaire going on a joyride. The privileges of wealth to be able to go and disregard all that could be done here on Earth. For me, there has to be some offset. We are not going to do this if we can't make a huge difference for the problems the world's faced with today, or we don't earn the right to go up into space.

'You definitely don't get into my position in life unless a couple of things went your way at the right time. And then you think about the extreme other end of the spectrum which is the families where nothing went right, they got dealt a horrible hand in life, and a lot of these kids [suffering from cancer] don't even grow up and have a chance to experience even one hundredth of what I've had the opportunity to experience, and it's an imbalance that sucks and it's terrible and we should do something about it … If we are going to eventually live in a world where everybody is capable of going out and journeying amongst the stars then we better fight childhood cancer along the way.'[3]

It was decided that St Jude Children's Research Hospital, in Memphis, Tennessee, would be the official beneficiary of the Inspiration4 mission. St Jude, founded in 1962 by beloved entertainer Danny Thomas, is a world leader in childhood cancer research, particularly leukaemia. The aim was to raise $200 million for the hospital.

With this in mind, Isaacman offered two of the remaining three seats to St Jude. The hospital selected Hayley Arceneaux, a staff member who is herself a cancer survivor and had been treated at St Jude. She went on to qualify as a physician's assistant and returned to the hospital to work with leukaemia and lymphoma patients.

St Jude opted to raffle the second seat, which eventually went to Christopher Sembroski, a US Air Force veteran with a background in the aerospace industry. Ironically, as a college student, he had volunteered with a company named ProSpace that lobbied government to open up space travel and pave the way for companies such as SpaceX.

Isaacman decided to offer up the fourth seat in the form of a contest. The person who came up with the best business idea for an online shop incorporating the ecommerce services of his company, Shift4 Payments, and the online store Shift4Shop, would win the final seat on Inspiration4. That honour went to Dr Sian Proctor, a geoscientist whose father had worked for NASA during the Apollo missions. She also shares Musk's vision of opening up space to all. As an artist and poet, she promotes what she calls 'JEDI Space' – Just, Equitable, Diverse and Inclusive – for all humanity as part of her Space2inspire initiative. She used the Shift4Shop to sell her artwork.

These four individuals represented a keen balance between privilege and pioneering, but Isaacman took this a step further. For the four seats he had purchased, he assigned each a symbolic trait. As mission commander, his seat symbolised leadership. The other traits were generosity, prosperity and hope. Arceneaux sat neatly in the hope seat, while Sembroski filled the generosity seat and Proctor took the prosperity seat.

SpaceX's Falcon 9 rocket did the heavy lifting, and the Dragon

– the first privately owned spacecraft to transport astronauts to the ISS – spent three days in lower Earth orbit with its first all-civilian crew. They drifted at an orbital altitude of 585 km, which was the fifth-highest human orbital altitude in history. It was even higher than the ISS, which orbits the Earth at an altitude of 408 km.

Suddenly, a billionaire, a physician's assistant, an air force veteran and an entrepreneurial scientist were alone in orbit. For Musk, this was the critical moment in terms of getting the public excited about space again. This was now far beyond the nuts and bolts of sending rockets into space, winning CRS contracts, launching government satellites or even sending professional astronauts into space. This was science fiction made real. Where going into space was once seen as a question of national duty, it was now a personal bucket-list experience.

Musk had moved ridiculously fast, from building his own rockets to developing reusable rockets to transporting space cargo to astronauts and sending civilians into space. A timeline of 12 years from when Falcon 1 became the first privately funded rocket to reach orbit in 2008 to this moment. When you consider that it took the US nine years – and an enormous national effort – to land a man on the moon, Musk's 12 years is an incredible achievement. And he had done it as a private company. It was a giant leap that left his competitors, the so-called 'Space Barons', far behind.

The Billionaire Space Race, as it's become known, revolves around three individuals: Elon Musk (SpaceX), Jeff Bezos (Blue Origin) and Richard Branson (Virgin Galactic). Their combined net worth is a little more than the GDP of South Africa. But individually, they couldn't be more different in their visions of space.

Branson was probably the first to tout the appeal of spaceflight for paying customers and not just astronauts. He has long harboured dreams of his own to travel into space. Branson's vision appears more focused on space travel as a means of transport, with a vision of one day being able to fly people between cities and countries at a suborbital level, far faster than any commercial airline could.

Bezos wants to take this a step further. He has a vision of people travelling into space and living and working in spinning orbital space colonies. A moon base is also part of his grand vision, as is the plan to move much of Earth's industry into space as a way of keeping the planet clean. And, of course, space tourism.

Musk has plans to go the furthest of all – to Mars. Space tourism is also on the agenda. But Musk's ultimate aim is for humans not just to visit space but to live there. And he has targeted Mars as the 'new Earth'.

Branson and Bezos have been determined to beat each other as the first Space Baron to actually go into space. Branson took the first shot, on 11 July 2021, when he flew his suborbital spaceplane VSS *Unity* (SpaceShipTwo class) to what is defined by the Fédération Aéronautique Internationale as the agreed edge of space – the Kármán Line of 100 km altitude, or the boundary between Earth's atmosphere and outer space. *Unity* reached an altitude of 86 km during the trip. Although it can be argued that Branson's craft did not quite reach space, as he did not cross the Kármán Line, both the US Air Force and NASA place the boundary of space at 80 km, which does give Branson the title of first Space Baron in space.

On 20 July 2021, Bezos made his trip into space in his New Shepard 2 rocket (named for Mercury astronaut Alan B Shepard). New Shepard touched into outer space at 105 km altitude, just a shade over the Kármán Line, giving him bragging rights as the first Space Baron in space. Bezos took with him 82-year-old Mary Wallace (Wally) Funk, who became the oldest person to travel into space, and 18-year-old Dutch pilot Oliver Daemen, who became the youngest. Bezos's younger brother, Mark, also went along for the ride.

But in almost every sense, Musk is leading this three-way space race. SpaceX has transformed the rocket industry more than any other company. It has secured the necessary and highly lucrative contracts to fuel its expansion. And it is by far the most popular and perhaps most visible of the three in the minds of the general public – the result of Musk's own popular persona as well as his highly visible failed launches. Musk has not yet publicly stated if and when he will travel into space himself, apart from joking that he would indeed like to die on Mars one day, 'just not on impact'. On a more serious note, though, he has stated that his position at the helm of so many companies at present makes it too much of a risk for him to entertain space travel for now.

Yet while Branson and Musk appear happy to share in the dream of space, Bezos has been involved in court battles and public spats with both companies. Bezos's Blue Origin was quick to point out that Branson had not crossed the Kármán Line, even producing a detailed explanatory graphic and describing Branson's craft as a 'high-altitude airplane' rather than a rocket. Blue Origin has also taken repeated swipes at SpaceX, going so far as to declare its landing vehicles unsafe for astronauts. They were also at pains to point out that New Shepard 2 boasted 'the largest windows in space'.

Then, on Wednesday 15 September, Musk blasted past them all. His Inspiration4 mission made history in every sense as the first all-civilian crew surged past the highest points reached by Branson and Bezos, and even the ISS, reaching an altitude of 585 km.

And the records tumbled.

As listed on the SpaceX website, it was the first all-civilian human spaceflight to orbit, with the first black female spacecraft pilot (Proctor) and the youngest American in space (the 29-year-old Arceneaux, who also became the first person with a prosthetic body part to go into space, having lost part of her left thigh and knee to cancer at the age of ten), and it was the longest human spaceflight since the Hubble missions – and several other firsts. In a nod to Bezos, Musk and his team pointed out that Dragon's cupola provides a viewing area of over 2000 square inches, making it the largest continuous window ever to go into space. And finally, the Inspiration4 mission raised close to $154 million for the St Jude Children's Research Hospital.

But it's between Musk and Bezos that the most intense battle and most heated exchanges have occurred. Up until now, SpaceX has led the way. It has won the necessary government and NASA contracts against Blue Origin, and it has secured the prized launch sites. Although formed two years after Blue Origin, SpaceX quickly eclipsed its rival. Musk's ability to move at the speed of light has clearly been the differentiator, while Bezos is said to favour a more cautious approach. While Musk was printing 'Occupy Mars' T-shirts, Bezos encapsulated Blue Origin's approach as *gradatim ferociter* (step by step – ferociously).

And Musk appears to be winning the PR war as well. As they've competed for everything from government contracts to public support, Musk has come out ahead. Bezos's response has been to go to court. When NASA awarded the CRS contract to SpaceX, Blue Origin sued NASA on the grounds of 'unlawful and improper evaluation of proposals submitted'.

In the mind of the public, Musk is a billionaire offering the hope of a brighter future in which he wants to save the planet, save humanity and make spaceflight accessible to all – not just the super-wealthy. Bezos, on the other hand, seems to be portrayed as a billionaire taking jaunts into space while his company is under intense scrutiny over its treatment of its employees. Dragging the space race into court and suing NASA – essentially the hand that feeds – is hardly doing his image any good.

Musk summed up the advantage he has over Bezos when he

described the Inspiration4 mission: 'We're trying to make the dream of space accessible to anyone. This Inspiration4 mission helps bring awareness of spaceflight to a lot of people – makes it more personal. Hopefully as the name suggests, it inspires people about spaceflight.'[4]

Quite simply, Musk makes it personal and Musk inspires. Bezos does not.

The two have traded blows on Twitter, and at times it has appeared petty. But for all his flaws, for all his mistakes, for all the criticism of his business practices, the reality is that Musk resonates with people. The success of SpaceX and Tesla confirms this. He resonates so much that people are willing to overlook the negative in pursuit of his shared vision.

For both men, though, and any who follow, the risks are high.

On this scale, when things go wrong, the result is cataclysmic. Space travel remains a risky bet. Despite this, of the almost 600 people who have been into space, only 18 have lost their lives. And only three have actually died in space, namely, above the Kármán Line.

Accidents are bound to happen, but up to this point, the overwhelming majority of those who have given their lives in the pursuit of new horizons among the stars have been professional astronauts, often from the military, on government missions. Any loss of life remains tragic, but when professional astronauts lose their lives on government missions, it's something people can perhaps deal with.

However, when civilians die, that penetrates an entirely new area of the public psyche. The *Challenger* disaster of 1986 is an example; of the seven crew members who perished when the Space Shuttle exploded just over a minute after launch, only one was a civilian. Christa McAuliffe, a teacher, had been selected to become the first American civilian to go into space.

Millions watched in shock as *Challenger* broke up. The tragedy rocked American society and the world. President Ronald Reagan declared a week of mourning. But it's worth noting that the news reports that followed invariably mentioned that Christa McAuliffe was a schoolteacher. Everybody knew there was a schoolteacher on board.

The more space tourism becomes a reality, the higher the risk of tragedy involving ordinary citizens. Governments may well be able to absorb this impact, and the resulting backlash. But private companies are less able to do so.

Musk perhaps appreciates this more than most as a result of his experience with Tesla. In June 2021, the National Highway Traffic Safety Administration (NHTSA) opened investigations into 30 collisions involving Tesla vehicles, which had led to ten fatalities since 2016. The NHTSA pointed to Tesla's Autopilot system as 'suspected of use'. The investigations were not exclusively focused on Tesla, and also examined vehicles from other car makers using driverless technology. But the spotlight still fell first on Tesla.

SpaceX, and any other private space entities, will certainly face similar scrutiny in order to ensure that the space race remains a safe race for all.

Is Elon Musk Boring?

ON 17 December 2016, Musk summed up all of our frustrations when he tweeted, 'Traffic is driving me nuts.' But in the mind of Elon Musk, it didn't just end there: 'Am going to build a tunnel boring machine and just start digging,' he followed up. And, in case you were foolhardy enough to not believe him, he added, 'I am actually going to do this.'

Frustrated with the endless traffic problems of Los Angeles, Musk found himself dreaming up a tunnel system that would alleviate congestion on the roads. He decided to set up an infrastructure company, The Boring Company (quite literally, to bore tunnels), that would aim at doing just that. According to The Boring Company, the decision to go for tunnels rather than, say, flying cars – equally improbable but perhaps not out of the question when it comes to Musk – boils down to the fact that tunnels are 'weatherproof, out of sight, and won't fall on your head'.[1] For Musk, the fact that tunnels can be built in three dimensions – in that they could be stacked in what he refers to as a 3D network of tunnels – allows the creation of an almost endless network that can accommodate even the most aggressive expansion of a city. Albeit with the necessary regulatory approvals.

The vision of The Boring Company is to 'solve traffic, enable rapid point-to-point transportation and transform cities'. Simple as that. For most of us, Musk had us at 'solve traffic'. Once again, Musk had a grand vision for humanity, perhaps not on the scale of saving the planet but one that would certainly preserve the sanity of millions of road users in busy cities. All of us can get behind a cause that will make our daily commute that much faster and more pleasurable. Even more so when the company comes with a bit of marketing razzmatazz that includes a tongue-in-cheek name rather than something like 'Traffic Infrastructure Solutions'.

With The Boring Company, Musk yet again displayed one of the qualities that his fans love. He envisions something everybody has talked about, but he doesn't just talk about it. He actually gets things done. Even the most far-fetched idea becomes a reality in Musk's hands. Think what you will of Musk, there is no denying his ability – and general modus operandi – to identify an industry, pinpoint its flaws and then attack it with gusto. It is problem-solving, or engineering, of the highest order. Or perhaps a re-engineering of the structures that society has become so accustomed to that no new thought has been put into how they can be done better. And once Musk goes public with his plans and ideas, there follows a certain amount of scepticism. But in the background, Musk achieves two very critical goals. He reignites a conversation around a particular topic and becomes the stimulus that fast-tracks innovation and progress in this area. Musk said as much when he described one of the goals of Tesla as the acceleration of the shift towards electric vehicles becoming the norm and no longer just an emissions-control ideal that remains on the drawing board. In the case of The Boring Company, Musk's twofold goal is to dig tunnels faster and at a fraction of the current cost.

The Boring Company is certainly evidence of how Musk moves from idea to actualisation. After founding the company, Musk quite literally began digging. He and his team dug a hole in the SpaceX parking lot in Hawthorne. Initially, he was told it would take two weeks to dig a hole of any consequence. Musk's response was to start on a Friday afternoon and 'see what's the biggest hole we can dig between now and Sunday afternoon'.[2] This is not a man who wastes time overthinking big ideas. By 2018, members of the public could explore the first stretch of a 1.6-kilometre test tunnel.

He has developed tunnel boring machines (TBMs) that are named after famous poems and plays; the first was Godot, after Samuel Beckett's *Waiting for Godot*. After Godot came Line-Storm, so named after a Robert Frost poem. And then came Prufrock, named after TS Eliot's 'The Love Song of J Alfred Prufrock'.

Prufrock is touted as a major upgrade in tunnel boring technology, in that it is able to 'porpoise'. According to The Boring Company website, 'it launches directly from the surface, mines underground, and re-emerges upon completion. This allows Prufrock to begin tunnelling within 48 hours of arrival onsite and eliminates the need to excavate expensive pits to launch and retrieve the machine'. It is said to tunnel six times faster than Godot and Line-Storm. The Boring Company does note that it still moves 'four to five times slower than a garden snail ... but Prufrock is catching up'.

The Boring Company currently offers various tunnel products, from the Loop (an underground public transportation system) to utility, freight and pedestrian tunnels. It also sells a fifth tunnel option simply called Bare – 'We build the tunnel, you put what you want into it'.

Loop is one of the more interesting tunnel concepts because of the way it fits into Musk's ecosystem of companies. Loop is planned as an 'all-electric, zero-emissions, high-speed underground public transportation system in which passengers are transported to their destination with no intermediate stops'. It fits into the broader picture of the Hyperloop, a project being worked on by a number of companies, including Musk's. The Hyperloop is a proposed system of ground transportation for people and cargo that would facilitate travel at high speeds in tubes either above or below ground. In the case of public transport, these low-pressure tubes would carry people in pods moving at up to 1 200 km/h. The ultimate goal would be for this to replace traditional road and rail travel. The idea is not a new one, but Musk has been instrumental in reigniting the discussion around it. Followers of his version of Hyperloop have referred to it as 'Teslas in Tunnels!' It's a seamless integration – from building an electric car to building underground highways for your electric cars.

The first Loop was built for the Las Vegas Convention Center, and began operating in April 2021. It features two 1.2-kilometre tunnels in which chauffeur-driven Teslas whisk visitors around the less than one square kilometre of the convention centre. It's impressive, but a far cry from 'solving traffic'.

Much in the same way as he approached SpaceX, Musk has sought to redevelop the tunnelling value chain and decrease the costs associated with digging tunnels. Musk publicly declared that The Boring Company would aim to build tunnels at a cost of approximately $10 million per mile, as opposed to the current cost of between $100 million and $1 billion per mile. Among the most obvious cost-saving methods is enhancing current TBMs to make them more efficient, creating a more automated tunnelling system and making the tunnels themselves narrower to reduce their cost. It is worth noting that all of The Boring Company's tunnel offerings are a single diameter.

As with all of Musk's ideas and projects, The Boring Company has met with scepticism from critics. A number of deals have fallen through, and many promises seem too good to be true. And yet, both

Musk and The Boring Company keep digging. Musk is reported to have had inquiries for tunnels in Australia, Europe and China. But it remains in its infancy, and the leap from Loop to Hyperloop is also still a giant and very costly one to make.

The general reaction to Musk's plans remains muted. But Teslarati, a media company that focuses on all things Musk, Tesla and SpaceX, believes they've seen this all before. Under the headline 'The Boring Company skeptics are making the same mistakes as Tesla and SpaceX critics', writer Simon Alvarez argues that The Boring Company is following exactly the same historical pattern as all of Musk's previous ideas and companies: 'Elon Musk himself has proven over the years that even conventionally insane ideas – such as landing the first stage of an orbital rocket on a drone in the middle of the ocean or scaling the production of a mass-market electric car – could be feasible if enough work is put into them.

'It is easy to mock or dismiss the ideas of people like Elon Musk and his teams at The Boring Company, SpaceX, and Tesla. But inasmuch as Musk's companies make it pretty easy to target them due to their goals and nature, SpaceX and Tesla's history shows that more often than not, it is a mistake to bet against Musk and his team of visionaries, almost all of whom seem to have the tendency to think outside the box by default.'[3]

Or, in the words of Musk's former business partner Peter Thiel, 'Never bet against Elon Musk.' But many investors are also trying to answer the question of whether it is worth betting on Musk's getting it right every time.

Sitting behind a tab at the top right of The Boring Company homepage is a link to a product that has nothing to do with tunnelling but has created even more controversy, and even led to legislation: the Flamethrower.

Musk designed his own flamethrower, and used it to launch

The Boring Company. As someone in tune with contemporary pop culture, he knew that zombies and the apocalypse are wildly popular genres. Zombies as a cultural phenomenon have given rise to a billion-dollar industry in the US. So Musk produced 20 000 flamethrowers with the promise that the device 'Works against hordes of the undead or your money back!' He charged $500 per flamethrower. He sold out in less than a week. And with $10 million, The Boring Company suddenly had seed capital.

The New York State Senate wasn't impressed and passed a bill that made possession of a flamethrower for recreational activities a crime: 'Elon Musk's Boring Company released a new flamethrower which sold out of all 20 000 within days, without any concern to the training of the purchasers or their reasons for buying. Allowing the general public to access this type of machine is extremely problematic. These dangerous devices should not be sold to civilians, and use needs to be restricted to trained professionals,'[4] the lawmakers argued.

And yet it's still there on the company homepage. But a click on Flamethrower takes you to a page headed 'The Boring Company *NOT* a Flamethrower'. And it simply reports '20 000 Not-a-Flamethrowers Sold – fire extinguishers sold separately'. Below it is a tweet from Musk: 'The rumor that I'm secretly creating a zombie apocalypse to generate demand for flamethrowers is completely false.'

At the end of all of this remains the obvious question: is The Boring Company a success? The simple answer is no. Not now. The more intriguing answer, though, is not yet.

MUSK is equally intrigued with the 'tunnels' that make up the neural networks in the brain. But whereas most of the projects he undertakes hold some hope for the future, he has expressed darker thoughts about the one that concerns him the most – artificial intelligence.

Commonly known as AI, artificial intelligence is the rapidly growing field of computer science that keeps pushing the boundaries of building machines or programming them to be capable of performing human tasks. Or, put more plainly, creating robots that can do the same things human beings can.

For Musk, the greatest danger lies not in AI in itself, but rather AI that is left unchecked and unregulated. He has compared this scenario to rule by a dictator, but worse: 'At least when there is an evil dictator, that human is going to die. But for AI there would be no death. It would live forever, and then you'd have an immortal dictator from which we can never escape'.[5]

Musk is not just concerned about AI; he is genuinely frightened by it: 'I'm really quite close to the cutting edge of AI, and it scares the hell out of me. It's capable of vastly more than anyone knows, and the rate of improvement is exponential.'[6]

And he's most concerned that he appears to be one of the few individuals at his level of interaction who is so concerned about it. Even his own Autopilot technology at Tesla has shown the complex – and sometimes dangerous – relationship between humans and machines programmed to try and think like humans.

Musk has long spoken out about the dangers of AI. In fact, he believes governments not only have been too slow in regulating AI but are actually too late. Developments in AI are now moving faster than legislation can ever hope to keep up. As he says, 'When the robots are walking down the street with us, then it's too late …'[7] We have to figure out some way to ensure that the advent of digital super intelligence is one that is symbiotic with humanity. That's the single biggest existential crisis that we face, and the most pressing one.'[8]

Musk certainly appears to have a genuine fear of what AI could do to humanity, perhaps recalling the *Terminator* movies of his youth. Musk has often expressed concerns about DeepMind, a British company owned by Google parent Alphabet Inc that focuses on AI development. 'Just the nature of the AI that they're building is one that crushes all humans at all games,'[9] he has said. It doesn't seem a particularly harsh threat – a robot beating you at chess. But in Musk's mind, where he has often pontificated as to whether we are not all already living in some kind of artificial simulation that operates much like a game, the words 'crushes all humans at all games' are far more chilling. The rate at which AI learns chess and other games, moving to beating world champions within the space of a few months – what takes years for a human to learn – is what concerns him.

On a more basic level, Musk has expressed fears that AI will enable robots to perform tasks so much more effectively and cheaply than humans that humans will become obsolete, leading to mass unemployment on a scale that would require massive government assistance.

Musk has tweeted that humanity should be more concerned about AI than about North Korea, as AI is 'far more dangerous'. More dangerous than nuclear weapons. He sometimes speaks about AI in terms of an apocalypse of the machines, and has predicted that it will overtake humanity within five years.

Essentially, Musk is asking for greater regulatory oversight of AI, the lack of which he has described as 'insane'. Musk breaks this down as the difference between 'narrow AI' and 'species-level-risk AI'. An example of narrow AI would be the social media algorithms that control what you see on Facebook or Twitter. Species-level-risk AI is digital super-intelligence. Musk believes that a safer future lies in the symbiosis of humanity with AI, so that AI maximises humanity's freedom of action rather than completely replaces it.

Neuralink, another Musk company, defines itself as 'Breakthrough technology for the brain'. Through Neuralink, Musk and his team are planning to implant technology in the human brain that will enable paraplegics to perform certain tasks with the help of technology.

This will be controlled by a Neuralink device that sits behind a person's ear, much like a hearing aid. Future goals are to manipulate brain function for Alzheimer's patients and possibly help to improve other disorders in the brain and spine. Maximising the freedom of action of humanity.

For Musk, Neuralink is not a contradiction in terms of his concerns about AI, it's a solution – the belief that a human brain should still control the machine through the Neuralink interface, and that the robots shouldn't be left to control themselves.

For the sceptical, the way Musk smoothly transitions from a doomsday prophecy about unregulated AI, pausing as he ends sentences such as 'This is the most important thing we will ever do', and then offers a solution, one that he happens to be the founder and owner of, is a wonderful sales tool. A realist would say he's seen too many science-fiction films and sometimes defaults a little too easily to the *Terminator* and *Matrix* scenarios, in which warnings are not heeded and machines ultimately take over the world.

Clearly, when a man who generally does not like government regulation, and who quite easily could profit from less of it, calls for tighter regulation, this should be a red flag. And before you drift off to sleep, you remember Musk's words: 'The nature of the AI that they're building is one that crushes all humans at all games.' If we are busy teaching AI how to play the game of life …

Whether it be in space, on land, in tunnels under the earth, or deep inside the human brain, Musk is having an impact at many levels.

And there is nothing artificial about his influence.

PART SIX

The Cult of Elon Musk

IN the 2012 blockbuster film *The Avengers*, the eccentric billionaire Tony Stark (aka Iron Man) turns to Captain America and nonchalantly says, 'Following's not really my style.' Elon Musk's fans have long held him to be the real-life version of Stark, and indeed the inspiration behind actor Robert Downey Jnr's portrayal of this character in the successful Marvel franchise.

Following is indeed not Elon Musk's style. But having followers certainly is. On Twitter, his most active social media platform, Musk has 61.3 million followers. These include everyone from professional golfers to politicians. He, in turn, follows 106 people or institutions.

Musk gets an average of almost 100 000 likes per tweet. His tweets can be obscure, funny, intelligent, market-altering, boastful or sometimes just plain strange. But they always move the needle. So much so that 52 of Musk's famous tweets have been immortalised in a colouring book created by one of his most ardent fans, the artist Salina Gomez. *The Illuminated Tweets of Elon Musk* is described on her website, Ill Ink, as 'Gonzo visual editorial journalism in the form of a coloring book'.[1]

Writing on the tech website *The Verge* in 2018 under the heading 'The Gospel of Elon Musk According to his Flock', Bijan Stephen recounts how Gomez, who was hospitalised after a failed suicide attempt, had stumbled on Musk's tweets, which convinced her that there were still people in the world doing good things. 'That was the only thing giving me hope, you know, to keep going,' she said.[2]

Musk has had songs written about him ('The Future Smells like Elon Musk' by Jim and Kathy Ocean), he's appeared on NBC's *Saturday Night Live*, he's been the subject of university studies and theoretical papers, and he has an army of Twitter followers who literally move at his command.

Musk has been described as a visionary, a charlatan, a genius, a conman and the saviour of humankind. For some, his technology and ideas make him a master disruptor, while others see him as a master deflector, using those same grand ideas to deflect attention from any negative criticism.

The rise of Elon Musk began with his attempt to revolutionise the financial services industry. But his critics will point to the role of Confinity and Peter Thiel in the founding of PayPal. They will also say that Tesla was already in existence and making electric cars, thanks to Martin Eberhard and Marc Tarpenning, before Musk invested in the company. While some describe him as an engineer, others say he is no more than a venture capitalist. Among the scores of YouTube videos about Musk, there is one that asks, 'Is Elon Musk a psychopath?' It appears on the Common Sense Skeptic channel, which offers a range of other clips about Musk and his companies.

A mainly online group known as TSLAQ (tslaq.org/) have made it their mission to gather data that they believe exposes the shortcomings of both Musk and Tesla. Their very name demonstrates their purpose: TSLA is how Tesla is listed on the NASDAQ, and Q is the NASDAQ notation for bankruptcy.

TSLAQ has gone so far as to label Tesla a fraudulent company. They are hardly alone. Tesla is one of the most shorted stocks in history. (Shorting is when investors literally bet on the failure of the stock.) And yet the company's value continues to climb. In October 2021, Tesla's stock value broke the $1 trillion barrier for the first time after car rental giant Hertz placed an order for 100 000 Tesla vehicles in a bid to bolster its fleet with electric vehicles.

Even the Hertz deal came amid ongoing investigations by the National Transportation Safety Board (NTSB) as to why Tesla was contining to manufacture vehicles incorporating its Autopilot technology when it had yet to fully respond to the NTSB's concerns and queries over the safety of this technology. Tesla has been involved in more than 1 000 lawsuits.

Another matter of debate is fatal collisions involving Tesla vehicles. On the TSLAQ website, under 'Tesla Safety', there is a link to TeslaDeaths.com, which records in detail fatalities 'that involved a driver, occupant, cyclist, motorcyclist, or pedestrian death, whether or not the Tesla or its driver were at fault'. As of 30 October 2021, it was claimed that ten deaths were related Tesla's Autopilot, out of a total of 210 Tesla-related fatalities. One of the main drivers of their research is to prove a supposed disconnect between Musk's claims about the safety of Tesla vehicles and the facts.

Dig further on the Internet, and there is an entire subculture questioning Musk. The website gotmusked.com is a good example, and once again its main focus is Tesla. It questions everything from the validity of Tesla's actual advantage in battery technology (it showcases the data to prove otherwise) to even Musk's perceived genius. In fact, it questions everything about Musk himself.

It was here that I discovered the questions surrounding Musk's claim that he attended Stanford University and dropped out. Evidence is presented in the form of court records from the legal case between Eberhard and Musk, affirming that there are no records of his having enrolled at Stanford. But this still doesn't discount the fact that Musk was indeed accepted by Stanford. This is not a fabrication.

Gotmusked goes so far as to declare in bold letters, 'Elon Musk is a charlatan, not a genius, and possesses no genius or expertise outside of marketing, sales, and pushing propaganda'. If you google 'Elon Musk Fraud' you are presented with 6 530 000 results. 'Elon Musk Conman' will call up 2 580 000 results. But 'Elon Musk Genius' brings forth 36 400 000 results, and 'Elon Musk Hero' 10 200 000 results.

Musk has many detractors, and they go to great lengths to make their point heard. Among them are Bernie Sanders, Sarah Palin, Bill Gates, Jeremy Clarkson, the SEC, Jeff Bezos and Mark Zuckerberg. All have very clear faults of their own. But it could be that Musk is the 'people's billionaire', at a time in history when people are feeling a significant disconnect from those who make the rules.

Yet some people seem to take it personally that Musk is playing in their fields of expertise, and allegedly without sufficient knowledge. Continue digging, and you will come across Piekniewski's Blog (blog.piekniewski.info/). Filip Piekniewski PhD describes himself as a 'researcher working on computer vision and AI'. He's a 'senior scientist' and 'software engineer' working for Accel Robotics, based in San Diego, California. His thoughts on AI in particular have seen him quoted in scholarly publications, on popular websites and also by the BBC.

On 28 December 2018, Piekniewski posted: 'I must admit, a few years back I thought he is literally the next Steve Jobs, only actually better, since he was onto so many things … I admired SpaceX, thought that Tesla cars had many great solutions in them …'[3]

But Piekniewski says he began to harbour suspicions when Musk ventured into the realm of AI, his own specialist field: 'At some point in 2015 or 2016 Elon started talking outrageous stuff in the domain of AI, a domain of my own expertise, which I could tell right away was total bullshit. And then I began looking at all this stuff in detail. Doing some math here and there. Reading various opinions. As a result, my opinion on Musk and many of his ideas has changed somewhat substantially. At this point, I can pretty much say with confidence that 90% of his stuff is utter BS, and the remaining 10% is perhaps impressive but still questionable.'[4]

In a post titled 'Elon and the Collective', Piekniewski addresses what he believes are the inconsistencies throughout Musk's career. He did this, he says, because he was tired of trying to explain it every time he met a Musk devotee. He starts with SpaceX's reusable rockets, arguing that the idea itself is not as revolutionary as Musk claims and has been in existence for some time. So why, you ask, hasn't it been developed further until now? Piekniewski believes the answer lies in the cost:

The space shuttle program had exactly the same aim: a reusable space plane with reusable boosters. Only the main fuel tank burned up in the atmosphere but that was not a huge sacrifice, since the tank did not have engines, which are by far the most expensive part. However, although good-looking on paper, it turned out to be a commercial disaster. The shuttle had to be essentially taken apart after every mission (and even then there were a few close calls and two full-blown disasters). Ultimately, lifting cargo on a shuttle was much more expensive than using a regular, disposable rocket.

The rocket as it performs ascent and then descent undergoes some serious accelerations (way higher than a typical plane), while being built extremely delicately to minimize the mass (much tighter margins than an airliner). The rocket engine undergoes much higher stress than a jet engine. Hence all that stress can cause material fatigue and small malfunctions, while the margin for error on a rocket is extremely small. Hence if e.g. it turns out that the risk of mission failure on these reused boosters increases substantially after every use, all the anticipated savings from reusability may be quickly wiped out by one or two lost missions. And it should be noted, that the cargo that goes into space is often MUCH more expensive than the rocket itself.

So essentially we are exploring here the amount of tail risk that we can shave to get some savings. And for that we need data. A lot of data. And the fact that someone did it once or even ten times is not sufficient to declare a victory. Each of the space shuttles flew dozens of times, when one of the SpaceX boosters will have flown 100 times with between flights maintenance at an economical level, then it will be an actual success. And we are not close to that yet.[5]

Piekniewski is more damning on Musk's goal of colonising Mars: 'This sounds very romantic, and I think that if we stretched ourselves quite a bit, we could probably send an Apollo-style mission to Mars, mainly to plant a flag and get some samples. That alone would be dangerous as hell and really technically difficult, but permanent structure, Mars city, colonization, these are just sci-fi musings.'[6]

He delves into the science behind his contention, science that he argues makes even the threat of mass extinction on Earth a less inhospitable proposition than living on Mars: 'The argument often brought up here is that humans need to go multiplanetary to avoid extinction. I'm willing to accept that argument, but the disaster necessary to make Earth less hospitable than Mars would have to be truly epic. If we detonated all the nukes ever made, we would not get even close. There would still be atmosphere, plenty of water, manageable temperatures. It would seriously need to be a planetary-scale cataclysm, way beyond the thing that killed the dinosaurs 65 million years ago. So this argument as it stands is bullshit.'[7]

But detonating all the nuclear weapons on Earth would indeed precipitate an environmental catastrophe, and the electromagnetic pulse from the combined blast power would likely shut down modern life as we know it.

Yet Piekniewski doesn't discount the need for space exploration, and supports Musk's belief that the future for humans as a species lies herein. But he'd far rather see a focus on the moon than Mars. He argues, quite simply, that the Moon is closer and we've been there before: 'We should just find some cave on the Moon and start building a permanent base there. Perhaps deeper under the Moon's surface we would find the necessary resources such as water and carbon dioxide (water seems to be present in the always shaded craters). If we learned how to kickstart manufacturing there, the Moon would be a great outpost for launching more distant missions further down the road. Aiming at colonizing Mars now is simply silly.'[8]

Yet Musk is sinking his entire fortune into chasing this 'silly' idea. He's not the only one, but he's certainly the most ambitious and has the greatest appetite for going into space. There is a difficult balance to strike between Musk's grandiose plan to save humanity and colonise Mars, and Piekniewski's retort that it would be better to rather find a cave on the moon and build a base there.

On the subject of The Boring Company, Piekniewski is once again ruthless in his assessment: 'This is advertised as a solution to mass transit. Now again, this is simply ridiculous. First of all, electric cars in tunnels carrying people en masse is an old idea. It is called a metro, and it has been known and used all over the world for more than 100 years. Now let's dig to some numbers: a typical metro car weighs some 40 tons and is able to take 175 people (probably more if they squeeze). It means the infrastructure mass is some 228 kg per passenger. A Tesla model X weighs 2.7 tons and takes 5 (max 7) passengers. That means the mass of the infrastructure is 380–540 kg per passenger. Right there, without even going any further into other things, the raw cost of mass of infrastructure carried, which translates to the amount of energy necessary to operate, is roughly 2x that of actual mass transit. A train does not need to carry a battery for example, just takes the energy from the third rail. In addition a train has much lower rolling friction, etc … This is just a tip of the iceberg. There is so much wrong with this idea that it is hard to know where to start.'[9]

In assessing the Tesla Autopilot idea, Piekniewski states the obvious. Cars will never drive themselves, and shouldn't, and any vehicle manufacturer that claims to have 'self-driving technology' is lying: 'Autopilot, as impressive as it is as a cruise control system, is not by any means autonomous driving ready. Anyone who thinks otherwise is an idiot, period, and should be rapidly taken out of the road because he is endangering innocent people. The fact that this technology has been released as "beta" to [the] general public is irresponsible and significant number of fatalities [have] already occurred.'[10]

On SolarCity and the solar roof tiles debacle, Piekniewski declares, 'like with many of Elon's promises the devil is in the mundane engineering details'. In fact, he seems to predict the fire hazard that Walmart had to deal with: 'The problem is electric connectivity. Each tile needs to be connected to others, these connections have to be element resistant (it is a roof after all!) and reliable. Getting that to work is not easy and fragile. Wind, tiny earthquakes or even birds walking along the roof displace the tiles ever so slightly and they lose contact. Once the circuit is broken it is difficult to find and fix the fault. Even worse a short circuit can lead to heating and fire danger.'[11]

On the Tesla front, Piekniewski wonders whether they are as far ahead of the traditional competition as claimed: 'Tesla has issues with stuff long solved by every other manufacturer: panel alignment, leaking seals, paint job blemishes, rattling plastics, all sorts of QA [quality assurance] things. And I'm not making this stuff up. Twitter, Tesla forums and even fan-based vlogs on YouTube are full of complaints and horror service stories. This may have been growing pains for a 4–6-year-old niche car company, but Tesla has been around for more than 15 years, burned through tens of billions of dollars (mostly debt, which Tesla has roughly $10 billion of) and is valued on the stock market above Ford and GMC … I won't even go into the mountain of issues the short sellers bring up – even if only one third of their findings are true, this company is in a complete management chaos. What is certainly true is the long list of executives departing one by one over the last few years, this is indicative of authoritarian management and toxic company culture to say the least. So all in all, certainly not everything is right about this company, and I'm sure all these short sellers are there for good reason, they smell bullshit.'[12]

At the end of his lengthy evaluation, Piekniewski declares, 'Although resistance to Elon and his fans is futile, and we will all be assimilated, I call bullshit. I think the crowds of people who think Elon is the savior of mankind will be in for a great disappointment. Extravagant entrepreneur, great salesman, dreamer he is. But second incarnation of Jesus, savior of the planet and genius engineer he is not. Time will tell if I was right.'[13]

The blog post yielded close to 60 replies, some praising him for pointing out the obvious, and others lambasting him for not being a believer. Yet the 2018 post also underestimates Musk. Piekniewski declares, 'As of the end of 2018 SpaceX hasn't flown a single human to orbit.' Two years later, Musk and SpaceX ticked this box.

I reached out to Piekniewski to ask whether this single achievement had perhaps changed his views on Musk. 'No. There was absolutely nothing that has changed my mind,' he wrote back. 'SpaceX? Yes, they launch rockets. Whether the economy of their process is any better than fully disposable rocket remains to be seen. As far as I know the company still requires external funds and does not operate at a profit. It's a bit of a long story but with rockets all that matters is price per kg to orbit. When a stage is reused, part of its fuel, which could give the payload a lot of extra acceleration, needs to be saved for landing. Which in turn causes that the total load to orbit be approximately half than if it was disposable. Which in turn means that the same payload sent to orbit with a reusable rocket can be sent into space with a smaller rocket. In the grand scheme of things, the gains from reusability, even if they exist at all, will be at the order of 20 per cent, nowhere close [to] the promised ten times. It's simply the math of this particular problem.'

Then I asked him about Mars. Much like Dr Moogega Cooper, Piekniewski believes Mars is a pipe dream: 'Mars is a delusion just like it was before. In fact Musk has sent absolutely nothing to Mars. One would expect the guy wholly interested in sending humanity to the Red Planet to use last year's opportunity and at least send some small probe? Three missions went to Mars in 2020 and none of them had anything to do with Musk.'

The Boring Company? 'Hyperloop is dead on arrival. The Las Vegas tunnel is a joke.'

Full Self-Driving (FSD)? (This is an upgrade on Autopilot with several extra features that require even less input from the driver.) 'FSD is the biggest vaporware [technology that has been advertised but hasn't been properly developed] in the history of mankind. Six years after sales started, it's nowhere near functional and will never be functional because the entire approach is flawed. This is my particular area of expertise and I'm 100 per cent sure of what I'm saying here. Their struggles in FSD are exactly like I predicted, and they have no clue how to get over the currently, completely unsafe state of the art. All the claims about cars having sufficient hardware for FSD were a criminal level bluff.'

The solar roof? 'Dead. Perhaps because it was never about having the tiles, as it was more about having a safe and non-fire-hazard connectivity. Also, it makes zero sense to put solar panels on shaded parts of the roof since they essentially don't produce any energy at all.'

Neuralink? 'This is a total scam. Let's just say I know that from a friend of a friend who happens to be working there. But even without that, I've had enough experience in neuroscience to know with certainty that their claims are complete fantasy.' (He didn't name the friend.)

Tesla? 'Clearly Tesla is nothing about cars as much as it is about stock price. The cars just seem to be a nice prop to keep the story going.'

Piekniewski presents a damning assessment of every one of Musk's companies, ventures and ideas: 'Really, the only thing this guy does is launching those rockets, and perhaps the real genius of his is to realise what the Cold War era governments realised too: rockets are more a tool of propaganda than they are a tool of space exploration.'

The reason I chose to quote Piekniewski at such length is that it reveals a common theme. Musk has his zealous fan base, and his equally zealous critics. Whether it's due to his great wealth, his perceived arrogance or the fact that he's doing what so many have talked about but never tried, a common response seems to be to either declare him the saviour of humanity or immediately discredit him as a charlatan, rather than adopt a more moderate approach to him and his ideas.

But while the business world and venture capitalists view Musk as having the Midas touch and are more than willing to take a gamble on him, the likes of Piekniewski remain unimpressed: 'In the department of propaganda, memes and market pumps, I think he is a truly one-of-a-kind genius and certainly will make the history books. Just not in the chapter most people expect. The rocket story gives credibility, serves to shut down skeptics and keep all the other balls in the air. But rockets could not save the Soviet Union and eventually they won't be able to save Elon.'

Musk could well come to represent the most audacious experiment in our modern culture's pervasive cult of personality.

His Future Among the Stars

WHEN I started this journey of Elon Musk, it was with the immediate realisation that anything Musk does has an exponential ripple effect.

The first interview I listened to was his appearance on *The Joe Rogan Experience* on 7 September 2018. It was a wide-ranging conversation, covering his thoughts on love, humanity, the sustainability of Earth, Mars and the danger of robots taking over the world, but it was overshadowed by a few seconds and a puff of smoke. 'Elon Musk smokes weed on Joe Rogan podcast' was the headline that went viral.

The second realisation was that any biography of Musk would be merely a snapshot of the man at a particular time. Musk moves faster than he tweets. You could quite easily add a chapter a month to a biography of him, such is his wide-ranging impact in a variety of fields. Anything he says is of consequence. Anything he does is captured and analysed.

At the time of writing, David Beasley, the director of the World Food Programme (WFP), was quoted in a CNN article as saying that two per cent of Musk's wealth would solve world hunger. Solve world hunger. It's the kind of comment that often involves Musk. You are the richest man on Earth, thus your money can solve Earth's problems.

Musk responded. And he responded in a way that most are never ready for: show me how, and I'll do it. More accurately, he tweeted: 'If WFP can describe on this Twitter thread exactly how $6 billion will solve world hunger, I will sell Tesla stock right now and do it'.

Right there lies the true genius of Musk. For the comic-book fans, his true superpower is beyond anything Iron Man represents.

Elon Musk will attempt anything he can get his head around. And he will attempt things in industries and realms that people have generally believed to be too big to change – be it financial services, the car industry or spaceflight. Or even world hunger.

This is exactly what people love about him. Elon Musk has a vision, and nothing is too big for that vision. And he expresses it with a sincerity that sometimes sees him tear up in interviews. As big and bold as his ego can be, he can also describe criticism he has received as 'hurtful'. His ideas, and sometimes even the man himself, appear almost naive. Others have described him as ruthless. His own brother has said he possesses many great qualities, but empathy for others is not high up on the list.

And yet it's in the simplicity of asking what nobody else has thought to ask that Musk seems to find new solutions to the complexity of issues nobody has ever thought to question. Much like his grandfather, Joshua Haldeman, he is a pioneer and an adventurer. Grandad Haldeman climbed into a plane and took his adventures around the world. Musk appears more interested in the adventures that lie within his own imagination. As such, he has great value to offer. In a short space of time, he has revolutionised several industries.

Whether you agree with him or not, whether you believe his companies to be a success or not, it cannot be argued that when Musk steps into an industry, change occurs.

Before Elon Musk, the move towards electric vehicles was still seen as a novelty and was moving at a glacial pace. Now, no major vehicle manufacturer can envision not having a viable electric vehicle in its product line. It's become an absolute necessity. Musk has, as he said all along, accelerated this change.

And he will continue to change.

This is a man who has world-shifting ideas in the shower, who finds it hard to sleep, who works ferociously. And this is a man who is far from finished.

Even as I write, Elon Musk is debating plans to solve world hunger and launching a constellation of satellites into low Earth orbit to help lower Internet costs as part of SpaceX's Starlink initiative. In February 2022, he reportedly provided thousands of Starlink satellite kits (including a router and satellite dish) to embattled Ukraine to help support their communications systems, which were severely affected by Russian bombing. He is cautioning against unregulated AI, pushing the boundaries of space exploration, furthering the technology of electric cars, drilling tunnels to solve traffic, seeking the hidden answers to human brain malfunctions, debating new forms of currency and even being asked what kind of system of government he'd like to see on Mars. And on top of all of this he places his Holy Grail – the preservation of human consciousness, that most rare of things in the entire universe.

And somewhere, perhaps he will finally find the true love he so desperately seeks and claims he cannot live or work without.

THE intention of this book was never to provide a comprehensive biography. Rather, it was to offer an overview of the life of a man with South African roots, and how his roots may have shaped him into becoming a colossus of our age.

There was a time when people looked to the far reaches of the planet. For adventurers, explorers and pioneers, the focus was on discovering far-off lands, climbing the highest peaks, exploring the depths of the oceans. And then the focus began to shift inwards. The great journey of discovery was the mind and the emotions, and of being rather than doing. Perhaps what Musk has done is to draw us back to the big, bold ideas. He has pulled us out of ourselves again, and made us once again look up. At a time when our focus has narrowed to the 16:9 frame on an Instagram screen, he has pulled us out again and reminded us all to dream big.

So I've tried to give some context to Elon Musk – where he's come from, and where he's going to.

It's been an incredible journey, and clearly, this is not where his story ends.

It's a moment of Musk.

Or, in the words of Elon, 'I'm just being me.'

Acknowledgements

WHEN it comes to Mars, as with any major project, it will take the collective effort of a number of people for that first man or woman to set foot on the Red Planet.

Similarly, the biography of a life as big as that of Elon Musk takes the collective help of several people to achieve.

To Jeremy Boraine, Gill Moodie, Alfred LeMaitre, Martine Barker, Paul Wise, Nicole Duncan and the incredible team at Jonathan Ball Publishers, thank you for the vision and the opportunity for me to be able to step into this space with Musk.

To all those who kindly responded to my questions and queries and helped to paint a picture of Musk from his childhood to becoming one of the most influential figures of our time, thank you for your valuable input.

To my wife, Ursula – my first reader – if you like it, then I always know we've got something special. Thank you for your advice and every cup of tea that goes into every single book.

And finally, to Buzz Lightyear, for that wonderful line that echoed in my head throughout the writing of this book: 'To infinity, and beyond.'

Notes

PART ONE
A Strange Child

1   Mary Alexander, 'The 16 June 1976 Soweto students' uprising – as it happened', South Africa Gateway, 15 June 2021, southafrica-info.com.
2   'June 16 Youth Uprising Casualties', South African History Online, 7 July 2021, www.sahistory.org.za/article/june-16-youth-uprising-casualties.
3   *The Joe Rogan Experience #1169*, 'Elon Musk', 7 September 2018, PowerfulJRE, youtu.be/ycPr5-27vSI.
4   Allen Drury, *'A Very Strange Society'*: A Journey to the Heart of South Africa, Trident Press, 1967.
5   *The Joe Rogan Experience #1169*.

A Family of Pioneers

1   John Vorster, 'Address at the official opening of the ASB Congress on 28 June 1971 in the Aula, Pretoria', South African History Online, 1 September 2019, www.sahistory.org.za/archive/address-official-opening-asb-congress-28-june-1971-aula-pretoria.
2   Maye Musk, *A Woman Makes a Plan: Advice for a Lifetime of Adventure, Beauty, and Success*, Jonathan Ball Publishers, 2020.
3   Ibid.
4   CTV, 'Maye Musk reveals the age she knew Elon was a special child', *Your Morning*, 21 January 2020.
5   XPrize.org, 'Elon Musk and Peter Diamandis LIVE on $100M XPRIZE Carbon Removal', livestreamed conversation, XPrize, 22 April 2021, www.youtube.com/watch?v=BN88HPUm6j0.
6   Sara Brooks Sundberg, 'A Farm Woman on the Minnesota Prairie: The Letters of Mary E Carpenter', *Minnesota History* 51, Spring 1989.
7   Eugene Smalley, 'The Isolation of Life on Prairie Farms', *The Atlantic*, September 1893.
8   Joseph C Keating and Scott Haldeman, 'Joshua N Haldeman, DC: The Canadian Years: 1926–1950', National Institute of Chiropractic Research, 1 June 1993. https://www.chiro.org/Plus/History/Persons/Haldeman/HaldemanJoshua-chrono.pdf.
9   Karin Hammerich DC, 'Canada's First Chiropractor', *Chiropractic Naturopathic Doctor*, 7 January 2008.
10 Ted J Kaptchuk OMD and David M Eisenberg MD, 'Chiropractic: Origins, Controversies and Contributions', *Archives of Internal Medicine* 159(20) (1998).
11 Jerome L Stam and Bruce L Dixon, 'Farmer Bankruptcies and Farm Exits in the United States, 1899–2002', United States Department of Agriculture: Agriculture Information Bulletin Number 788, 2004.
12 Keating and Haldeman, 'Joshua N Haldeman'.
13 Ibid, p 9.
14 Ibid.
15 Ibid, p 10.
16 Ibid, pp 10 and 11.
17 Ibid, p 11.

Don't Panic

1   Musk, *A Woman Makes a Plan*.
2   Ibid, p 13.
3   CBS News, 'Tesla and SpaceX: Elon Musk's industrial empire', *60 Minutes*, 30 March 2014. www.youtube.com/watch?v=cl1oQnzcwFg.
4   Ibid.
5   Keating and Haldeman, 'Joshua N Haldeman'.
6   Musk, *A Woman Makes a Plan*.
7   Postmedia News, 'Before Elon Musk was thinking about Mars and electric cars, he was doing chores on a Saskatchewan farm', *Regina Leader-Post*, 15 May 2017.

Broken Home

1–2   CBS, 'Full Interview: Maye Musk, Mother of Elon Musk, Talks About Her Extraordinary Life, CBS2, 25 August 2020, www.youtube.com/watch?v=nGQB6b1G940.
3   Musk, *A Woman Makes a Plan*..
4   CBS, 'Full Interview: Maye Musk'.
5   Ibid.
6   Musk, *A Woman Makes a Plan*.
7   Ibid.
8   CBS, 'Full Interview: Maye Musk'.
9   Musk, *A Woman Makes a Plan*.
10   Ibid.
11   CBS News, 'Tesla CEO Elon Musk: The "60 Minutes" Interview', *60 Minutes*, 10 December 2018.
12   Neil Strauss, 'Elon Musk: The Architect of Tomorrow', *Rolling Stone*, 30 November 2017
13   Errol Musk, Facebook post, 25 March 2018.
14   Barbara Jones, 'Inter-galactic family feud: Elon Musk has called his father "evil" ... so we tracked him down to South Africa where he says his son needs to "grow up" after "tantrums" over his child with new model wife, 30', *Mail Online*, 17 March 2018.
15   Errol Musk, Facebook post, 25 March 2018.
16   Strauss, 'Elon Musk: The Architect of Tomorrow'.
17   Errol Musk, Facebook post, 27 July 2020.
18   Ibid.
19   Errol Musk, Facebook posts, 27 July 2020, 4 August 2020.
20   Errol Musk, Facebook post, 27 July 2020.
21–23 Ibid.
24   Jeremy Arnold, 'I Talked to Elon Musk about Journalism and the Blood Emeralds Story', Substack post, The Save Journalism Committee, 9 March 2021.
25–27 Ibid.
28   Errol Musk, Facebook post, 4 May 2019.
29   Errol Musk, Facebook post, 8 June 2020.
30   Ibid.
31   Strauss, 'Elon Musk: The Architect of Tomorrow'.
32   CBS, 'Full Interview: Maye Musk'.
33   Ibid.

Educating Elon

1   André du Plessis, 2003. 'Chapter 3: Hatfield in Context', in *Gautrain Station, Hatfield*, MArch dissertation, University of Pretoria, 2003.
2   Kerry A Dolan, 'How to Raise a Billionaire: An Interview with Elon Musk's Father, Errol Musk', Forbes, 2 July 2015.
3   Errol Musk, Facebook post, 18 September 2018.
4   *The Money Show with Bruce Whitfield*, Radio 702, 6 May 2015.
5   Musk, *A Woman Makes a Plan*.
6   Strauss, 'Elon Musk: The Architect of Tomorrow'.
7   Julian C Stanley, 'In the Beginning: The Study of Mathematically Precocious Youth (SMPY)', 1996, files.eric.ed.gov/fulltext/ED423110.pdf.
8   Vanderbilt University Television News, 15 September 2017, Vanderbilt Peabody College. www.youtube.com/watch?v=XkPQHIUHWwc.
9   Staff Writer, 'Researchers Confirm Link Between High Test Scores in Adolescence and Adult Accomplishment', *Duke Today*, 2 June 2016.
10   Ibid.
11   Tom Clynes, 'How to Raise a Genius: Lessons from a 45-Year Study of Super-Smart Children', *Nature* 537, 7 September 2016.
12   Vanderbilt University Television News, 15 September 2017, Vanderbilt Peabody College.
13   Errol Musk, Facebook post, 8 June 2020.
14   CBS, 'Full Interview: Maye Musk'.
15   'Elon Musk: "I Don't Give a Damn About Your Degree"', interview, *AutoBild.TV*, 5 November 2014, YouTube, www.youtube.com/watch?v=CQbKctnnA-Y.

16   Ibid.
17   *The Joe Rogan Experience* #1169.
18   Ibid.
19   *The Money Show with Bruce Whitfield*, Radio 702, 6 May 2015.
20   Ibid.
21   Foundation 20, 'Elon Musk', interview with Kevin Rose, 8 September 2012, www.youtube.com/watch?v=L-s_3b5fRd8.
22   Ibid.

Broken Bones

1   CBS News, 'Tesla CEO Elon Musk'.
2   Strauss, 'Elon Musk: The Architect of Tomorrow'.
3   Alec Hogg, 'Errol Musk: 'Elon was beaten so badly, I couldn't recognise him'', *BizNews*, 22 July 2015.
4   Ibid.
5   Errol Musk, Facebook post, 26 May 2013.
6–8   Ibid.
9   Strauss, 'Elon Musk: The Architect of Tomorrow'.
10   Ibid.
11   *The Joe Rogan Experience* #1169.
12   Staff Writer, 'Bryanston High School saddened by Elon Musk bullying', *News24*, 23 July 2015.
13   Ibid.
14   Ibid.
15   'Lie about Elon Musk's Pretoria Boys High School donation exposed', *MyBroadband*, 11 January 2021.
16   Comments taken from Bryanston High School SA Alumni, Facebook group, 4 August 2021.

PART TWO
Canada Calling

1   Associated Press. '4 Die in Worst South Africa Bombing in a Year', *The New York Times*, 4 June 1988.
2   Peter Dickens, The Observation Post: South African Modern Military History, samilhistory.com/.
3   Graeme Callister, 'Patriotic Duty or Resented Imposition? Public Reactions to Military Conscription in White South Africa, 1952–1972', *Scientia Militaria, South African Journal of Military Studies* 35(1) (2007).
4   Peter Dickens, 'Ride Safe', The Observation Post: South African Modern Military History, 23 December 2017.
5   'End Conscription Campaign (ECC)', South African History Online, 30 March 2011.
6   'International Conscientious Objector Day – Notice to the Press', press statement, 15 May 1990, University of Johannesburg Historical Papers.
7   Foundation 20, 'Elon Musk', interview with Kevin Rose, 8 September 2012, www.youtube.com/watch?v=L-s_3b5fRd8.
8   Interview with Charlie Rose, PBS, 8 November 2009, charlierose.com/videos/12550.
9   Ibid.
10   Postmedia News, 'Before Elon Musk was thinking about Mars'.
11   Melissa Rosales and Nebraska Public Media, 'How a robot could keep farmers out of grain bins', Harvest Public Media, 27 May 2021.
12   Postmedia News, 'Before Elon Musk was thinking about Mars'.
13   Eric Berger, *Liftoff: Elon Musk and the Desperate Early Days that Launched SpaceX*, William Collins, 2021.
14   Robin Keats, 'Rocket Man', *Queen's Alumni Review*, issue no 1, 2013.
15–18   Ibid.
19   *The Joe Rogan Experience* #1169.
20   SXSW, 'Elon Musk Answers Your Questions!' interview with Jonathan Nolan, SXSW 2018, 12 March 2018, www.youtube.com/watch?v=kzIUyrccbos.
21   *The Joe Rogan Experience* #1169.
22–23   Ibid.

24   Strauss, 'Elon Musk: The Architect of Tomorrow'.
25   Ibid.
26   Helena Wasserman, 'Elon Musk's dad has had a baby with his stepdaughter, who is 42 years younger than him', *Business Insider South Africa*, 23 March 2018.

The American Dream

1   Justine Musk, '"I Was a Starter Wife": Inside America's Messiest Divorce', *Marie Claire*, 10 September 2010.
2   Justine Musk, 'Visionaries Are People Who Can See in the Dark', TEDx talk, 1 June 2017, www.youtube.com/watch?v=OxA0LESuUDE.
3   Musk, '"I Was a Starter Wife"'.
4   Ibid.
5   Elon Musk, Twitter, 30 August 2020.
6   Ibid.
7   Errol Musk, Facebook post, 8 August 2020.
8   Ashlee Vance, 'Elon Musk: The College Years', *Esquire*, 5 June 2015.
9   Foundation 20, 'Elon Musk', interview.
10   Superior Court of California, *Martin Eberhard v. Elon Musk et al.*, case no CIV484400, 1 October 2009.
11   'Elon Musk's Vision for the Future', interview with Steve Jurvetson, 7 October 2015, podcast, Stanford eCorner.
12   Foundation 20, 'Elon Musk', interview.
13–14   Ibid.
15   Elon Musk, 'History of Zip2', video address, 8 October 2003, Entrepreneurial Thought Leaders series, Stanford eCorner.
16   XPrize.org, 'Elon Musk and Peter Diamandis'.

PART THREE
Zip2

1   Foundation 20, 'Elon Musk', interview.
2   Interview with Charlie Rose.
3   Walter Isaacson, *A Benjamin Franklin Reader*, Simon and Schuster, 2003.
4   Strauss, 'Elon Musk: The Architect of Tomorrow'.
5   'Elon Musk's Vision for the Future'.
6   Ibid.
7   Ibid.
8   'Elon Musk on Tesla, SpaceX and Why He Left Silicon Valley', *Wall Street Journal*, 9 December 2020, www.youtube.com/watch?v=V1nQFotzQMQ.
9   'Elon Musk's Vision for the Future'.
10   'The Beginning of PayPal – Elon Musk in 1999', www.youtube.com/ watch?v=ezQLq5kJ9sA.
11   'Elon Musk's Vision for the Future'.
12   'Elon Musk's 2003 Stanford University Entrepreneurial Thought Leaders Lecture', 8 October 2003, www.youtube.com/watch?v=afZTrfvB2AQ.
13   'Entrepreneur Elon Musk: Why It's Important to Pinch Pennies on on the Road to Riches', podcast interview, Knowledge@Wharton, Wharton School, University of Pennsylvania, 27 May 2009.
14   Benjamin Franklin, *The Way to Wealth*, Simon and Schuster, 2011 (1758).
15   'Entrepreneur Elon Musk: Why It's Important to Pinch Pennies'.
16   *The Joe Rogan Experience* #1169.
17–18   Ibid.
19   Strauss, 'Elon Musk: The Architect of Tomorrow'.
20   Ibid.
21   'Elon Musk's 2003 Stanford University Lecture'.
22–23   Ibid.
24   Mark Gimein, 'Fast Track: Elon Musk is poised to become Silicon Valley's Next Big Thing. What put him in the driver's seat?' *Salon*, 17 August 1999.
25   Ibid.
26   'Elon Musk's 2003 Stanford University Lecture'.
27   Staff Writer, 'What does it take to start a business?' Private TechHub, 16 April 2018.

28	Ibid.
29	Lisa Napoli, 'Compaq Buys Zip2 to Enhance Altavista', *The New York Times*, 17 February 1999.
30	'Elon Musk's 2003 Stanford University Lecture'
31	Gimein, 'Fast Track'.
32	Strauss, 'Elon Musk: The Architect of Tomorrow'.
33	Gimein, 'Fast Track'.
34–35	Ibid.
36	Robert Payne, *Leonardo*. Robert Hale Limited, 1979.
37	'An Evening with Elon Musk', interview with Alison van Diggelen, 'Revolutionaries', season 2, Computer History Museum, 2 January 2013.
38	Gimein, 'Fast Track'.
39	'Entrepreneur Elon Musk: Why It's Important to Pinch Pennies'.

PayPal

1	'Entrepreneur Elon Musk: Why It's Important to Pinch Pennies'.
2	Elon Musk, 'Founding of PayPal', video address, 8 October 2003, Entrepreneurial Thought Leaders series, Stanford eCorner.
3	'Young Elon Musk featured in documentary about millionaires (1999)', YouTube, 24 October 2015, www.youtube.com/watch?v=eb3pmifEZ44.
4	Ibid.
5	Musk, 'Founding of PayPal'.
6	David O Sacks, 'Why did PayPal merge with X.com?' response to Quora post, 2011.
7	*Inc. Magazine*, 'A Conversation with Tesla CEO Elon Musk', interview with Max Chafkin (2008), YouTube, 13 November 2015, www.youtube.com/watch?v=Xcut1JfTMoM.
8	Julie Anderson, 'How was the rivalry between PayPal and X.com before/after the merger?' response to Quora post, 2016.
9	'The 50th Anniversary of the Internet, 29 October 2019: Debate – Has True Innovation Stalled?', www.youtube.com/watch?v=qDa8SRzGrcg&list=PLAt9_m6WVp2y68peOC2NO0TU8w4dveqwN.
10	'Peter Thiel Speaks at Center on Capitalism and Society's 2015 Conference', The Center on Capitalism and Society, 24 November 2015, www.youtube.com/watch?v=Y11uX8X6iz4.
11	Ibid.
12	Foundation 20, 'Elon Musk'.
13	'Peter Thiel Speaks'.
14–22	Ibid.
23	Berger, *Liftoff*.
24	'Elon Musk interview from Air Warfare Symposium 2020', Air Force Association, 2 March 2020, www.youtube.com/watch?v=sp8smJFaKYE.
25	XPrize.org, 'Elon Musk and Peter Diamandis'.
26	'Mohammad Al Gergawi in a Conversation with Elon Musk during WGS17', 13 February 2017, www.youtube.com/watch?v=rCoFKUJ_8Yo.
27	Elon Musk, 'SpaceX Starship Live Update', SpaceX, 29 September 2019, www.youtube.com/watch?v=sOpMrVnjYeY.
28	'Elon Musk addresses National Governors Association Summer Meeting', National Governors Association, 15 July 2017, www.c-span.org/video/?431119-6/elon-musk-addresses-nga.
29	'Mohammad Al Gergawi in a Conversation with Elon Musk'.
30	XPrize.org, 'Elon Musk and Peter Diamandis'.
31	Ibid.
32	'Peter Thiel Speaks'.
33	Ryk van Niekerk, 'Q&A with Sequoia Capital's Roelof Botha', Tech Central, 16 May 2016.
34	Ibid.

PART FOUR
The Break-Ups

1	Musk, '"I Was a Starter Wife"'.
2	Justine Musk, 'Mean Girls, Leadership + The Problem with Sandberg's "Ban Bossy"

	Campaign', blog post, JustineMusk.com, 16 March 2014.
3	Musk, 'Visionaries Are People Who Can See in the Dark'.
4	Ibid.
5	'Young Elon Musk featured in documentary about millionaires (1999)'.
6	Musk, '"I Was a Starter Wife"'.
7	Elon Musk, Twitter, 30 August 2020.
8	Musk, '"I Was a Starter Wife"'.
9–12	Ibid.
13	Justine Musk, blog post, JustineMusk.com.
14–15	Ibid.
16	'Elon Musk Very Awkward Moment', Elon Musk Motivation channel, 25 June 2018, YouTube, www.youtube.com/watch?v=sL1gqHDer9E.
17	Ibid.
18	Elon Musk, Twitter, 18 January 2012.
19	Hannah Elliott, 'Elon Musk to Divorce from Wife Talulah Riley', *Forbes*, 18 January 2012.
20	Emily Kirkpatrick, 'Elon Musk Thinks Johnny Depp and Amber Heard Should "Bury the Hatchet"', *Vanity Fair*, 18 June 2020.
21	Strauss, 'Elon Musk: The Architect of Tomorrow'.
22	Musk, 'Visionaries Are People Who Can See in the Dark'.
23	Justine Musk, 'Wounded People Tell Better Stories', TEDx talk, 26 January 2016.
24	Musk, 'Visionaries Are People Who Can See in the Dark'.
25	Ibid.
26	'Elon Musk: "I Don't Give a Dam About Your Degree"'.

PART FIVE
Ad Astra

1	This chapter draws on a *60 Minutes* profile of Elon Musk, presented by Scott Pelley; CBS News, 'SpaceX: Elon Musk's Race to Space', *60 Minutes*, 18 March 2012, www.youtube.com/watch?v=23GzpbNUyI4.

Sputnik and the Space Race

1	Samuel Willard Crompton, *Sputnik/Explorer 1: The Race to Conquer Space*, Milestones in American History series, Chelsea House, 2007.
2	Roger D Launius, 'Sputnik and the Origins of the Space Age', NASA History Division, 2 February 2005.
3	Daniel J Boorstin, *The Americans: The Democratic Experience*, Vintage, 1974.
4	Walter A McDougall, ... *the Heavens and the Earth: A Political History of the Space Age*. Basic Books, 1985.
5	Musk, 'Opportunities in Space: Mars Oasis', video address, 8 October 2003, Entrepreneurial Thought Leaders series, Stanford eCorner.
6	Ibid.
7	David Shiga, 'Neil Armstrong criticises new space plan in Congress', *New Scientist*, 12 May 2010.
8	CBS News, 'Tesla and SpaceX'.
9	Musk, 'Opportunities in Space'.
10	'Elon Musk's Vision for the Future'.
11	Musk, 'Opportunities in Space'.
12–13	Ibid.
14	Elon Musk, mission statement, SpaceX website.
15	'Mohammad Al Gergawi in a Conversation with Elon Musk'.
16	Richard Branson, 'Elon Musk, in 'The 2013 TIME 100', *Time*, 18 April 2013.
17	Arwa Mahdawi, 'Of course billionaires like Elon Musk love outer space: The Earth is too small for their egos', *The Guardian*, 27 May 2020.
18	*Metaphysical Milkshake*, 'Dr Moogega Cooper: Should We Colonize Mars?', podcast episode, 31 August 2021.
19	Carl Sagan, 'Carl Sagan's Message for Mars', 1996, The Planetary Society, www.planetary.org/video/20180727-carl-sagan-message-to-mars.
20	*Metaphysical Milkshake*, 'Dr Moogega Cooper'.
21	Ibid.

22   Carl Sagan, *Cosmos*, Ballantine Books, 1985.
23   Musk, 'Opportunities in Space'.
24   Elon Musk, Twitter, 13 July 2021.
25   Gene Gregory, 'Is the Space Effort a Waste of Money?' *The UNESCO Courier*,
        March 1970.
26   'Elon Musk's Vision for the Future'.
27   Ibid.
28   'Elon Musk's 2003 Stanford University Lecture'.

SpaceX

1   Musk, 'Opportunities in Space'.
2   'Elon Musk's 2003 Stanford University Lecture'.
3   *Planetary Radio*, 'A Conversation with Elon Musk of SpaceX', podcast episode,
        The Planetary Society, 16 February 2009.
4   Ibid.
5   CBS News, 'SpaceX: Elon Musk's Race to Space'.

Falcon 1

1   *Ask a Spaceman*, 'How to Build a Rocket ... or Not', podcast episode, 13 June 2018.
2–4   Ibid.
5   'Tom Mueller (SpaceX) explains the Merlin rocket engine', Livescribe pencast,
        3 June 2016, Burn Hard Zen channel, YouTube, https://www.youtube.com/
        watch?v=UqF8lKBlPqY.
6   Ibid.
7   Eric Ralph, 'SpaceX crushes rocket engine world record during Raptor test',
        Teslarati.com, 18 August 2020.
8   Berger, *Liftoff*.
9   C-SPAN, 'NASA Officials Hold SpaceX Crew Dragon Post Launch News
        Conference', Kennedy Space Center, 30 May 2020.
10   Dmitry Rogozin, '"This is their war, not ours": Dmitry Rogozin responded to the
        launch of Elon Musk's Crew Dragon', *Forbes* (Russian edition), 8 June 2020.
11   'Dinner Program – To Infinity and Beyond: Jeff Skoll Talks with Elon and Kimbal
        Musk', Milken Institute, 12 July 2013, www.youtube.com/watch?v=T55CcN5c5as.
12   Elon Musk, 'Challenges in the Space Industry', video address, 8 October 2003,
        Entrepreneurial Thought Leaders series, Stanford eCorner.
13   'Elon Musk's 2003 Stanford University Lecture'.
14   Berger, *Liftoff*.
15–16   Ibid.
17   CBS News, 'Tesla and SpaceX'.
18   Berger, *Liftoff*.

Musk's Christmas Miracle

1   CBS News, 'Tesla and SpaceX'.
2   *The Joe Rogan Experience* #1169.
3   CBS News, 'Tesla and SpaceX'.
4   'Elon Musk Very Awkward Moment'.
5   Ibid.
6   Interview, 1 April 2015, BTV.
7–9   Ibid.
10   CBS News, 'Tesla and SpaceX'.
11   Berger, *Liftoff*.
12   Bethany McLean, '"He's Full of Shit": How Elon Musk Fooled Investors, Bilked
        Taxpayers, and Gambled Tesla to Save SolarCity', *Vanity Fair*, 25 August 2019.
13   XPrize.org, 'Elon Musk and Peter Diamandis'.
14   Interview with Charlie Rose.

Tesla

1   'Tesla's Founders on Elon Musk and the Early Days', CNBC, 6 February 2021,
        www.youtube.com/watch?v=eblPwXFb7TE.
2–4   Ibid.
5   Interview with Charlie Rose.

6   'Tesla's Founders on Elon Musk and the Early Days'.
7   Ibid.
8   Catherine Clifford, 'Elon Musk: This is the "why" of Tesla', CNBC, 4 February 2019.
9   Ibid.
10   Intel Newsroom, 'Intel Predicts Autonomous Driving Will Spur New "Passenger
        Economy" Worth $7 Trillion', news release, Intel Corporation, 1 June 2017.
11   Ibid.
12   'Tesla's Founders on Elon Musk and the Early Days'.
13   Joseph B White, 'Tesla CEO Elon Musk Battles Car Dealers Over Company Stores',
        The Wall Street Journal, 22 October 2012.
14   Elon Musk, statement, August 2009.
15   Edward Niedermeyer, *Ludicrous: The Unvarnished Story of Tesla Motors*, BenBella
        Books, 2019.
16   Patrick McGinty, 'Review: In "Ludicrous," Elon Musk is a hoaxer for the 21st century',
        Pittsburgh Post-Gazette, 1 December 2021.
17   'A Grain of Salt', press release, Tesla Motors, 9 June 2016
18   Ryan Mac, 'Elon Musk Can't Lose', *BuzzFeed*, 30 January 2020.
19–22   Ibid.
23   Chris Isidore, 'Tesla's dirty little secret: Its net profit doesn't come from selling cars',
        CNN Business, 1 February 2021.
24   Elon Musk, Twitter, 6 November 2021
25   'Tesla's Founders on Elon Musk and the Early Days'.

The Space Barons

1   CBS News, 'Tesla CEO Elon Musk'.
2   'Elon Musk interview from Air Warfare Symposium 2020'.
3   Part of this chapter draws on the five-part documentary series produced by
        Netflix and Time Inc on the Inspiration4 mission: *Countdown: Inspiration4 Mission to
        Space*, Netflix, 2021.
4   Ibid.

Is Elon Musk Boring?

1   This chapter draws extensively on The Boring Company's website:
        www.boringcompany.com.
2   Strauss, 'Elon Musk: The Architect of Tomorrow'.
3   Simon Alvarez, 'The Boring Company skeptics are making the same mistakes as
        Tesla and SpaceX critics', Teslarati.com, 29 November 2020.
4   Jesse Pound, 'Elon Musk's flamethrower incenses New York lawmakers: State
        Senate passes bill banning the weapon', CNBC, 21 June 2019.
5   Ryan Browne, 'Elon Musk warns A.I. could create an "immortal dictator from which
        we can never escape"', CNBC.com, 6 April 2018.
6   SXSW, 'Elon Musk Answers Your Questions!'
7   'Elon Musk talks Twitter, Tesla and how his brain works — live at TED2022', 14 April
        2022, www.youtube.com/watch?v=aV_IZye14vs.
8   SXSW, 'Elon Musk Answers Your Questions!'
9   Maureen Dowd, 'Elon Musk, Blasting Off in Domestic Bliss', *The New York Times*,
        25 July 2020.

PART SIX

The Cult of Elon Musk

1   Salina Gomez, *The Illuminated Tweets of Elon Musk Coloring Book*, Ill Ink, 2020,
        www.salinamariegomez.com/.
2   Bijan Stephen, 'The gospel of Elon Musk, according to his flock', *The Verge*, 26 June
        2018.
3   This chapter draws on a Musk-sceptic blog maintained by Filip Piekniewski, and on
        my correspondence with its author: see 'Piekniewski's blog'.
        blog.piekniewski.info/.
4–13   Ibid.

Index